# John Donne

# and the

# Metaphysical Gesture

# JOHN DONNE AND THE METAPHYSICAL GESTURE

BY

*JUDAH STAMPFER*

*Funk & Wagnalls New York*

Library of Congress Catalog Card Number: 70–98526
Published by Funk & Wagnalls,
*A Division of* Reader's Digest Books, Inc.
Printed in the United States of America

*For Lucy Greene*

# Contents

## *Part* IV

## *Special Subjects*



## *Part* V

## *The Religious Poems*

# Introduction

Current definitions of metaphysical poetry, by one or another poetic device, of Ramist logic, correspondences, unified awareness, emblems, eccentric images, etc., have loomed up, and then fallen into question. A fresh, undetected device may yet be hit upon; yet to us, something in the metaphysical poem has always suggested, not any stylistic device, but some essential plot. There is a peculiar personal poignance, one not of unfolding imagination, but in his pinched immediate situation, in the poet's grasp for salvation, love, order, sexual fulfilment, against a crumbling universe of reference. The catharsis may be comic, equivocal, a downright illusion; but in contrast to Eliot or Yeats, it characteristically remains deeply private. Whether he wants a recalcitrant mistress, as in "Womans Constancy," or the "Three-person'd God" in the Holy Sonnets, the poet's predicament is personal, his being small and uncertain, as he rises, body and intellect, to a confrontation. Indeed, his catharsis lies in reducing the arbitrary, immediate to personal indifference or mastery. Our first chapter, "The Metaphysical Shudder," will develop our argument, and contrast the metaphysical plot with that of other modes of poetry. Our second will sketch in some suggestive events in Donne's life. We will then consider the lyrics of John Donne as illuminated by their elements of plot.

Yet such words as "plot" and "catharsis" give us pause. The general bent of current criticism, whether clarifying ambiguities, multiple meanings, imagery, etc., or exploring institutions, word derivations, theologies, publishing practices, etc., engages in word analysis. The word is the brushstroke of the poet; as the brick is of the construction engineer. Deftly piling word on word, he shapes his poem, constructs his building. The critic's concern is with the shape of words, their texture, their solidity, their weight, how they fit together.

The analysis of words certainly carries weight in criticism. A sure knowledge of their ways can illuminate all aspects of a poem. Nevertheless, word analysis has often left us bewildered and frustrated. What justifies the exact freight of analysis on this or that word? Syntax alone? Some intuition about the meaning? Or just convention? How significant is the poetic situation, aside from its word associations? Does imagery warrant study simply by a fascination with imagery, as the impressionists suggest? Then the poem may be only a collage of vivid fragments. Does the image bear on the totality of the poem? And what constitutes such a totality? An idea? But not all poems build around ideas. An experience? Then we return to the situation of the poem. And in what sense is the poet related to the speaker—the "I"—of his poem? Certainly such problems are open to exploration by word analysis; yet the problem remains, What constitutes the unity of the poem?

However we formulate our misgivings, they return to a mistrust of words as the units of construction of a poem. Words no more shape a poem than bricks a large structure. Certainly an architect uses brick, wood, glass, steel, and concrete; but he also builds by space, height, the rhythm of an interior, and his grasp of human needs. So lyric poetry tends to have a skating quality, as its words skim off non-verbal material. Indeed, the metaphysical poets habitually use words they mistrust to achieve non-verbal effects, as a wounded man senses his scar tissue in flexing his muscles. The poem works with and against the grain. Donne's imagery seldom stands at face value. Sometimes he is reinforcing by an image, sometimes secretly scoffing, sometimes saying something particular, sometimes loosely meshing diverse ideas to air out his mind.

In considering the uses of words, we recall many years ago

first reading William Empson's *Seven Types of Ambiguity* with a gathering excitement evoked by few books of criticism. Suddenly the most distant periods opened to one another. Poetry seemed flush with human nature, yet structured firm as a bridge, outside the damp of history, each usage running like a vegetable shoot from the usage that preceded it. Since then, however, we sensed uneasily that we had imposed our own functions on the book. *Seven Types of Ambiguity* remains a primary tool in exploring the density, variety, and vitality of a poetic line; it does not render the process of the poem in all its intimacy. As electricity is not metal, though metal conduct it; so inaudible inner gestures that words convey are its units of construction. A head-on consideration of ambiguity is only a window on the complexity of spirit that is the core of a lyric poem, surging through its dense cake of ambiguity.

We then considered the landscape of poetry by the criticism of Northrop Frye. Indeed, his work strangely recalls Seventeenth Century systems of correspondences, unfolding word tapestries of human experience. Yet his approach seemed more illuminating in fiction and drama. In lyric poetry, there remains that mysterious entity of the private self of the poet, whose hesitations cannot be slighted, nor can his pinched occasions, his unpredictable equilibrium of the rhetorical and the dramatic, his rendered episodes and direct addresses to his reader be denied. The possibilities of reticence, duplicity, self-assertion, and self-effacement grow as the person of the poet is grafted onto the texture of his poem.

We then returned to Kenneth Burke, whose early study of *Samson Agonistes*, with its close parallels to Milton himself, also "eyeless, in Gaza, at the mill with slaves," expressed the shaping contour of the poet in his poem, the very structure of his psyche. We first mistrusted so great a degree of self-projection as a possible flaw in the poem, a failure of sublimation. But it seemed increasingly clear that poetry can express at most only a fractional sublimation, as the act of writing seizes and shapes the poet's psyche. Utter sublimation is simply beyond the human animal. A poem then shows wherein the poet transcended himself, what his price, and what remains intransigent in his poem.

Indeed, such concerns with fractional sublimation and the consciousness of the poet particularly apply to Donne, a man of many voices, prickly situations, turbulent self-discoveries, and brooding monologues in verse. Word analysis alone would expose only exemplars of poetic devices with no sense of their bent or purpose. Thus the compass metaphor in "A Valediction: Forbidding Mourning" is a far conceit; but in that forced situation, any intelligent, downright man might utter it. To isolate it as a bizarre conceit blurs what is imaginative flight, what is emotional warp, and what is dramatic intent. So "The Flea" is a minuet of his words and her actions, that reads as a drama.

And yet despite our terminology, a lyric poem is neither a short story nor a simple confessional. Its peculiarity lies not simply in its dense language, but also in the person of the internalized speaker. When Wordsworth writes, "I wandered lonely as a cloud," the poetic "I" has affinity to Wordsworth, perhaps as an imp, an alter ego, even a wish fulfilment; but regardless of its psychological origins, its presence is inescapable. Yet, even written in the third person, a lyric poem will contain the speaker by his style, his sensuous grasp, his concerns—ubiquitous and all-significant.

The idea of the speaker rids us of a critical dilemma. On the one hand, the poem reverberates with its author's temperament. Indeed, if his life is an allegory, his poetry and biography interweave in one vast tapestry. Thus Donne looms amid his poems, sermons, and letters, a great verbal body, his tissue of literary marvels ineluctibly mingled with his frustrations and delayed career. But such a reading violates Donne's own artistic detachment, his very vocation as a poet, reducing his poems to antiquarian items. He wrote discrete, living poems, shaping situation and character, not to be blurred on one another. But when we withdraw to discrete, structured poems, their author should fade as an architect from his buildings; yet John Donne speaks in his poems.

A focus upon the speaker resolves this dilemma. As a shaped element, he comes on afresh in each poem. Separate poems do not automatically blur together. And yet, by partial sublimation, the speaker will be exceedingly close to the poet.

Indeed, the speaker may expose the poet's temperament more than the episodes in his life. For poems are not simply art objects, but successive grapplings with the concerns of the poet's imagination; they cluster together. So Donne's promiscuity poems show an astonishingly parallel temperament, despite their various moods.

The speaker also helps distinguish the lyric plot from other modes of plot. By our understanding, every lyric poem is a monodrama. It may have a setting, but the setting exists as it is grasped by the speaker and permeates his consciousness. A novelist also shapes his setting—Dickens a rainfall, Stendhal a landscape, Tolstoy a forest—yet we brush aside the novelist while we read. In a lyric poem, the opposite takes place; our participation is always through the speaker's consciousness. His awareness is the setting of the poem, its very grace. Hence the heightened importance of language in a lyric poem, for language is the texture of its lyric world. So other characters exist in a poem as the speaker grasps them. They form the dialectic of his consciousness: a woman to his man, a king to his need to serve, a comrade when he needs a friend.

This is not to say all lyric action is in the mind. The speaker imagines, he improvises; but he also bears witness. Sudden, free elements constantly surprise us. At the cry, "Oh stay," in "The Flea," we suddenly realize this is a detailed, actual scene, the woman fixing the flea on the table with her fingernail. And is "The Message" spoken directly to the woman, as is "The Flea," or meditatively, as in "The Legacie"? We rejoice in the speaker's lilting masculinity, our ignorance of the scene a part of our wonder. The language can thus shift back and forth from objective to subjective. Magic occurs; but without supernatural paraphernalia, it is perhaps only as a lyric flight of the speaker. So the god of courtly love hangs in the speaker's imagination; yet it is somehow also real. In a novel, verbs like *die*, *collapse*, *rise*, *kill*, can stretch a certain distance beyond literal reality, but with clearly indicated limits. A lyric speaker can glide from death to collapse, to boredom, murder, suicide, saintliness, and back to his mother's parlor with sturdy resilience.

This lyric plot simultaneously occupies a man's consciousness, and has some objective reality, yet its reality need not be that clearly determined. This stands in contrast to Aristotle's *Poetics*, where characters enact their destiny in a fairly well-defined setting. When Tolstoy and Proust move characters about, we can distinguish a man's thought from the setting of his action. So Dostoevsky, for all his projected demons, his first person narrator, his tirades chapters long, belongs essentially in Aristotle's world. With Kafka came the break. Whatever its earlier uses, Kafka first opened the lyric plot to modern fiction. His setting is simultaneously the consciousness of the speaker and the flat he lives in. Action flickers in his consciousness, words hang suspended; yet they are somehow in the world. A Kafka beginning, "As Gregor Samsa awoke one morning from uneasy dreams, he found himself transformed in his bed into a gigantic insect," recalls Blake's:

> Piping down the valleys wild,
> Piping songs of pleasant glee,
> On a cloud I saw a child,
> And he, laughing, said to me . . .

The clinching persuasiveness of the lyric plot lies in the hard presence of the speaker, his immediate grip of experience. So Donne's colloquialism, his tone of immediacy, surprise, a brisk vibrancy of music, all ground his poem in an immediate, personal situation, "I wonder by my troth, what thou, and I/Did, till we lov'd?" The ego, the strong consciousness of the speaker, anchors the poem amid sudden immediacy and jarring changes, allowing no break with ordinary experience. Terms borrowed from engineering best establish such equilibrium: disruption, grounding, centrifugal force. In "Loves Exchange," Donne's most extreme depiction of the incarnate, raging god of love, a tough, downright veteran, confronts Love as a familiar rascal:

> *Love*, any devill else but you,
> Would for a given Soule give something too.

The colloquial usage and narrative pace grounds the disruptive scene in immediacy. Only at the end of Stanza 4, in the full smack of his desperate outrage, does the speaker betray the actual scene.

Gothic fiction also calls for a strong style, violent nouns, turbulent surges of passion, characters larger than life, but in a special area of experience outside the here and now. So Edgar Allan Poe begins "The Black Cat" with a double insistence on a faraway tale, yet one that actually happened to someone: "For the most wild, yet most homely narrative which I am about to pen, I neither expect nor solicit belief." So experiences in Gothic fiction come in a bottle, from a decayed manuscript, a dead man's lips, their settings flooded, crumbling into ruins, under fire and plague. By contrast, the lyric plot suggests no tale, however high and gripping, but is grounded in immediate experience, though on a lyric plane.

Nor is the lyric plot allegory, as *The Divine Comedy* is, among other things, an allegory. The *Inferno* begins:

> Midway in our life's journey, I went astray
> from the straight road and woke to find myself
> alone in a dark wood.

Such adjectives—"*life's* journey"—"*straight* road"—"*dark* wood"—do not make their nouns more shockingly immediate, but abstract and stylize them for the core road of experience, without any chance impingements. Precisely because no earthly road is straight, Dante took the straight road. Spenser begins *The Faerie Queene* on a tone of allegory:

> A Gentle Knight was pricking on the plaine,
> Y cladd in mightie armes and silver shielde,
> Wherein old dints of deepe wounds did remaine,
> The cruell markes of many'a bloody field.

These adjectives—"*gentle* Knight"—"*mightie* armes"—"*silver* shielde," "*old* dints"—"*deepe* wounds"—stylize the nouns to a mode of knight, not a specific knight.

In the lyric plot, nothing is stylized; all is delivered in spontaneous immediacy. If characters in allegory are embodied concepts, characters in lyric poems are embodied impulses. They are what the speaker grasps of them, simultaneously real and a factor in a dialectic of his spirit. So Wordsworthian characters—Michael, the old Cumberland beggar, the cottage girl of "We Are Seven"—exist, not as detached figures, but rather in the experience of grasping them by a swift, unpredictable consciousness. So, in Donne's "The Apparition," the speaker describes some woman; she exists, but only as he grasps her. Indeed, the impulse a character embodies can be quite random. In Harold Pinter's *The Homecoming*, no actual daughter-in-law turns to prostitution on a London visit, nor does an actual husband allow it. Some gesture, an inclination to looseness, a word of disengagement, is simply blown up on stage to enact the impulse behind it. *The Homecoming* is realistic in that real impulses are projected on stage; but its plot is lyric, not narrative.

It would be well here to correlate our terms by contrast to the narrative plot in Aristotle's *Poetics*. The lyric plot, then, is a rendering, in words of a closely rhythmic texture, of a complete movement of awareness. It begins as an imbalance of spirit precipitates the speaker into words. It continues as the lyric work of testing, tasting, itemizing, and defining gradually realigns his spirit, and concludes with the attainment of clear knowledge or a finely crystalized predicament. Its closing clarity of spirit is the catharsis of the poem. Hence the cathartic finality of these closing lines:

> If our two loves be one, or, thou and I
> Love so alike, that none doe slacken, none can die.
> ("The Good-Morrow," ll. 20–21)
>
> This bed thy center is, these walls, thy sphere.
> ("The Sunne Rising," l. 30)

Our defining terms are psychic, rather than narrowly poetic, but our intent is not outside the domain of literature. The reverse is true; we conceive of aesthetic transport, the impulse of creative joy, as the principal factor in a lyric resolution. But poetry is a representational, not an abstract art, a complex, "dirty" art, full of personal strategies and rationalizations. Its words have moral reverberations; its harmonies have a psychic pace; its structure is a grasp of spirit. Indeed, that is the mysterium of poetry. Language is one among many plateaus of human experience; the psyche slips among them all, never engulfed, never blocked out. It tastes about, grows silly, slumbers away its fears of hypocrisy, loneliness, triviality, then grows spasmodically triumphant. The grace of poetry is its illusion of wholeness, its ability to encapsulate, structure, and render eternal the very motion of a psyche's awareness, to reverberate with what it touches, yet remain serenely afloat above what it ignores. Its attainments are literary, not by its subject matter, but by its largesse of language as it fuses the experience of awareness in the finished poem.

Indeed, our terms, though generally applicable to lyric poetry, are peculiarly relevant to John Donne, who all his life felt a restless irritation at his pinched situation, and allowed his personal material on any level to smack into words. His lyrics are peculiarly an imbalance of spirit precipitated into words:

> Busie old foole, unruly Sunne,
> Why dost thou thus,
> Through windowes, and through curtaines call on us?
> ("The Sunne Rising")
> For Godsake hold your tongue, and let me love . . .
> ("The Canonization")

This approach gives us a clue to the structure of the *Holy Sonnets*. On first reading, their unity seems of the loosest, with a various subject matter, and abrupt shifts in mood. One sonnet lays down no clear foundation that the next builds on. Indeed, the same octave and sestet seem to be joined together with no inescapable necessity—two moods, flung one on the other, and called a poem. But the *Holy Sonnets* offer a psychic unity and structure, as the speaker's spirit gradually meshes to God's will. After a formal opening, that establishes only alienation and disengagement, sonnet after sonnet proceeds to engage the speaker, clarify his inner environment, and articulate the factors in his disposition. The *Holy Sonnets* end when he and God have one will. Any psychic factor, any shift in mood or subject, is valid in achieving this end.

Donne's sonnets tend to follow a dialectic of thesis, antithesis, and synthesis. Sonnets 1 and 2 have an antithesis in lines 9 and 10, and their synthesis in lines 11 to 14. While not theoretically necessary, the dialectic brings to equilibrium the psychic factors in a sonnet, for a 14-line poem is too long for a single statement, and too irregular for a series of stanzas.

Given an instinct for structure, a thesis would of itself evoke its antithesis, then a synthesis to resolve the disparity. Shakespeare's sonnets are characteristically structured thus.

The correlation between the content of the poem and the person of its author is never trivial. Creative writing is, among other things, passion poured on paper. Where should the poet's plot constructions come from, his polarities of tension, his very catharses, if not from the structure of his own psyche? What energies move a poem if not the poet's, grasped and harmonized in a lyric structure? Such concepts as detachment, universal reference, and a common ground of poetry are exceedingly complex (in the next chapter, we will discuss Eliot's formulation in "Tradition and the Individual Talent"); but the groundwork of any poem is the structure of its author's psyche. The purists who would see the lyric poem as a detached verbal construction are at the least exceedingly naive about how they use words.

We will, in any case, confine ourselves to "the speaker" in discussing Donne's lyric plots, thus avoiding the antiquarian question of John Donne's intents in his poems. Yet their development, their lyric plots, their modes of fulfilment will show a considerable unity, and even shadow forth the poet who was their author. We will confine ourselves in Chapter 2 to a sketch of the tensions in John Donne's career. It is one of the starkest drama—an allegory—touched to poetry in his writing. The various genre, defined by convention, of the elegies, satires, epistles, etc., valuable as they are, would complicate the development we envision of his poetic career. We will therefore confine ourselves to the lyrics, discussing them by their concerns and affinities of mood.

Our groupings are by no means rigid. Thus, "A Valediction: of My Name, in the Window" could be moved from Chapter 12—"The Fragility of Art"—to Chapter 9—"Poems of Parting." Yet it is noteworthy that certain aspects of the subject matter suggest a closeness of date. Thus, the "Promiscuity Poems" project an apprentice lover, with no fixed way in life, as do also the "Misogyny Poems" and "Poems of Rejection." Together, they suggest the mentality and concerns of a first lyric period, mellowing to experience in "The Compromise of Love."

Two radically different groupings, "The Structure of Love" and "The Marital Poems," grapple with the experience of commitment. Courtly love overrode, in the first poems, the sense of threat, immaturity, a questionable cosmos, even demonic seizure. These poems are more aggressively secular, with a theory of libido, a fresh dynamic of love, a careful neo-Platonic framework that serves as a scaffolding for the exorcism of demons. Such a drastic break in theme and plot suggests some break in Donne's life, such as his courtship and marriage with Anne More. By this reading, "The Good-Morrow," "The Sunne Rising," "The Anniversarie," and "The Canonization" form a stark, heart-rending sequence, recording Donne's marital experience.

Helen Gardner cites evidence from Prof. Praz that would date "The Sunne Rising" and "The Canonization" after the accession of James I; but we shall consider Prof. Praz' evidence, which we find open to question. So long a pause after his marriage suggests such a lag in poetic temperament, that firmer evidence seems called for not to date them with their manifest content, Donne's marriage. Despite the disagreement in this or that poem, however, the striking parallels in our sequences—though Helen Gardner's grounds are their stanzaic and philosophical complexity, ours the lyric plot—tend to support our more detailed groupings as offering recognizable stages in Donne's life, not autobiographically, but in terms of his concerns of spirit.

Our intent is not only to add a reading to Donne's poems, but to give body to this most elusive poet. Never establishing a career as a poet, Donne's poems project no clear persona. Nevertheless, his craggy presence is everywhere present—the skeptic, the fanatic, the evasive metaphysician—poems welling up in his trough of spirit. By our reading, Donne looms in his youth as a premature modern of astonishing talent, who carved out a solitary, secular destiny, until demands and perils made his position untenable. His secular life destroyed, he set about in a slow, skeptical, wilful path, still fanatic, still austerely truthful, to find an utter union with God. Other poets offer their limpid music, their sensuous immediacy, their mystical rapture. Donne overbears us by his presence, his lash of disbelieving truth, his sour debunking skepticism, his gargantuan laughter, his hunger for intimacy and dignity, his grasp of his immediate condition, his knowledge of what the price of change, and what the alternatives. This is a slow, sober force —for all his lashing wit—engaged in a race for intimacy against every caution of safety. Periodically, he flashes out sudden poems that illuminate his strong presence, bearing witness to a rage against all stations, and a resilience against all circumstances.

Our text in the love poems follows Sir Herbert J. C. Grierson's edition, *The Poems of John Donne* (London: Oxford University Press, 1912), Vol. I. In the religious poems, however, we follow Helen Gardner's edition, *John Donne: The Divine Poems* (London: Oxford University Press, 1952); as we follow her definitive rearrangement of the *Holy Sonnets* in our reading. I would also here express my appreciation to Alfred Kazin, with whom several early discussions helped open the subject, to Thomas Kranidas, whose careful reading of some of the material helped clarify my meaning, to Robert Voitle for his suggestions on bibliography, and to Maya Sharma, who helped with some research during its preparation.

# *Part I*

## *The Poet and His Craft*

# I

# The Metaphysical Shudder

Metaphysical poetry eludes definition;[1] yet many a group has oddly assorted characteristics. Quick speech, a bent for politics, and large blue eyes may characterize one family, starchy desserts and a need to be self-employed another. Not every designation requires a genus and a species. So we associate the truculent learnedness of the metaphysical poets, their sinewy music, strong lines, impassioned confrontations with large issues, distant conceits, colloquial speech, and a bent for religious experience. Seventeenth Century poets came in families—these were not "sons of Ben." No more definition may be possible, or necessary. Dryden's impatience, in the opening of his *Essay on Satire*, that Donne "perplexes the mind of the fair sex with nice speculations of philosophy," is simply what jarred Dryden. Salt does not define a heavily salted soup, though a dinner guest may only remark that flavor.

Yet we remain dissatisfied. A family need not be closely analyzed—willy-nilly the family remains; but why cluster Crashaw with Vaughan, and not Milton? Did their common vocation associate Donne and Herbert? Donne's friendship with Herbert's mother? Their colloquial speech? We seek structuring elements, not just a list of club rules. There was, after all, no club.

Samuel Johnson imprinted on metaphysical poetry an identity of style, finding a "discordia concors," where "the most heterogeneous ideas are yoked together; nature and art are ransacked for illustrations, comparisons, and allusions." This approach has, indeed, shaped their subsequent definition, in one or another element of style: imagery, language, logical devices, or what have you. Yet a style a bit narrowly defines a school of poetry. Wordsworth's stylistic innovations depicted experiences to which they were appropriate; but the experience characterizes him, not simply his style. T. S. Eliot, in his essay, varies Samuel Johnson's formulations: "Donne, and often Cowley, employs a device which is sometimes considered characteristically metaphysical; the elaboration (contrasted with the condensation) of a figure of speech to the farthest stage to which ingenuity can carry it." But we remain wary. Johnson couched his argument in a discussion of wit; Eliot was establishing a context for his innovations in sensibility. Strong creative minds will illuminate their concerns by their criticism. So each element of style singled out for definition has proven unsure. Given Seventeenth Century discipline in decorum, we are at least disposed to seek other elements to justify an innovation in style.

Speaking most simply, even a bit naively, they may have been metaphysical poets because metaphysics worried them. Certainly Donne, Herbert, Crashaw, Vaughan, and Traherne confronted religious commitments that had metaphysical implications. And even in Donne's love poetry, geographical restlessness, ranging wit, a cataloguing of modes of experience bespeak a mental force seeking deep stability. The song, "Goe, and Catche a Falling Starre," offers covert allusions to love experience: falling bodies to be caught—if the bodies of stars; feet to be cleft—if the feet of devils; female songs to be heard—if the songs of mermaids; hair—if aged and white. Its speaker, aloof, disdainful, is interested in love, but contemplates it from afar with harassed fascination. The poem is a temperamental gesture then, not a commitment to passion. Donne's solitary, regal spirit will not be pushed. Indeed, the poem involves not one, but two Donnes, as the lover asks the metaphysician to "Goe . . . catche . . . tell me . . . teach me . . ."

But surely if concerns of subject matter make a metaphysical poet, then why not Pope, Lucretius, Wallace Stevens? But we have in mind worries, and not simply concerns. No specific metaphysic binds our Seventeenth Century poets; yet they had strikingly parallel positions—embattled conservatives, projecting religious universes in a vast backwater of faith, the groundwork of their universe steadily undermined by experiment and skepticism. Small wonder that they appealed to T. S. Eliot, also a learned religious conservative in an age of radical doubt, helpless before discoveries he could not anticipate, nor humanize once arrived at. These temperamental concerns shaped their style. Hobbes and Newton may have shaped the coming tone of literary English; but its most stately utterance came from Sir Thomas Browne and Robert Burton, who worked under the wrenching advances of Galileo and Francis Bacon, their language burdened with ponderous concepts and charged words, whose structure was not the firmest.

These were metaphysical poets, then, in that the metaphysics they inherited was breaking up into elements of decor. So, in our own day, Wallace Stevens, a very conscious craftsman, varies broken iterations of metaphysics. Yet our criterion is too large. Wallace Stevens is not a metaphysical poet, nor was Milton (though his metaphysics was also crumbling). A metaphysical unsureness may have charged their language; but we sense in some elusive way it related to their egos, as it did not to Milton or Wallace Stevens.

We remark here a curious coincidence. This is the one movement in English poetry with ordained clergymen as its leaders, not as the perfunctory gesture of a Ben Jonson (reciting his verse to save his skin), or the aborted religious vocation of Milton (who shifted directly to poetry), but as the committed vocation to which they dedicated their lives—Donne, Herbert, and Traherne, dean, parson, and chaplain, Crashaw an exiled Catholic priest. It is no coincidence that Hopkins, again an ordained priest, most clearly resembles them among the moderns. When a man undertakes a new life stage, becoming the instrument and vessel of some mystic substance of grace, then metaphysics is, as it were, the raw material of his spirit, not simply an idea he ponders. He reshapes his ego around it, confronts it radically afresh, as Wordsworth confronted a meadow. Even the young Donne had religious exiles, saints, and martyrs in his family with whom to identify. Can we imagine Bishop Bloughram's own lines, rather than Browning's for him? Or Wordsworth's, were he literally a priest in some pantheistic church, and not simply a guide and a wayfarer into the wilderness? His passions might then have been more precipitous.

Milton confronted their problems of fundamental knowledge, but with another temper. In *Paradise Lost*, Raphael responds to Adam's perplexities by leisurely exhorting humility, not by harassed, broken answers:

> To ask or search I blame thee not, for Heav'n
> Is as the Book of God before thee set,
> Wherein to read his wondrous Works, and learne
> His Seasons, Hours, or Days, or Months, or Yeares;
> This to attain, whether Heav'n move or Earth,
> Imports not, if thou reck'n right; the rest
> From Man or Angel the great Architect
> Did wisely to conceal, and not divulge
> His secrets to be scann'd by them who ought
> Rather admire . . .
>
> (VIII, 66–75)

The uncertainty of Donne's *Anniversaries* is here, but not his stark unease. When Donne writes, in his Holy Sonnets:

> At the round earth's imagin'd corners, blow
> Your trumpets, Angells, and arise, arise
> From death, you numberless infinities
> Of soules . . .
>
> (IV, 1–4)

he impossibly, simultaneously grasps a finite and infinite world. This involves not only his poetic temperament, his freedom from the "dissociation of sensibility," as Eliot would have it, but his thrust at reality, his grasp at bewildering contradictions. The word "imagin'd" fuses impossible structural elements. The trumpets are literally blown at an imagined place. This assertion of reality in the teeth of bewilderment we call the metaphysical shudder. By it, we mean, a grasp at complex truth in a universe crumbling to bewilderment and triviality.

In this sense, Crashaw is a metaphysical poet. His elaborate Baroque imagery, pushed to "play on, that from excess of it, the imagination may sicken and so die," would in another poet merely decorate an emotion; but Crashaw is after God's body, not merely an emotional catharsis. His excesses of language, like Donne's "At the round earth's imagin'd corners," struggle to affirm an elusive yet literal truth in untrustworthy language. They reverberate with a metaphysical shudder. These men lunge, shift, and tramp about, confronting, suggesting, and relating to metaphysical mysteries with uncertain language.

Milton characteristically had only a moral shudder:

> The hungry Sheep look up, and are not fed,
> But swoln with wind, and the rank mist they draw,
> Rot inwardly, and foul contagion spread:
> Besides what the grim Woolf with privy paw
> Daily devours apace, and nothing sed,
> But that two-handed engine at the door
> Stands ready to smite once, and smite no more.
>
> (*Lycidas*, 125–131)

Suspense grips this passage, a shudder of unnamed horror, a mysterium in the present tense that rises to an implied menace, the more awesome for remaining unsaid. Such suspense on matters of faith, in direct relationship to his selfhood, would make Milton a metaphysical poet; but in matters of faith, Milton is never the harassed participant, only the omniscient, believing observer. Under eternity, no suspense is possible, nor any present tense. So, in *Paradise Lost*, in a moral challenge, we are with Abdiel, the participant, but in metaphysical obscurity, we are with Raphael, not Adam. So Milton's creation unrolls in a tapestry like a vast Rubens painting, with vivid immediacy, but from too Olympian a point of view to allow suspense. His panorama of creation stands in contrast to the starkly personal and immediate confrontation in Donne's "Goodfriday, 1613. Riding Westward." And even brief personal lyrics like "On His Blindness" have narrowly moral confrontations, characteristically rounded out in a dedicated resolve, not a shudder of metaphysical tumult, like

Donne's defiant close, "Death/thou shalt die." "Lycidas" ends with the uncouth Swain rising "to fresh woods and Pastures new," "On His Blindness" with the affirmation, "They also serve who only stand and wait," *Paradise Lost* with Adam chastened and reconciled to a life of alienation, all moral gestures.

This is not to find metaphysical poetry ridden with anxiety; yet even in their most exuberant fulfilment, they are forever, as it were, poking pillars in all directions, so as to hold firmly, however supported.[2] So "The Extasie" and "Aire and Angels" define the components of love. So "The Good-Morrow" and "The Sunne Rising," both poems of glorious love fulfilment, articulate geography, history, even their universes; they are witty exercises, while hammering out a stability and order. Little is taken for granted in their celebration of love.

Herein, T. S. Eliot is closer to metaphysical poetry than is Milton. *The Wasteland* also opens with a metaphysical shudder:

> April is the cruelest month, breeding
> Lilacs out of the dead land, mixing
> Memory and desire, stirring
> Dull roots with spring rain.

So Donne begins:

> Where, like a pillow on a bed,
>   A pregnant banke swel'd up, to rest
> The violets reclining head,
>   Sat we two, one anothers best.

Both settings transcend a pathetic fallacy, overflowing emotion and suspense in a charged quiescence in the mysterium of nature. By contrast, Milton's "On His Blindness" is thoroughly subjective, personal, inward, reserved. Milton is in doubt, his universe never. His poem breathes few metaphysical mysteries.

Yet despite his metaphysical concerns, Eliot is far from a metaphysical poet. Indeed, his self-conscious association with them has obscured metaphysical poetry by obscuring their lyric plot. The imponderables of the lyric plot, by contrast to the more straightforward narrative plot, curiously encroach on contemporary fiction and drama. Lacking the survey of an Aristotle, its ramifications are peculiarly baffling; yet the lyric plot is finally, quite simply, that experience whereby a recognizable personality arrives at self-knowledge or a catharsis of spirit in the poem. Thus, in "The Extasie," a couple courting in the field achieves sexual love. In "To a Daisie," Wordsworth, wandering, lost and disconsolate, contemplates a flower and absorbs "Some steady love, some brief delight."

Two aspects of the lyric plot, by contrast to the narrative, are relevant here, the immediacy of speaker to reader, and the merging of literal and subjective. Even a narrative plot has no absolute barrier between speaker and reader. If only by his tone of voice, his order of episodes, the items he allows in a description, a speaker establishes his own rapport with the reader; yet traditional fiction gives the illusion of clear, objective ground. Yet in a lyric plot, the poet has such personal force, he pales his action to triviality. Control is virtually impossible. Words like "life" and "death" can mean anything literally. Yet some experience remains, some gesture, some movement. Indeed, every poetic age has evolved its own decor for the lyric plot, its coherence of episode, the way in which the poet intrudes on his own poem.

Thus, *The Wasteland* offers no clear hero, but a nervous aura of disembodied presences, Marie, a frightened young girl, and a sailor at Mylae in "The Burial of the Dead," a flicker of "I"s in "A Game of Chess," male, female, rich, poor, the fisher-king, the Phoenician sailor, the mythic bisexual prophet and seer, Tiresias. Eliot has appended a footnote:

> Tiresias, although a mere spectator and not indeed a "character," is yet the most important personage in the poem, uniting all the rest. . . . What Tiresias *sees*, in fact, is the substance of the poem.

But how literally is this meant? Is the action of *The Wasteland* the activities described, or Tiresias' process of seeing? Is the wasteland of the poem a real world, or in his eyes? Who is finally to be washed clean by rain, the fisher-king or Tiresias? Is the final catharsis one of emancipation—"Know the truth, and the truth shall set you free"—or in submission to natural forces of cyclical renewal? If the latter, why is Tiresias more than just a chorus? And what has cyclical renewal to do with Apollonian clarity of vision? The manifold ambivalences are exceedingly murky; but all boil down to one ambivalence: Do we as readers identify with Tiresias, the visionary, or with the fisher-king, the impotent man of action? And if they are one, wherein lies their unity?

The solution must be that they slowly fuse and become one; as futility in action brings the healing redemption of vision. So, in *Burnt Norton*, the impulsive rush into the rose garden, the peering into the pool, becomes futile as the "cloud passed, and the pool was empty." Only later is it healed by the release of vision:

> Words, after speech, reach
> Into the silence. Only by the form, the pattern,
> Can words or music reach
> The stillness, as a Chinese jar still
> Moves perpetually in its stillness.

So the murky strands in *The Wasteland* are resolved as the fisher-king becomes Tiresias. But this solution is only a plot construct, not our felt experience reading. *The Wasteland* has an awareness, a pain, a charged sensitivity, a flickering of presences, but no palpable defined persona, and therefore no real risk, only its atmosphere. Tiresias is nowhere in any danger. We don't know where to find him to begin with.

This divided persona underlies Eliot's poetry. His lyric plot is typically a dilemma between an action and a vision, a fisher-king and a Tiresias, the final and correct choice being the vision. So, in "The Love Song of J. Alfred Prufrock," a lifetime of futile visits to interminable soirées resolves itself, not in decisive action, but in a sudden clarity of vision: "No! I am not Lord Hamlet nor was meant to be":

> I grow old . . . I grow old . . .
> I shall wear the bottoms of my trousers rolled.

Here, the shift from futile gesture to a grasp of reality shapes its plot, its hero, Prufrock, a querulous, fussy male spinster, delicate of taste, in an uneasy, futile eagerness for company.

In "La Figlia che Piange," another early poem, the conflict is again between action and vision. The lovely lady wishes a young man to climb an outdoor staircase to her; but the poet, in the first person singular, would separate them to sustain the scene. He has pangs of doubt—"I wonder how they should have been together!"—but resolves it—"I should have lost a gesture and a pose." The vision is not of his reality, as in "Prufrock," or religious witness, as in *The Wasteland*, but a purely aesthetic gesture and pose. Nevertheless the choice is between action and vision, with two men, the hesitant lover and the poet, not one Prufrock, whose vision of truth replaces his futile gesture. And here also, the seer finally dominates the poem, not the man of futile gestures.

So, *The Wasteland* has, in a variety of guises, two men, the young man, hesitant before participation, and the visionary, Tiresias, who sees all. The "small house agent's clerk" may have intercourse with the spinster typist; but the gesture is as loveless a futility as Prufrock's conversations with women who ". . . come and go/Talking of Michaelangelo." And at the house agent's clerk's sexual encounter is Tiresias—"I too awaited the expected guests"—who afterward visited:

> where the walls
> Of Magnus Martyr hold
> Inexplicable splendour of Ionian white and gold.

We have the same two men, the choice, the mode of resolution.

The double hero muddies the ending of *The Wasteland*. Clearly, the fisher-king says:

> I sat upon the shore
> Fishing, with the arid plain behind me
> Shall I at least set my lands in order?

But who says:

> These fragments I have shored against my ruins
> Why then Ile fit you. Hieronimo's mad againe.

More likely Tiresias, who "foresuffered all"—the delinquent king has state business at hand, and can ill afford to shore up ruins with fragmentary runes.

Yet *The Wasteland* advances Eliot toward the *Four Quartets*. "The Love Song of J. Alfred Prufrock" is sharply focused, with one hero, one setting, one occasion. "La Figlia che Piange" has an apparent scene, the outdoor stairway parting the two lovers; but the bent of the poem suggests that everything is projected in the poet's imagination. So it begins with a series of imperatives, suggesting a stage setting, the director ordering roles and stage gestures:

> Stand on the highest pavement of the stair—
> Lean on a garden urn—
> Weave, weave the sunlight in your hair—
> Clasp your flowers to you with a pained surprise—

Indeed, this couching of the poem in the poet's imagination altogether differs from the use of imagination in the Romantic poets. When Keats evokes the nightingale in "Ode to a Nightingale," it is not luminously clear where reality yields to Keats' imagination; but the opening stanza couches his flight of imagination in a specific moment, gesture, person, with all of him engaged. There is no nonsense about:

> My heart aches, and a drowsy numbness pains
>   My sense, as though of hemlock I had drunk,
> Or emptied some dull opiate to the drains
>   One minute past, and Lethe-wards had sunk:

By contrast, the oblique imperative of "Stand on the highest pavement of the stair—/Lean on a garden urn . . ." only implies a speaker. The location of the poem is tenuous; there is not a whole person, but a detached imagination, with even a flavor of wistfulness, of subdued poignance, of disengagement. One uneasily mistrusts how much he really knows.

Eliot has rightly been praised for his grasp of reality; but his fresh aesthetic is equally striking. The early poems are pervaded by a staged imagination. He mentions newspapers, chimney pots, coffee stands; but his wash of easy city music drains them of particularity. He renders Eighteenth Century cityscapes, not hard, documentary realism, moods, not substantial hard things. Even the famous image:

> When the evening is spread out against the sky
> Like a patient etherised upon a table;

is no more objective than "My love is like a red, red rose." What it establishes is Prufrock's mood, who often went home from a soirée feeling "like a patient etherized upon a table." So the "one-night cheap hotels/And sawdust restaurants with oyster shells" are stylized renderings, not specific houses with blocked plumbing and bedbugs:

So Eliot is celebrated for the moody perceptivity of:

> I am aware of the damp souls of housemaids
> Sprouting despondently at area gates.

But that very poem, "Morning at the Window," ends with the figure:

> And tear from a passer-by with muddy skirts
> An aimless smile that hovers in the air
> And vanishes along the level of the roofs.

This smile, of a passer-by of wisdom and taste, is in the style of a Chagall painting, enjoying the scene by the roofs, but not a part of it.

So "Burbank with a Baedeker: Bleistein with a Cigar" has a wholly theatrical artificiality, a sort of simplified *Tales of Hoffmann:*

> Burbank crossed a little bridge
> Descending at a small hotel;
> Princess Volupine arrived.
> They were together, and he fell.

Style changes in musical comedy. These poems seem dated in a way "The Love Song of J. Alfred Prufrock" does not. I personally have never seen a "meagre, blue-nailed, phthisic hand," nor would I be jarred if I did. His poem is no real world, but a miniature to be savored and enjoyed, a bit campy, like a fine old operetta. Victorian commitment would only be gauche here.

So "Sweeney Erect" begins with a stage director's orders:

Paint me a cavernous waste shore
  Cast in the unstilled Cyclades,
Paint me the bold anfractuous rocks
  Faced by the snarled and yelping sea.

So operatic stagecraft pervades "Sweeney Among the Nightingales":

The circles of the stormy moon
  Slide westward toward the River Plate
Death and the Raven drift above
  And Sweeney guards the hornèd gate.

These poems remain, quite simply, in the poet's imagination. So, with no circumlocution, "The Hippopotamus" and "Whispers of Immortality" piece out the mental processes of T. S. Eliot.

But this early aesthetic, recalling Paris, Switzerland, and the low countries in the Twenties, becomes murky with portentous change in *The Wasteland*. Stage and wings change perspective, as Eliot reduces all characters not to two, but to one, Tiresias, the man of vision, from whom all characters more or less proliferate. The stage front occasions still flicker from character to character, but with the seer, Tiresias, vicariously participating. And his felt presence, the visionary poet, dignified and personalized, pervades the *Four Quartets*. Without a name, Eliot's speaker calmly testifies:

I do not know much about gods; but I think the river
Is a strong brown god—sullen, untamed and intractable,
Patient to some degree, at first recognised as a frontier . . .

This underlying plot structures Eliot's poems. His speaker, the witty visionary and subtle believer, renders experience with a dazzled poignance, never raw, but paced, stylized, with Klee's enigmatic ease, the muted torment of Ensor—not simply "Sketches," but "Preludes," not "A Windy Night," but "Sketches on a Windy Night," études, disembodied smiles, grotesque witchery, gliding from the trivial participant to the encompassing seer.

In the early poems, this gesture of stagecraft is projected

with simple harmony, as in "La Figlia che Piange." So, late in "Preludes," the poet intrudes in one couplet:

> I am moved by fancies that are curled
> Around these images, and cling:

But in *The Wasteland*, the scene is becoming cluttered with:

> . . . empty bottles, sandwich papers,
> Silk handkerchiefs, cardboard boxes, cigarette ends
> Or other testimony of summer nights.

Fragmentary, congested scenes pile on one another. The stage gesture has little charm. So, in "The Hollow Men," it thins to its dead bones. And in "Ash-Wednesday," we have only the seer, no stage setting, no prelude, no rhapsody, but the experience of conversion:

> Because I do not hope to turn again
> Because I do not hope
> Because I do not hope to turn
> Desiring this man's gift and that man's scope
> I no longer strive to strive towards such things . . .

Actual incident, actual social engagement, the risk and drama of occasion has left us—indeed, it was never more than a sterile gesture. Now all time is our occasion:

> Because I know that time is always time
> And place is always and only place
> And what is actual is actual only for one time
> And only for one place
> I rejoice that things are as they are and
> I renounce the blessèd face
> And renounce the voice
> Because I cannot hope to turn again
> Consequently I rejoice . . .

In the *Four Quartets*, Eliot's poetic hero is simply the engaged visionary, overflowing his sensibility. Indeed, the *Four Quartets* loosely echoes the epic mode. In each quartet, after the moment of ultimate mystical attunement, he discusses the clumsiness of words, exhibiting his wounds, as it were, like an epic hero in war games after the supreme encounter:

So here I am, in the middle way, having had twenty years—
Twenty years largely wasted, the years of *l'entre deux guerres*—
Trying to learn to use words, and every attempt
Is a wholly new start, and a different kind of failure
Because one has only learnt to get the better of words
For the thing one no longer has to say, or the way in which
One is no longer disposed to say it. And so each venture
Is a new beginning, a raid on the inarticulate
With shabby equipment always deteriorating
In the general mess of imprecision of feeling,
Undisciplined squads of emotion.

Eliot's basic lyric plot, the dialectic between specific action and universal vision, pervaded modern poetry until some twenty years ago. So Yeats, in "To the Rose upon the Rood of Time," struggled between "common things that crave," and his "Red Rose, proud Rose, sad Rose of all my days." Later, in "Sailing to Byzantium," he journeys from the land of fertility, where he is a sterile gesture, "A tattered coat upon a stick," to Byzantium, for a form beyond daily process:

. . . such a form as Grecian goldsmiths make
Of hammered gold and gold enameling
To keep a drowsy emperor awake.

So Ezra Pound, in "E. P. Pour L'election de son Sepulchre," keeps blandly silent as Mr. Nixon pins him down in particularities of fashion. So Wallace Stevens would surmount congested particularities, be the Man with the Blue Guitar:

A. A violent order is disorder; and
B. A great disorder is an order. These
Two things are one. (Pages of illustrations.)

Even Robert Frost, locked on a sparse Vermont farm, feels the tug of vision and play, though submitting to more pedestrian wills, his neighbor in "Mending Wall," the professional woodchopper in "Two Tramps in Mud Time," his horse in "Stopping by Woods on a Snowy Evening." Frost sticks with Vermont, the "country of old men," though it offers few enough "fish, flesh, or fowl." Only William Carlos Williams self-consciously resisted this core plot, and became more recently seminal.

The underlying tension of the early moderns, the surge to universal perception against the tug of small, particular occasions, has nothing whatever to do with metaphysical poetry. Indeed, if anything, it is its polar opposite. Yet metaphysical poetry was reexplored during the early modern period, when Eliot found the wit, enigmatic invention, and fused sensibility that might emancipate him from particularities of self and situation for his poetic vision. Such an emancipation was the last thing the metaphysical poets ever dreamed of in their lyrics. They wanted no vista of salvation, but the thing itself. No universal presence teased, fascinated, and absorbed them—the bard, Tiresias, Fergus the Druid, an eternal bird of hammered gold and gold enameling, the Man with the Blue Guitar. Locked in a particular here and now, they remained flesh and blood, limited men, who wanted salvation, sex, love, power, self-assertion, fulfilment, the body of God—forever Jack Donne, George Herbert, Henry Vaughan—educated, ambitious, alienated, difficult believers, perverse pounds of flesh. They shared some freight of learning with the early modern period, the malaise of a reality with no tailored solutions. More basically, in some obscure way, they had their respect. But there one draws the line. The modern period struggled for some universal plateau; these men were in a fix, not that their brains were befuddled, but their souls were in a jam. Their lyric poems groped for a strategy; if the strategy of a vision worked, well and good.

Their strategy determined the scope and quality of their catharsis. Both the metaphysical poets and the early moderns wanted personal fulfilment; yet Yeats, struggling to arrive at a plateau of universal expression, did not complete "Sailing to Byzantium" with his arrival at Byzantium. That occurred at the end of Stanza 2. He then went on to delineate the quality of its universal vision, to have:

> . . . such a form as Grecian goldsmiths make
> Of hammered gold and gold enamelling
> To keep a drowsy Emperor awake;
> Or set upon a golden bough to sing
> To lords and ladies of Byzantium
> Of what is past, or passing, or to come.

His catharsis lay in his destiny on the singing platform larger than and indifferent to his private self. Herbert, struggling in *Love* to arrive at the home of love, ended his poem with the words, "So I did sit and eat." Nothing remains to be said, once the personal need is satisfied.

This sense of a plateau of universal vision gives exaggerated emphasis to Eliot's essay, "Tradition and the Individual Talent." The essay valuably explores the autonomous activity of poetry, its existence, as it were, on a plateau of poetic matters in communication with one another, as if the Jungian concept of "the collective unconscious" were a peculiarly literary location. Our private lives struggle for personal fortune; but as creative artists, like catalysts we render the traditions and tensions about us.

Indeed, Eliot's very contrast of "feeling" and "emotion" in his essay distinguishes private fortune from public material. His terms remain undefined; but it seems tolerably clear that by emotion he means a flow of feeling under the grip of personal, half-fulfilled hungers, ongoing personal rhythms that trammel a man's ego. By feeling, he refers to awarenesses, intuitions, sentiments, fleeting memories, and muted emotions a man need only participate in, what we generally mean by sensibility. Two aspects of feelings make them most suitable for poetry. Firstly, they are more flexible than emotions, and can be shaped to the needs of one's creation. Secondly, they are not suspect, as are emotions, as engendered by personal hungers that have nothing to do with poetic values. Feelings are, as it were, emotions without ego.

Insofar as Eliot detaches and makes autonomous aesthetic judgment, the act of creation from the act of simple self-assertion, his essay is salutary reading. Writers are too prone to self-indulgence and sentimentality in their public performances. But the functioning of the ego is exceedingly slippery, nor its detachment to be leaned on with any security. Too much humility has rested on pride, stood fortified by a docile content, for self-transcendence to be trusted. Certainly a poet must express common feeling in the grip of creation; but what achieves transcendence is not his blanking out his emotions, but his force in fusing them into a poem, indeed, the bind and autonomy of his lyric plot.

To speak specifically of Eliot, his core plot is the process of transcending the particular, private self to arrive onto a plateau of universality. His essay, "Tradition and the Individual Talent," is therefore a theoretical justification of his own lyric plot, where again and again, he engages in a grand gesture of self-transcendence. But the metaphysical poets had a vastly different lyric plot, one with a large element of self-assertion, fusing and embedding their own emotions, the knot of their egos, into their own poems.

The overpowering presences of Eliot and Yeats swept away all perspective on their core plot. Hence the ongoing definitions of metaphysical poetry by Ramist logic or what have you —each stylistic device embarrassed by its spotty use, by parallels in Jonson and Milton, by its long antecedents suddenly, mysteriously flaring up, by the paucity of tight evidence in criticism of the period, by the varied usages of the metaphysical poets themselves, leaving us with statistical counts of usages, differences of degree that lead nowhere. But *ab initio*, we mistrust the definition of a poetic work by a stylistic device. Hairdressers and seamstresses work in this way. Our concern is not to hit on the key device in a metaphysical poem, but to intuit its unique structure, how it differs from the Elizabethans, the Romantics, the Victorians, the Moderns, its presumptions of character, its catharsis, and the price paid.

We have distinguished the metaphysical poets from the moderns; but our distinction would seem to identify them with the Romantics, particularly Wordsworth—their most programmatic leader—who also, in a pinch of moody, urban estrangement, sought communion with nature, as Donne sought communion in bed with his mistress, in the bridal chamber with his bride, or in chapel with his God. How then do their plots differ?

Wordsworth is not an easy poet to come to terms with. He irritated Keats, and a good many sensitive men. Where other poets traced the life of Adam, Don Juan, the Red Cross Knight, he traced the life of William Wordsworth. Yet John

Stuart Mill found his work healing. He served somehow as a poetic priest, where broader talents simply wrote poems. Indeed, we revere him for evoking a bountiful source of communion in the expanse of nature, dangling wafers of secular communion in "A presence that disturbs me with the joy/ Of elevated thoughts." This has superficial analogies to the Holy Spirit of Donne and Herbert; but Donne, an actual priest, never wrote lyric poems as a priestly service, but simply recorded his struggles with faith, talking to one person (if only himself), not to a flock. His minor poems are never testimonials. So the quieter poems of *The Temple* suggest an impersonal religious experience, a source to be tapped, like Wordsworth's Lake District; but the floor, the altar, the holy days are only its instruments. At the catharsis itself, in "Love," "The Pulley," "The Collar," the Holy Spirit addresses one man, George Herbert. Like Donne's, his catharsis is a private one.

A curious result of this is that religious experience, to the metaphysicals, is exceedingly sexy; the experience of nature to Wordsworth is at most motherly. Wordsworth never flirts with nature; he only, as it were, drinks from its bosom. Even Herbert, the most serene of the metaphysicals, wrote a minuet of courtship:

> Love bade me welcome; yet my soul drew back,
>   Guilty of dust and sin.
> But quick-ey'd Love, observing me go slack
>   From my first entrance in,
> Drew nearer to me, sweetly questioning,
> If I lack'd anything.
>
> A guest, I stammered, worthy to be here:
>   Love said, you shall be he.
> I the unkind, the ungrateful? Ah my dear,
>   I cannot look on thee.
> Love took my hand, and smiling did reply,
>   Who made the eyes but I.

Here the gentle Herbert. The more passionately tumultuous Donne finished one *Holy Sonnet:*

> Take mee to you, imprison mee, for I
> Except you'enthrall mee, never shall be free,
> Nor ever chast, except you ravish mee.

As for Crashaw, his identification with St. Theresa, dying as her bloody heart is pierced by the dart of her savior, is charming.

This is not to snicker, from a more secular vantage point, at the religious dimension of their experience. Sexual allusions are exceedingly frequent in metaphysical poetry; but there is some presumption in dissolving a metaphor into a rationalization. What is indisputable about sexual experience, however, is its personal, private quality. The marriage ceremony may require a communal priest; in the bridal chamber, he is surely superfluous. So the metaphysical poets wanted an immediate, private experience, with God their sweetheart, God their savior, God their father and mother, God their gift of grace and object of love—all experiences agreeable to the sexual metaphor. To Wordsworth's more public experience, the sexual metaphor is an embarrassment, an oral regression, if not a regression to the womb. Indeed, it simply does not apply.

This psychological dynamic fundamentally distinguishes the metaphysicals from the Romantics, matters of poetic technique then following. For lack of better, we shall use a Freudian term—though carefully qualified—in saying Wordsworth wrote essentially "id" poetry. By this we mean nothing narrowly sexual—metaphysical poetry was much sexier. But Wordsworth saw redemption and renewal in contact with a large, semi-personal entity, vast, unplumbed, mysterious, which he touched and flowed into, essentially the experience of establishing contact in classical analysis, where the id is not flirted with, but communed with. The id lives in an oceanic, limitless way, with no separate self that one can seduce, fight, and come to terms with, only a presence to tap and enter into. In this sense, Wordsworth wrote id poetry, in his sources of renewal and the dynamic of their attainment.

Shelley's "Hymn to Intellectual Beauty" suggests that such another "unseen Power/Floats though unseen among us," a large, impersonal, boundless entity, alive, yet above life, vast, unplumbed, mysterious, that he taps, joins, participates with, is dedicated to, yet never absorbs or makes his own; as Wordsworth only participates with Nature. In this sense, "Hymn to Intellectual Beauty" is another id poem. Indeed, the sense of an immanent, free-floating force, wind, or presence, elemental, yet in some sense alive, that he can commune with, runs through Shelley's most vivid lyrics; the "Ode to the West Wind," "The Cloud," "To Night." So in "To a Skylark," he ends by asking the skylark:

> Teach me half the gladness
> That thy brain must know,
> Such harmonious madness
> From my lips would flow
> The world should listen then—as I am listening now.

This is not to question the intrinsic message of these poems, the Platonic overtones of "Hymn to Intellectual Beauty," the inherent zest of a moving cloud, a bird song. But the parallel plot structure, whatever the immediate subject, is arresting, invoking a source of life, power, or inspiration, to be tapped by some gesture of harmonious rapport. This we call id poetry. So Keats' "Ode to Psyche," "To a Nightingale," "To a Grecian Urn," even the "Ode to Autumn."

Indeed, such an id poetry is not surprising during the Romantic period. The impersonal, mathematical entity of the Newtonian universe does not lend itself to personal relatedness. One must be quite mystical to feel a flow of oneness with a universal natural force that has no consciousness. Indeed, our sense of a universal nature grew steadily more alien and complex through the century. Darwin, Nietzsche, and Freud each pulled pegs from under the Romantic movement. A common charge against the Romantics, that of the pathetic fallacy, is not an entirely honest accusation. Yeats' identification with the Druids has not been attacked, to my knowledge, because the critic does not believe in Druids, nor is the problem of the pathetic fallacy insurmountable. It was the core plot of Romantic poetry that fell into disfavor, due to shifts in temperament, the depersonalization of the Newtonian system, fresh modes of going at truth. Another core plot then emerged in the work of Pound, Eliot, and Yeats, one equally alien to the metaphysicals, too pinched in their personal situation for nightingales, clouds, skylarks, and daisies to offer them fountains of inspiration.

From this, we advance our grasp of metaphysical poetry another notch. By contrast with Wordsworth, the metaphysical poets—we speak preeminently of Donne—wrote ego poetry, that is, the poetry that expressed a conscious mind, coming to terms with the reality about it. He is not cut off from id, superego, or aught else; but such elements are grasped in his consciousness, in the situation at hand, as he comes to terms with it. The poem takes place in a situation, a particular here and now to be assessed and worked with. Its meaningful grasp and resolution in sexual pleasure, love, self-respect, a relationship with God, or simply truth—that is the catharsis of the metaphysical poem.

Hence their striking beginnings, their plunges *in medias res*. The metaphysical lyric is not a set-piece, as often with the Victorians, but an event to be mastered. As Shakespeare's contemporary, Donne had the deepest sense of drama in his bones.[3] His poems begin in a life situation, attempting to grasp what is going on. Hence his stabbing attempts at assessment:

> I wonder by my troth, what thou, and I
> Did till we lov'd?

> Now thou hast lov'd me one whole day,
> To morrow when thou leav'st, what wilt thou say?

> Busie old foole, unruly sunne,
> Why dost thou thus,
> Through windowes, and through curtaines call on us?

Hence the stabbing out anywhere for an analogy, a correspondence. For the ego works thus in actual bewildering situations. Hence the colloquial language, speech in the present tense; as particular situations are being resolved:

> *Love*, any devill else but you,
> Would for a given Soule give something too.

This sense of its more open psychology distinguishes metaphysical from Elizabethan poetry. Indeed, not until the Seventeenth Century could ego poetry in this sense be written. Given a massive world view, a process of salvation, the linkage of soul to soul in society, the superego was too fixed to be redefined, reshaped, and assimilated. At his best, the poet came to terms with it. But once Bacon and Hobbes questioned the structures of faith, structure was no longer a given. Indeed, only during this twilight period, when the old cosmological structure was undermined, and the Newtonian structure not yet systematized, was metaphysical poetry possible.

In this sense, Ralegh's poem, "The Lie," anticipated metaphysical poetry, not in its techniques of imagery or colloquial speech, but in his situation, an aristocrat, like Donne, refusing to come to terms with the fabric of society. His is still a social, not a metaphysical shudder; but affirming his indestructible soul, he affirms his ego as supreme judge of social truth:

> Goe, soul, the body's guest,
> Upon a thankless arrant.
> Fear not to touch the best;
> The truth shall be thy warrant.
> Go, since I needs must die,
> And give the world the lie.
>
> Say to the court, it glows
> And shines like rotten wood;
> Say to the church, it shows
> What's good, and doth no good:
> If church and court reply,
> Then give them both the lie. . . .
>
> So when thou hast, as I
> Commanded thee, done blabbing,
> Because to give the lie
> Deserves no less than stabbing,
> Stab at thee he that will,
> No stab the soul can kill.

The most enigmatic parallel to metaphysical poetry is contemporary poetry. I recall once asking a young figure painter, who rendered simplified, stylized figures, why today no serious painter attempts Michaelangelo's heroic warriors, patriarchs, and archangels. He replied, "Man just isn't that important; why look at him that hard?" He paused, then added, "Only a fink would paint like Michaelangelo today." His remarks suggest a decorum of minimal statement and veracity to private, immediate sensibility. His subject gets as much attention as the man in real life. By it, William Carlos Williams also characteristically renders a fragmentary episode, an attitude, and no more.

The parallel to metaphysical poetry is illuminating. As metaphysical poetry flowered when structures of ideas came into question, so contemporary poetry when the uses of language are no longer trusted. Robert Creeley entitled his book, *Words*, precisely because words cannot be taken for granted, just as Donne wrote metaphysical poetry in a mistrust of metaphysics. Indeed, much current poetry could be retitled, not *Words*, but *Anti-Words*. It expresses what we may call a "communication shudder." So Duncan begins a poem with a flat sentence—but with no subject or verb, "Only passages of a poetry, no more." Evidently, communication evokes a queasy misgiving, a withdrawal, a minimal attempt, more extreme that Eliot's, who felt poetry a "raid on the inarticulate/ With shabby equipment always deteriorating/In the general mess of imprecision . . ." Eliot sensed his verbal equipment was shabby, but at least felt himself on a raid. But the purposive implications of the word "raid" are no longer self-evident when one uses words.

This mistrust, grounded in the ersatz intimacy of our mass media, has its roots in the peculiar implications of the common noun. Ideally, common nouns designate classes of experiences, the word "horse" any horse, light or dark, tall or short. Thus exceedingly particular experiences break into proper nouns, just as a particular horse has its name, not just "horse." In a love relationship, the designation, "girl," surely gives way to "Mary" or "Jane." The use of common nouns bound in syntactical sentences suggests a plateau of language experience at some remove from life experience, however vividly rendered. Language is, in this sense, a diversion of attention, "emotion recollected in tranquility." Experience at its heat calls for grunts, shrieks, name-calling, signs, curses, not syntactical renderings of common nouns in organized sentences.

This plateau of language is precisely what contemporary poetry finds suspect. The word today is a cliché, not trusted at a distance from experience. The slogan, "no ideas except in things," rejects not so much ideas per se, as structures embodied in words. The experience demands a maximum of immediacy.

This mistrust of syntactical language takes two opposing, yet related directions. On the one hand, if words are mistrusted as referents, they remain a *Ding-an-sich*, as in projectivist poetry, not structured evocations of experience, but themselves a structure of experience, to be grasped on its merits, like minimal sculpture, real in and unto themselves. This is suggested by Duncan's "Structure of Rime XXIII":

> Only passages of a poetry, no more. No matter how many times the cards are handled and laid out to lay out their plan of the future—a fortune—only passages of what is happening. Passages of moonlight upon the floor.
>
> Let me give you an illusion of grieving. In the room at the clean sweep of moonlight a young man stands looking down. An agony I have spoken of overtakes him, waves of loss and return.
>
> But he would withdraw from the telling. We cannot tell whether rage (which rimes) of grief shakes him. Let me give you an illusion of not grieving.

The opposite reaction is to keep words simple and close to actual experience, render language virtually as it is happening, almost as a sign, now that its symbolic functions are suspect. So William Carlos Williams offers here only the grace note of a small particular experience:

> I have eaten
> the plums
> that were in
> the icebox
>
> and which
> you were probably
> saving
> for breakfast
>
> Forgive me
> they were delicious
> so sweet
> and so good.

This poem has a clean ring. Donne's lines, by contrast, fork about, structure up in spines, tense into suggestive reverberations that hold only so much weight. To Donne, words were still magically charged, with an enormous freight of categories, correspondences, and allusions, though no longer grounded in a stable structure of order. Williams, by contrast, is limpidly casual. The charge has gone out of his language. Words unto themselves have at most a moronic clobber. Only the gesture remains, the imprint of spirit, the immediate experience. So Williams' poem is a gesture washed clean of allusions. Indeed, to anticipate our conclusions, whereas Donne's lyrics are, in a sense, metaphysical gestures, establishing the poet in the here-and-now of his situation, Williams' lyrics are psychic gestures, rendering in words a particular impulse in the here-and-now of experience.

Two implications are worth exploring in Williams' poem, relevant to metaphysical poetry. One is the breakdown of syntax in the language, the other the breakdown of poetic conventions. Thus, there is no punctuation, since a gesture is being rendered, not a meaning. The one word capitalized, "Forgive," indicates not a new sentence, but a change in gesture, a lifting of the eyes, as it were. The word "they" in the next line is not capitalized, though it could begin a new sentence, since its direction is the same. This breakdown in syntax, so mild here, is carried to extremes in current poetry, where phrase is often laid on phrase, with no clear relationship to one another save by their juxtaposition. But the poetic conventions also break down. No meter is used, no rhyme, no images. The apparent title, "This Is Just to Say," flows into the poem as part of its text. Lines are not capitalized. Their break seems intended to keep the poem completely casual, so that thought does not pause with the line break. Indeed, this poem seems so stripped of poetic conventions, we have only a list of negatives.

And yet, Williams' poem does magically reweave poetic conventions. First of all, each line begins at the same indentation, rather than scattered about the page. Each has at most three words. The first two stanzas, each of four lines, expresses a falling gesture, the third its rising response, giving the gesture suavity. And somehow the extreme brevity of the lines suggests extraordinary attention. In general, poetic lines, one under the other, can suggest parallel importance in content.

By using exceedingly short, even one-word lines, the poet freights every word with enormous value. By having a line, "and which," with only a conjunction and a pronoun, he suspends the entire poem in the simultaneity of a single small gesture. Indeed, this structuring of the poem by weight of emphasis may bear on the capitalization of "Forgive," not to begin a sentence or a stanza, but for solidity and weight. The entire poem is an apology, rising to "Forgive," capitalized as one stands up and doffs one's hat, out of courtesy.

This fusion of language and experience lies behind many stylistic devices of the metaphysical poets. Thus their mechanical or learned imagery, while avoiding classical images, suggests not so much an arresting "hit" or conceit, but the thinking process of an intelligent person in a jam. To speak personally, in an actual problem, I am most unlikely to fish for a solution in stories of Zeus or Apollo; but I might well speculate on how a compass moves. The metaphysical image is only a far-fetched conceit as a literary convention; in relationship to the thinking process, classical allusions are far-fetched, learned and mechanical images habitual and close at hand. An analogy to Zeus is, in this sense, rhetorical, an analogy to a compass ratiocinative.

This juncture of language and the experience it expresses, its simultaneity with its gesture, clarifies Donne's colloquial speech, his rough meter, his extraordinary inventiveness of stanza form. Colloquial English is supremely in the spoken present tense. Its use in print, in the past tense, is a sentimental self-indulgence. Its use in the present tense in the wash of a situation, gives the bite of immediacy. Wordsworth's doctrine of poetry as "emotion recollected in tranquility" may suggest the acceptance and release he seeks in poetry. The metaphysical poets had other hungers in mind. Indeed, a colloquial expletive might begin a lyric to shake up the placidity of words on paper. "I wonder by my troth" and "For God sake hold your tongue" are the opposite of emotion recollected in tranquility. They are, as it were, "see-it-now" poems, in the heat of immediacy, without the amplitude of the past tense.

The action in the poem expresses the same immediacy as its language. Here, again, style only reflects essential movement, the lyric plot. Donne's "The Flea" has as its action the killing of the flea after line 18, beginning Stanza 3. But there must be some gesture between Stanzas 1 and 2 that shifts the poem from a witty analogy to the sudden plea beginning Stanza 2: "Oh stay, three lives in one flea spare." Clearly she has placed her nail down, pinning the flea, in response to his conceit in Stanza 1, just as its actual killing begins Stanza 3. The poem is, then, highly dramatic, with three speeches by a man, attempting to seduce a woman, and two responding gestures, as she gradually kills a blood-laden flea. He finally refuses to capitulate; but delicate, wilful, and wildly witty, he is utterly ineffectual, the adolescent dandy, attempting a seduction[4] by an absurd conceit, marching on in his arguments after she kills his analogy. In her gesture, she symbolically kills him, reducing him, by analogy, to a flea who only wanted her drop of virginal blood. But the flea was killed for his pains, while the ineffectual dandy only remained stranded in his wit. I would speculate that the poem ends with a third gesture, a snort of triumphant indifference and renewed flirtatious conversation, as *la ronde* continues.

And yet the speaker does not capitulate at the end. Nowhere is his stanza broken. He has all the language, she all the action. He plays for her blood in a seduction; she draws his blood in the flea. He has all the wit; she all the effectiveness. At the end, he retains his style; she, alas, retains her content. Is the poem a robust laughter at ineffectual conceit in wooing, or a celebration of style in defiance of circumstance? Whatever one's attitude, the poem is simultaneous with its experience, as on a stage. Its experience is its very sinew.

Indeed, Donne's rough squaring-off of accent to meter, his complex stanzaic structures, at times purely architectural, to be grasped as large slammed-down units, suggest this same impact of experience. They resemble the brushstrokes of an impassioned painter—a Van Gogh or a Gauguin—slamming down units that blend because of his visionary grasp, with the very smack of immediacy.

One last implication worth exploring in the Williams poem is its casually taking for granted the entire person of the speaker. His selfhood is never defined. Contemporary lyric poetry is, in this sense, post-Freudian. It renders episodes, gestures, attitudes; but what of the ego? The uses of that cliché are slippery, illusory, trivial, its brushstrokes heavy-handed, attempting too much. Metaphysical poetry, by implication, and often explicitly, always defines its ego, where and what it does, what it wants, what its chances are for basic fulfilment. It is existential, which contemporary poetry is not. Clearly, then, the contemporary poets shared the metaphysicals' consuming sense of particularities and immediacies. They generally lack their totality, where the entire person is at stake, defining his environment in the gesture of establishing it.

Donne is exceedingly evasive, sometimes exasperatingly so. He does not establish his own point of view in "The Flea" with the clarity of Keats in his lyrics. Yet this is appropriate to ego poetry, where the ego is so guarded and tentative. Yet Donne's selfhood remains in his poems, but on their fringes, aristocratically aloof, guardedly there. His poems, then, are metaphysical gestures, each establishing a personal order in a blurry chaos. Donne has gone somewhat out of fashion. Once admired for his daring techniques, his fused sensibility, his temperament was then found too disruptive and harassed. But so was Hamlet's; yet who would exchange him for Brutus? Donne's rhetorical excesses, his driven logic, his poseur affrontery, had Hamlet's temperament, fencing verbally while he sniffed about the establishment. So Donne hung between Catholicism and the Anglican Church, scholasticism and sexual license, university, church, and empire. But in that sustained ambiguity, he wrote the first uncompromising ego poetry in our tradition; and who after him was his equal? So his irritable evasiveness and tumultuous casting-about has a charismatic magnificence. By our reading, only his "Hymn to God my God, in My Sickness" brought his temperament to a stasis. But this he thought his death-bed poem.

Indeed, the Oedipal elements in Donne's temperament are so abundant as to embarrass long scrutiny, his father's death when he was four, his mother's remarriage six months after the funeral, his thrashing about for a poetic model in love or in faith, his secret and disastrous marriage, his abandonment of his mother church to be dean in a church that oppressed it.

More directly pertinent here, the trauma in Donne's career found a metaphysical compensation. Quite simply, his ambition for a secular career, cut off by his indiscreet marriage, was finally compensated by a second career in the ministry. What he could not resolve in relationship to the state, he finally resolved, as it were, in relationship to the infinite.

But so Herbert abandoned the more admired career open to him and pursued by his brother, to settle in service as a village person. So Crashaw abandoned country, family, and faith in a foreign priesthood. So shadowy Vaughan remained suspended between this-worldly service as a doctor and a longing for immediate union with eternal light. This is, indeed, what we may call the metaphysical trauma, characteristic of these poets. Unable to define and fulfil their egos in secular terms, they plunged for resolution into a direct relationship to metaphysical entities. In this sense, they were metaphysical poets because metaphysics offered them elemental sustenance in a shifting, wounding, and insecure world.

Indeed, the driving force of this metaphysical trauma can account for the extraordinary personal catharsis so frequent at the end of their poems, the enormous sense of arrival, as after a long pilgrimage. The suggestion is that the world hurt them, befuddled them, alienated and bewildered them, offered them no security for its vivacious presence. Typically, their egos came massively to rest in the securities of a large metaphysical anchoring. So Herbert achieved the anchorage of grace in "The Collar" after a wandering of secular thrashing:

> But as I raved, and grew more fierce and wild
> At every word,
> Methought I heard one calling, "Child!"
> And I replied, "My Lord!"

So Crashaw reduced an uncontrollable world to a sensuous metaphor, living and dying for his personal arrival:

> For while Thou sweetly slayest me,
> Dead to myself, I live in thee.

So Vaughan blurs the earth to a shadowy reality, proclaiming:

My soul, there is a country
Far beyond the stars
Where stands a wingëd sentry
All skillful in the wars.

The huge shudder of arrival in the catharsis of a metaphysical poem is extraordinarily winning. One senses a sigh of relief, a trauma of intimately personal anchorage. Indeed, insofar as the catharsis of a lyric poem clarifies and settles the speaker's feelings, these poems offer an enormous freight of catharsis.

The use of language is always in harmony with non-verbal experience. Thus, a civil servant's words reverberate as he uses them, in his career and nowhere else. The function of scientific language is to reverberate with non-verbal laboratory data. Indeed, the variety of areas with which language can reverberate is extraordinary and inexplicable. The problem of decorum in lyric poetry is not simply a matter of what vocabulary is permitted, but also what areas of psychic experience the poet permits his work to reverberate with. Thus, T. S. Eliot's essay, "Tradition and the Individual Talent" simply articulated Eliot's decorum, one that, among other things, blocked out a narrowly personal lyric catharsis. His personal arrival, insofar as the poem expresses it, is rendered transparent, a way-station on his true pilgrimage to a plateau of universality. His lyric catharsis is enormous and far-reaching, but it lacks the extraordinarily intimate privacy of being, the serenity and lyric relief of the metaphysical lyric, as in Herbert's close:

You must sit down, says Love, and taste my meat.
So I did sit and eat.

## NOTES

[1] Helen Gardner, the editor of *The Elegies and Songs and Sonnets of John Donne* (Oxford University Press, 1965), in her introduction to *John Donne, a Collection of Essays* (Englewood Cliffs, N.J., Prentice-Hall Inc., 1962), gives a résumé of various attempts made to define metaphysical poetry on either side of the Channel, moving through the Augustan attitudes of Dryden and Pope, to Romantic responses up to Grierson's edition of Donne's poetry in 1912. In her review, she gives an account of T. S.

Eliot's enthusiasm for metaphysical poetry, and includes his later retraction in "The School of Donne," delivered as part of the Clarke Lectures, 1926. The Augustan voice, expressed by Johnson, the Romantic period's essayist Hazlitt, and the modern critic Eliot all approach metaphysical poetry in terms of the rigors of poetry of their age.

This critical situation has moved little since then. Thus, Louis Martz, in *The Poetry of Meditation* (New Haven, Yale University Press, 1954), still stands behind Grierson's list of devices and mannerisms, but adds to it Eliot's concept of a unified sensibility in syncretic fashion:

> Those qualities, some thirty years ago, received their classic definition in the introduction to Grierson's anthology, *Metaphysical Lyrics and Poems*, and in Eliot's essay inspired by that volume. Developed in a series of influential books issued during the 1930's, the definition views Donne as the master and father of a new kind of English poetry, with these distinguishing marks: An acute self-consciousness that shows itself in minute analysis of moods and motives; a conversational tone and accent, expressed in language that is "as a rule simple and pure"; highly unconventional imagery, including the whole range of human experience, from theology to common details of bed and board; an "intellectual, argumentative evolution" within each poem, a "strain of passionate paradoxical reasoning which knits the first line to the last" and which often results in "the elaboration of a figure of speech to the farthest stage to which ingenuity can carry it"; above all, including all, that "unification of sensibility" which could achieve, "a direct sensuous apprehension of thought, or a recreation of thought into feeling," and made it possible for Donne to feel his thought "as immediately as the odour of a rose."

J. B. Leishman, in *The Monarch of Wit*, as Gardner indicates, sets a new tradition, attempting to see Donne against the background of his age, to define Donne by his private and individual use of Seventeenth Century contexts:

> Donne has been too often considered as a so-called metaphysical poet and too little as a Seventeenth Century poet (many characteristic Seventeenth Century poets began to write during the reign of Elizabeth); let us begin, then, by trying to reach some not too inadequate conception of the principal differences and varieties within that fundamental identity. *The Monarch of Wit*, J. B. Leishman (New York, Harper Torchbooks, 1966), p. 12.

This present work attempts to build upon Leishman's foundation, and define metaphysical poetry as growing out of the attitude of mind that resulted from what Marjorie Hope Nicolson called, "the breaking of the circle." (For a background to the problems of the age, see Marjorie Hope Nicolson's book, *The Breaking of the Circle;* for Donne's awareness of these problems, see C. M. Coffin's book, *John Donne and the New Philosophy*, The Humanities Press, 1958.) Donne's attitude of acceptance and rejection at once of old material and new possibilities gave rise to a strain which resulted in what we call the metaphysical shudder. Here, the corpus of Donne's lyric poetry is seen in this light.

2 Some of these pillars were *The Leviathan*, *The Laws of Ecclesiastical Polity*, and *The Anatomy of Melancholy*—all attempts to hold firm in the crumbling cosmologies of the period. Yet the men who wrote these works were constructive men and within their works they respond to the challenge of the age. The doubts that were inherent in the age ushered in by Galileo, Copernicus, Kepler, Moor, and Harvey are embedded in the sinews of their reasoning, revealed, for example, in the debating quality of Hooker's prose in "Talking of Law" in Book I in the following:

> Laws, as all other things are many times full of imperfection; and that which is supposed behoveful unto men, proveth oftentimes most pernicious. The wisdom which is learned by tract of time, findeth the laws that have been in former ages established, needful in order later to be abrogated. (*Of the Laws of Ecclesiastical Polity*, London, J. M. Dent and Sons Ltd. New York, E. P. Dutton and Co. Inc., 1954, vol. I, pp. 421–422.)

Hooker recognizes the need for change; yet the Law was perfect. By introducing the idea that Law might be imperfect—imperfect as men—he raises the terrifying head of insecurity. The effect in social and psychological terms is summed up by Hooker in:

> Notwithstanding we do not deny alteration of laws to be sometimes a thing necessary; as when they are unnatural, or impious, or otherwise hurtful unto the public community of men, and against that good for which human societies were instituted. (*Ibid.*, pp. 421–422.)

But he warns against indiscriminate change, changes made too quickly without a penetrating study of situations that seem to demand change.

> . . . We will conclude, that as the change of such laws as have been specified is necessary, so the evidence that they are such must be great. If we have neither voice from heaven that so pronounceth of them; neither sentence of men grounded upon such manifest and clear proof, that they in whose hands it is to alter them may likewise infallibly even in heart and conscience judge them so: upon necessity to urge alteration is to trouble and disturb without necessity. As for arbitrary alterations, when laws in themselves not simply bad or unmeet are changed for better and more expedient; if the benefit of that which is newly better devised be but small, sith the custom of easiness to alter and change is so evil, no doubt but to bear a tolerable sore is better than to venture on a dangerous remedy. (*Ibid.*)

Hooker's argument about change is systematically erected against an insecure age. And though he asks for change—even recognizes its necessity—he is conscious that things are happening too fast and too quickly. There is no time to grasp all the implications, no time for shaping and sorting out these ideas that have grown so suddenly. The new ideas should be taken cautiously. Hooker urges that one should not change to their demand simply because of their newness for "to bear a tolerable sore is better than to venture on a dangerous remedy." Hobbes was more radical.

And for Hobbes the world was no longer a reflection of divinity—the microcosm represented the heavenly macrocosm God. Man is seen as a machine by Hobbes:

> Nature, the art whereby God hath made and governs the world, is but the art of man, as in many other things, so in this also imitated, that it can make an artificial animal. *For seeing life is but a motion of limbs*, the beginning whereof is in some principle part within; why may we not say, that all automata (engines that move themselves by springs and wheels as doth a watch) have an artificial life? *For what is the heart, but a spring; and the nerves, but so many strings; and the joints, but so many wheels, giving motion to the whole body, such as was intended by the artificer?* Art goes yet further, imitating that rational and most excellent work of nature, man.
>
> (Sir Thomas Hobbes, *Leviathan*, New York, Collier Books, 1962, p. 19.)

The attitude that the age engendered is given powerful expression by Sir Thomas Browne:

I condemn not all things in the Council of Trent, nor approve all in the Synod of Dort.

(Sir Thomas Browne, *Religio Medici and Other Writings*, p. 4, New York, E. P. Dutton and Co. London, J. M. Dent and Sons, 1951.)

He was a doctor, a man of science, and a man of reason. But he felt the necessity for religion and expressed it thus in the opening of the *Religio Medici:*

For my Religion, though there be several Circumstances that might persuade the World I have none at all, (as general scandal of my profession, the natural cause of my Studies the indifferency of my Behavior and Discourse in matters of Religion, neither violently Defending one, nor with that common ardour and contention opposing another:) yet, in despight hereof, I dare without usurpation assume the honourable stile of a Christian.

(Browne, p. 1.)

Reason was not enough. He also felt the need to affirm faith:

I love to lose myself in a mystery, to pursue my Reason to a O altitudo: 'Tis my solitary recreation to pose my apprehension with the involved Enigmas and riddles of the Trinity, with Incarnation, and Ressurection.

(Browne, p. 9.)

In his desire for religion he does not ask for facts and explanations nor does he wish to see to believe, instead he says:

I can answer all the Objections of Satan and my rebellious reason with that odd resolution I learned of Tertullian, Certum est, quia impossibile est. I desire to exercise my faith in the difficultest point; for to credit ordinary and visible objects is not faith but persuasion. Some believe the better for seeing Christ's Sepulchre; and, when they have seen the Red Sea, doubt not of the Miracle. Now, contrarily, bless myself and am thankful that I lived not in the days of Miracles, that I never saw Christ nor His Disciples.

(Browne, p. 9.)

Thus the scientist, in expressing his desire to affirm the Unknowable by faith in the face of doubt, cast at the old ways of belief by the "new philosophy," seeks to come to terms with experimental knowledge and given knowledge. Hooker is cautious of change and yet cognizant of its necessity. Hobbes turns to new ways of thinking, breaking out of the old in bold statement; and Browne the scientist, shaken by the new changes, seeks to erect the way of faith in the way of radical discovery. The sense of insecurity was steady in the period.

[3] Pierre Legouis in his essay, *The Dramatic Element in Donne's Poetry*, excerpted from his book, *Donne*, *The Craftsman*, in *John Donne: A Collection of Critical Essays* (Englewood Cliffs, New Jersey, Prentice-Hall Inc., 1962, ed. by Helen Gardner), defines Donne's sense of drama in terms of craft. Having eschewed the method of the "Tableau Vivante," and the purely psychological conception of the dramatic, Legouis says:

I shall take the word dramatic in a third sense: in many of the "Songs and Sonnets" there are two characters; the second is indeed a mute: or rather his words are not written down; but we are enabled to guess how he acts and what he would say if he were granted utterance. The way in which Donne gives us those hints is both very clever and very modern. More important still for us here is the effect produced on the speaking character by the presence of a listening one, whom he tries to persuade and win over. What seemed at first disinterested dialectics, indulged in for truth's sake, or at least as "evaporations" of wit, sounds quite differently when the reader realizes this dumb presence.

(p. 38.)

4 Legouis sees the action of *the flea* differently. He says:

. . . in the second stanza the mingling of the lovers' blood in the flea's belly is said to be almost a marriage, yea more than that; the insect becomes at once woman, man, nuptial bed, and wedding church; in killing it the poet's mistress would commit, not only murder on him, a crime she is inured to, but suicide and sacrilege.

(*Ibid.*, note 3, p. 47.)

# 2

# John Donne

The personal drama of a reticent craftsman is not easily fer-reted out. A lawyer develops his cases, a doctor his world of medicine; we catch an aura of subject matter, the pace of a career. But of a creative writer, whose words crackle in our intestines, we demand more. Grasping his endless smash-ups, abandoned children, a tearing of city air—all so cool, easy, and casual—we want some control of the mysterious stranger, before we allow a laying on of hands.

With a novelist we can come to terms. Vivid as is his personal drama, the edge of "see-it-now" in his work, his stance of bearing witness, yet his story remains self-contained, approachable on its merits. No author confronts us on every page, refusing to be ignored. But lyric poetry is too alive with the act of its writing to allow such terms. Under its icing of words, everywhere flicker binding threads of illusions and non-verbal energies. Confronting the speaker of the poem, we grope for the poet who projected him. Wordsworth may have been a self-involved, reactionary career-builder with an illegitimate child in Paris; yet his poems project a presence of breath-taking immediacy and simple communion. We would have a writer in the shaping presence of his poem.

Donne's many confused voices vary in intelligence, suavity, and vocabulary of experience, self-infatuated women, harassed warriors, jouncy boys, all speaking with lyrical immediacy and directness. Yet as Donne matured, his lyrics simplified and clarified their presence. Indeed, the pace of Donne's development can be measured in terms of the clear immediacy of his speaker's voice. Thus, his early poems are a medley of voices. The late love lyrics project a remarkably even voice, though it does not quite grip its speaker inescapably. There is a tease, a reticent withdrawal, a forlorn, stylized music, not the vibrance of a total man. The Holy Sonnets keep changing direction with a strong pulse of commitment; yet sudden, fresh impulses keep breaking in. The lyrics still struggle to clarify their voice toward the last hymns.

As for the early love lyrics, their varied voices can obscure the poem. We tolerably grasp the point of view of "The Good-Morrow" and "The Sunne Rising," fresh, ardent marital poems, persuasive as Botticellis, or of "Breake of Day," expressing the harassed accommodation of a mildly pretentious lady. But how do we read the tired, over-extended image of the heart in "The Legacie?" Did Donne write this with a surly pout? Or is a stuffy aristocrat being ridiculed?

In Browning, the problem never arises. The speaker in "My Last Duchess" is so carefully shaped that his mask holds good; the poem is a dramatic monologue, not a lyric. The setting is too carefully defined, the occasion, the speaker and person addressed shaped like characters in a novel. But Donne's elusive voices breathe with utter intimacy. We grope for the source of their insistent authority. Why is the poet so evasive? Indeed, we can hardly gauge the seriousness of intent in Donne's early lyrics. Here, Donne stands apart, fitfully writing, never publishing, never founding a literary career, hardly distributing his lyrics. Was he clearing ground for a career in law or diplomacy? Did some esoteric commitment bind him? His upbringing in a condemned religion, trained from infancy to secretive reticence? We have no sure answers among an embarrassment of explanations.

These considerations bear on such problems as the dating of Donne's poems. Helen Gardner, in her edition, *The Elegies and the Songs and Sonnets of John Donne*, divides the songs and sonnets into two groups, before 1601 and from 1602 to 1605, based on theme and stanza complexity. Her criteria are cogent, given the fitful evidence; but obscure variables becloud the issue. Perhaps a slighter stanza was simply dashed off to vent some personal irritation. Perhaps Donne slowly narrowed himself to more psychological studies. We are not disputing Miss Gardner's sequence; on the contrary, our own suggested sequence remarkably agrees with hers. But we first need a close grasp of the man's working habits; and they elude us.

Indeed, Donne's literary career is so obscure, the man comes clearer in the texture of his poems, for whatever large, easy suggestions their contours offer. Thus, we note that their skin is tongue-tied, their adjectives few and tame; but hard verbs pivot their lines with force. Strong lines move as in a Dürer engraving, with instinctual structure. Periodically, a string of verbs thrashes about in agitation. Stiffly outlined presences, human, demonic, angle up in caricature. The flesh experience is kept starkly Gothic. Sensuous experience does not flow here with classic grace. The Renaissance rendering of a stylized hedonism with classical body proportions did touch England, but only lightly. Marlowe's *Hero and Leander* moves with dignified pleasure through classical flesh experience; but Marlowe was a programmatic iconoclast. So Spenser unfolded an elaborate tapestry of a continuum of experience. Donne's Gothic bodies were more angular, elongated, abrupt, strained to a situation, smells and perfumes to betray an affair, books and clothing to slow up the love-making, pinched, unnatural movement, the sign of the cross incised all over a landscape. A rounded body never rests in a halo or an eggshell, its landscape rolling in easy, vegetable largesse.

To ground a context for Marlowe, Spenser, and also Donne, a book like *A Mirror for Magistrates*, reprinted with numerous expansions from 1559 to 1610, might be considered, with its heavy, repetitive morality, its flight from any sensuous command of human experience, its fascination with death, its hollow, intangible atmosphere, full of visionary spirits, winter, and the grave. Its steady drag of preoccupation bears on the atmosphere of the Holy Sonnets. Donne reacted against this, not by any stylized, sensuous expression, but by his eccentric iconoclasm, his strong lines. If we suspend all doctrinal argument, and consider only temperamental dispositions, Burton's *Anatomy of Melancholy* and Sir Thomas

Browne's *Religio Medici* both taste of learning in the lees of life. Such a backwater could produce meditative poetry—and in Donne's later work, it did—but also constriction, intellectualism, and melancholia. Marlowe reacted by a direct, classical song of innocence. Donne's reaction was more complex. It had something of Dürer's sudden line, a taut gesture incising what he had to say.

Donne, then, was the most Gothic of the Seventeenth Century poets, ferociously inventive in his structures, thrashing among gargoyles, angels, and essences. His poems of misogyny exceed those of promiscuity. His compromises of love, "The Flea," "The Baite," though comic, melodious, have an edge of asperity, even sado-masochism. His mistrustful, Hobbesian world crackles lists of verbs, with a gamy avoidance of adjectives and sensuous nouns. He rarely basks in the feeling-tone of experience. He expresses nothing of Italy, nor any stylized living. His promiscuity poems are ribald ideas, not wallowings in flesh, his committed love poems chaste as sheeted wind. A high, strong Renaissance ego in life as in his poetry, he never relaxed to nature, or the roll of the seasons. And after his long, penitential marriage, he withdrew into his holy poems. Always a dualist, he detached himself from the world altogether.

Donne flung poetic gestures in a high, hard, mental fever, his lines locked in his thought. Even his Elegy XIX, with its grand march into bed, ends not with felt sexual pleasure, but a last argument:

> To teach thee, I am naked first; why then
> What needst thou have more covering than a man.
> (ll. 47–48)

At their most sensuous, his lyrics suddenly grasp at experience with taut equilibria and clumsy magnificence. And his radiant love lyrics are chaste and Gothic, with arched, flying implications of heady enlightenment. A dandy and an aristocrat, of strong, precise reserve, he never wallowed or dissolved in Dionysiac pleasures, but forged out a structure with Apollonian clarity, while rendering its grotesque underpinning.

So contours begin to sketch themselves in. An elusive figure stands there to be grasped, frustrated, violent of mind, with a proud reserve, a trenchant disbelief, a talent for mimicking voices, rendering cracked, virginal mentalities with a clench of words, taking positions so outrageous we feel our leg pulled. The autonomous ego, that proud, slippery, evasive self, is no easy presence to establish. John Donne, who attempted it again and again, was not simply practicing colloquial English or parsing out images by Ramist logic, but flexing his instrument in willful abandon in poem after poem of the metaphysical gesture.

Yet we traverse Donne's lyrics with choked dissatisfaction. After the Gothic springtime of "The Extasie" and "Goe, and Catche," evasive, scattered withdrawals register a botched career, occasional agonized gestures of self-expression, a few brilliant, abortive exercises. A poet's life need be no simple allegory; but Donne's seems a caprice of accidents.

Our initial set is in error. Secular moderns, to whom Keats is the model young poet discovering himself, we blink about bewildered after Donne's radiant love lyrics. But Donne was no boyish innocent, awakening into easy adulthood, but of a secretive, aristocratic Catholic family, learned, doctrinal, tough, a family of high aspiration, conservative solidity, revolutionary menace, and an unbending spine of honor. And over their mixed aspiration and anxiety hung menace from the government, the church, and natural sources. Sir Thomas More, the utopian statesman and martyr, was Donne's great granduncle. His grandfather, Thomas Heywood, died in exile. His two uncles, Elias and Jaspar Heywood, visited England under mortal risk with the first English Jesuits. When Donne was two, his grand-uncle, another Thomas Heywood, "Sir Thomas the Parson," was arrested for saying secret mass and publicly executed at a ceremony horrible in every detail. Donne's younger brother, Henry, with whom he went to college, died in prison before reaching adulthood for hiding a Jesuit.

Nor was Donne's family life secure. When scarcely four, his father, John Donne the elder, about to be appointed Master of the Ironmongers Company, suddenly took sick, drew up his will, and died, leaving a fortune of between 3,000 and

4,500 pounds. Within half a year, his mother, Elizabeth Drury, remarried with another wealthy and well-established Romanist, Dr. John Symings, president of the Royal College of Physicians; and they changed homes. Life was full of menace and abrupt shifts. God the Father dangled large blessings, but had inexorable demands.

An ambition for a secular career crossed Donne's religious groundwork, and controlled the first period in his life. Its basis perhaps lay in his father's early death, his mother's hasty remarriage, a revulsion against the family history, a search for power where security lay—in the state. We fish in vain for a clue; yet the turn was large, oblique, and irreversible. In October, 1584, he and Henry, aged twelve and eleven, matriculated at Hart Hall in Oxford, a secret Catholic center without a chapel, whose students avoided graduating to escape the oath of allegiance. So, coming before he reached sixteen, he needn't take the Oath of Supremacy on entering. The customary training in the trivium and quadrivium at Oxford would accord with the vehement disputations of his early love lyrics. He explored no new horizons in those passages, but fell back on schoolboy habits in a radically new situation. At this time, Oxford was a center for Spanish study, after the humanist teacher, Juan Luis Vives. Donne's first surviving portrait has a Spanish motto. Perhaps he pursued then an acquaintance with the rash of Spanish mystics, whose works resemble his own later in his career.

In 1587, at fifteen, Donne transferred to Cambridge University. In itself, the move was understandable. Another year at Oxford would have brought up the problem of the degree and the oath. Yet the shift was from a secret Catholic center to a militant Protestant school, and a center for scientific skepticism. This was congenial with a secular career in the Anglican establishment, a position Donne labored for against every setback until his ordination in his middle years. During this period, he gestated the open attitude to religious dispute that found expression in Satyre III. The Grand Armada was destroyed in 1588, the year Donne's stepfather died. In 1591, three years after the Armada, England still seethed with empire and the fear of assassination. Donne then returned to

London and entered Lincoln's Inn, to prepare a career in law and public service.

At Lincon's Inn, Donne was unremittingly hard-working, turbulent, well-connected, yet with a firm sense of building the basis of a career. He had good reason to be secretive about his Catholic background. His brother, Henry, was arrested and died in prison in 1593. Meanwhile Donne studied daily from four to ten A.M., leaving a record of 1,400 authors. What did he want to be? A poet? With ferocious patience, he pursued another goal, carving out a secular career in his native London. Born on Broad Street, like John Milton, close by the Mermaid Tavern, his father warden of The Ironmongers Company, his was no simple bourgeois ambition, a London Shakespeare, assaying a literary career when the family business faltered. He came rather from a family of high bourgeois, that had ruled England and dominated its stage. His intense ambition has abundant testimony, as does his social mastery, in his serving as Steward of Christmas at Lincoln's Inn in 1594 and in 1595 as Master of the Revels.

Then came the multiple voices and evasive ego of the earliest poems. Such painstaking withdrawal and reestablishment precluded a single, resonant, self-assertive voice. He rather wrote poems as trial balloons, testings of possibilities, strong self-assertions, investigations of integrity, savage, harassed barks of annoyance—witty, funny, ardent, perverse, experimental. Given his background and ambition, he had little margin for error in mastering the ways of the world.

Mornings, Donne studied; but the London amusements were open to university students. The afternoons offered plays at the theaters outside the city walls, the evenings feasts and revels. Donne's early characterization is well known; "not dissolute, but very neat; a great visitor of ladies, a great frequenter of plays, a great writer of conceited verses." So, in the Lothian portrait, an elegantly dressed melancholic has his hat swept off his face at a rakish angle to exhibit his long, sensitive face. The studied pose has a hint of the self-absorption and high style of a young dandy in his poetry. We see no reason to mistrust this characterization; yet it does not preclude deeper strata in his nature.

From the early songs and sonnets emerges an untested young stylist in the world of affairs, one of a high guarded bravado toward women, a joyous zest on the move, but also threat and harassment. The female figure, while flirtatiously engaging, too often exceeds him in size, age, security, and presence, her person blurring with the god of love. Insofar as a maternal dimension is suggested, it offers threat and insecurity. Nor, given Donne's peculiar development in his career, would we expect otherwise, with the unrelentingly masculine bent of his early career, pursuing knowledge, a career in law, diplomacy, war, acquiring trusted male friends, at the same time that he mistrusted and repressed his female component, his ties to home, mother, and family, as a potential disaster. Increasingly estranged from his family roots, the Catholic mass, his mother, the church, the angelology of Mother Mary and the saints, Donne forged a masculine independence and domination. So, in the early poems, the attitude to women is charged with uneasy mistrust.

In 1596, Donne participated in the greatest expedition of Queen Elizabeth's rule, the attack on Cadiz, the leading Spanish port, an undertaking so keen that just to be accepted in Essex' company was a great honor. There were 150 ships of every kind, manned by 5,000 sailors, with 6,000 soldiers, including 1,000 "gentlemen voluntaries," "covered with feathers, gold and silver lace." And the foray was an utter success. They surprised Cadiz early on a Sunday morning, when four great galleons and eighteen galleys guarded some forty merchantmen loaded with cargo. The galleons ran aground. The commanders of two, the *St. Philip* and the *St. Thomas*, set theirs on fire, consuming many of their crew alive. The English soldiers then climbed over the unfinished city fortifications, and opened the gates to plunder and burn the city. The West India merchant fleet negotiated for ransom, then burned themselves rather than submit to the English terms. Faro in Portugal was then raided, the library of the Bishop of Algrave taken as booty to found the Bodleian Library at Oxford. On the expedition, Donne befriended Thomas Egerton and Francis Wooley, son and stepson of Sir Thomas Egerton, Lord Keeper of the Great Seal and member of the Privy Council. A second expedition in 1597 under Essex foundered in storm and calm. In 1598, at twenty-six, Donne became chief secretary to Sir Thomas Egerton, a lord and statesman of England who took a place in processions and ceremonies over everyone but the Archbishop of Canterbury, whose protégés included Francis Bacon and Essex himself. Donne's public path was open before him.

Donne had arrived, but amid unforseeable menace. Long estranged from his own home, Egerton's household became Donne's foster home, not of exile and martyrdom, but of seeming success and security. He openly referred to Egerton in a letter as his father. "Nor did his Lordship in this time of Master Donne's attendance upon him account him so much his servant as to forget he was his friend and to testify it, did always use him with much courtesy, appointing him a place at his own table, to which he esteemed his company and discourse to be a great ornament." In this environment, Donne relaxed his guard.

At Sir Thomas' table intermittently lived Anne More, niece of his second wife, Elizabeth, and daughter to Sir George More of Losely in Surrey, a hot-tempered anti-Catholic, destined to be Keeper of the Tower. From October 1, 1599, to March 20, 1600, Essex, returned in disgrace from Ireland, was incarcerated in Essex House. Sir Thomas, his gaoler and prosecutor, was ridden by state duties. In January, 1600, Elizabeth Egerton died; and Anne, at sixteen, took over the household. Essex, Egerton's protégé, was executed in 1601. Upon Egerton's remarriage, Anne was summoned home to Surrey. That year, she and Donne secretly married, at twenty-nine and seventeen respectively. Queen Elizabeth was aging toward her death in 1603, the country in confusion, the aristocracy fumbling for a successor.

Without poking among biographical obscurities, Donne's marriage has incestuous overtones that suggest a giddy self-indulgence in a situation of concealed menace. His own home had been a forbidding one. Here, in his foster home, all things were reversed, all boundaries heightened and blurred, the forbidden permitted, the sinful a blessed opportunity. God poured an unending largesse of opportunity. From the age of four, with his mother's speedy remarriage upon his father's death, he was and wasn't a son at table. And then, in 1600, a virginal sixteen-year-old child-woman, his house companion for over a year, became his new mistress. Sir Thomas, a widower, was distracted by state affairs. The incestuous pressure bound him as the family scene attained a miraculous opening.

The area of love, as projected in Donne's promiscuity poems, was no garden of easy fleshly indulgence, but a challenge to his bravado and freedom to shift about. The women in them flickered teasingly about, with demonic authority behind them, in no solid, defined relationships. His revulsion and death wish there were strong, also his shaping ambition. Again and again, he blocked out their presence. His projected female speaker in "Breake of Day" speaks idiotic nonsense. The woman in "Loves Diet" projects a "cumbersome unwieldiness" her lover secretly feeds on. The speaker is harassed, elegant, with high-keyed mastery, but evasive, on the move. And then it happens. His lady-of-the-house is suddenly permissible, a wisp of a girl who loves him. He marries her, and in the most inept manner, sends a note to her father. The walls collapse on his life.

The early lyrics are flamboyant, but scattered, fitful, overshadowed by insecurities. Only the lyrics of "The Structure of Love" and "Emotional Marriage" offer an epiphany and self-transcendence, when the speaker grasps his universe with clear forbearance. "The Extasie," "The Good-Morrow," and "The Sunne Rising" avoid their shifty fluidity of relationship, their transient flirtatious play. They rather carefully measure and nail down the structure of new relationship. The ego of the speaker at last becomes manifest with Apollonian clarity and detachment, joined to his beloved in radiant exaltation and mystical fulfilment. By our understanding, these poems belong around 1601, during his marriage and before his career finally collapsed.

The argument Helen Gardner cites from Prof. Praz, dating "The Sunne Rising" after James I's accession from his habit of rising early for his sport of hunting, is a tenuous external coincidence that offers no more than a suggestion. On its own merits, the date is dubious. Lord Keeper Egerton, a member of the Privy Council, knew very well of his coming ruler, and would judiciously discuss him at table. His chief secretary, Donne, was long familiar with James' temperament. In contrasting a male world with a female oasis of love, Donne would hardly make a female his emblem of male scheduling. His poem required a male figure. So, in "The Canonization," "The Kings reall, or his stamped face" appropriately depicts the entrenched masculine world assaulting his female oasis of love. And given Donne's personal condition after 1603, when James took the throne—such a date is most dubious—two years married, his career in ruins with long months in prison, living on friends' bounty, writing petition after petition for any legitimate occupation. Men in such circumstances are not prone to such a pitch-point of expansive glory and optimism. By then, he had felt the weight of his newfound anchor of transcendent love. His epiphany of euphoric surprise was over.

An earlier date also seems dubious for these poems. Donne could have loved before; but these psychic elements seem too fundamentally restructured. Not only does the voice clear; but its plot tensions change. Gone is the hanky-panky of being involved and uninvolved, innocently all-knowing, reserved yet fully in the experience, a veteran with a bright, eager face and clean hands. Something comes into sharp focus here as out of an evasive blur.

Indeed, those early poems of courtly love express an attunement of considerable tenacity. From an early involvement like "The Paradox" to the full-blown deification of "Loves Exchange," the supple suavity of "Loves Deitie," the rebellious self-assertion of "The Message," Donne confronted a detached, superior power of love in the rejecting woman. So the promiscuity poems offer a *modus operandi* in a shifting world. But "The Extasie," "Aire and Angels," as do the poems of emotional marriage, spell out a changed structure that permits commitment. Indeed, ambition and empire now bow before an emotional marriage. The young groom, with radiant, open-eyed exaltation, indifferent as Lear, shrugs his shoulders to "pacts and sects of great ones/That ebb and flow by the moon." A tough apprentice warrior, one who sailed with Essex to sack Cadiz, wrote the promiscuity poems; but here their constellation of values is attuned to a marriage so exalted it made the sun a servant and elevated them to:

> . . . two better hemispheares
> Without sharpe North, without declining West?
> What ever dyes, was not mixt equally;
> If our two loves be one, or, thou and I
> Love so alike, that none doe slacken, none can die.
> ("The Good-Morrow," ll. 17–21)

This reading gives dramatic pace to the calm commitment of "The Anniversarie," already suggesting death, "The Canonization," a statement embattled in a choked disgust before the implacable world. Somehow the same voice speaks here, as it did not in the promiscuity poems, one intelligent, responsible, not trapped in abortive romances, but harassed and at large in the world. We take as literal the surrender of a statesman's role, a "peece of Chronicle" for a love death:

> We can dye by it, if not live by love,
> And if unfit for tombes and hearse
> Our legend bee, it will be fit for verse;
> And if no peece of Chronicle wee prove,
> We'll build in sonnets pretty roomes;
> As well a well wrought urne becomes
> The greatest ashes, as halfe-acre tombes,
> And by these hymnes, all shall approve
> Us *Canoniz'd* for love.
> (ll. 28–36)

This closes the first epiphany in Donne's lyric poetry, a fusion of voice, person, and occasion in utter, exalted arrival. It is carefully secular, an arrival among autonomous forms of life. The happiest, "The Good-Morrow" and "The Sunne Rising," join the lovers in a fresh, indestructible universe. In "The Extasie," the embattled male and female souls fix quiescent the accidents of meeting, to allow structure to be established in a great negotiation. Exploring it, Donne grasps the very nature of the libido, the temper of sexual love as shaping two people into a unique entity of marriage. For a moment, the splintered dualist arrives at fusion, earthly, autonomous, at peace in an ordered world.

The epiphany was faulted. The woman in "The Extasie" is extraordinarily muffled, a voiceless reflection of a clear, strong bond; but no free, loving companionship is apparent. Moreover, both "The Good-Morrow" and "The Sunne Rising" note reality as dancing, and far away. The young lover properly bids his waking bride "good-morrow," but as a diplomatic secretary, he need not consign all else to a dream. In "The Sunne Rising," we take "nothing else is" as literal, his awakening psyche his only reality. So Shakespeare's Antony greeted Cleopatra, and soon lost his empire. So intoxicated an epiphany is touched with hubris.

Anne More's period as a chaperoned lady of York House continued from January, 1600, to October. Sir Thomas Egerton then again remarried; and Anne returned to her father's house, her grandfather having died. During the fall of 1601, Anne came to London with her father, who attended Parliament. She met Donne secretly and married him shortly before Christmas. Soon thereafter, in February, 1602, by an intermediary, the Earl of Northumberland, Donne sent the following letter to his father-in-law:

Sir,

If a very respective fear of your displeasure, and a doubt that my lord (whom I know, out of your worthiness, to love you much) would be so compassionate with you as to add his anger to yours, did not so much increase my sickness as that I cannot stir, I had taken the boldness to have done the office of this letter by waiting upon you myself to have given you the truth and clearness of this matter between your daughter and me, and to show you plainly the limits of our fault, by which I know your wisdom will proportion the punishment.

So long since as her being at York House this had foundation, and so much then of promise and contract build upon it so, without violence to conscience, might not be shaken.

At her lying in town this Parliament I found means to see her twice or thrice. We both knew the obligations that lay upon us, and we adventured equally; and about three weeks before Christmas we married. And as at the doing there were not used above five persons, of which I protest to you by my salvation there was not one that had any dependence or relation to you, so in all the passage of it did I forbear to use any such person, who by furtherance of it might violate any trust or duty towards you.

The reasons why I did not fore-acquaint you with it (to deal with the same plainness I have used) were these: I knew my present estate less than fit for her. I knew (yet I knew not why) that I stood not right in your opinion. I knew that to have given intimation of it had been to impossibilitate the whole matter. And then, having these honest purposes in our hearts and these fetters in our consciences, methinks we should be pardoned if our fault be but this, that we did not, by fore-revealing of it, consent to our hindrance and torment.

Sir, I acknowledge my fault to be so great, as I dare scarce offer any other prayer to you in mine own behalf than this, to believe this truth—that I neither had dishonest end nor means. But for her, whom I tender much more than my fortunes or life (else I would, I might neither joy in this life nor enjoy the next). I humbly beg of you that she may not, to her danger, feel the terror of your sudden anger.

I know this letter shall find you full of passion; but I know no passion can alter your reason and wisdom, to which I adventure to commend these particulars;—that it is irremediably done; that if you incense my lord, you destroy her and me, that it is easy to give us happiness, and that my endeavors and industry, if it please you to prosper them, may soon make me somewhat worthier of her.

If any take the advantage of your displeasure against me, and fill you with ill thoughts of me, my comfort is that you know that faith and thanks are due to them only that speak when their informations might do good, which now it cannot work towards any party. For my excuse I can say nothing, except I knew what were said to you.

Sir, I have truly told you this matter, and I humbly beseech you so to deal in it as the persuasions of Nature, Reason, Wisdom, and Christianity shall inform you; and to accept the vows of one whom you may now raise or scatter—which are, that as my love is directed unchangably upon her, so all my labours shall concur to her contentment, and to show my humble obedience to yourself.

Yours in all duty and humbleness,
J. Donne.

From my lodging by the Savoy,
2nd February 1602.
To the Right Worshipful Sir George More, Kt.

Donne left York House in expectation of his reply. His reference to his sickness in Paragraph 1 was not an exaggeration. He was subject to nervous sickness for the remainder of his life. But once he had married Anne More in this fashion, this was a loser's letter. He admits his careful plan, his caution about whom to use, his awareness of their responsibility to Sir George, also that he married so because only thus could he bring it about. In Paragraph 6, he warns of the consequences of Sir George's opposition, making himself a measured, sober schemer in head-on conflict, with no mitigating ardor, no youthful urgency, no discreet omission of the insult, only a dry articulation of the fact of marriage, and to an irascible anti-Catholic and public figure.

Sir George's reply was unrelenting. He had Donne dismissed and thrown into prison, together with Christopher and Samuel Brooke, who had managed the secret wedding, and petitioned the Court of the Archbishop of Canterbury to have the wedding annulled. Donne was so sickly that he was soon transferred to his lodging under house arrest. There were memories of his brother Henry, who had died in prison. The clerical court then declared the marriage valid, and Sir George back-tracked and requested Sir Thomas to take Donne back in his employ. Sir Thomas had said at his dismissal, "He parted with a friend, and such a secretary as was fitter to serve a king than a subject." He now replied, "Though he was unfeignedly sorry for what he had done, yet it was inconsistent with his place and credit to discharge and readmit servants at the request of passionate petitioners." Anne returned to her husband; and Donne began his family life.

Donne spent two years, from 1602 to 1604, at the estate of Anne's cousin, Sir Francis Wooley, at Pyrford in Surrey, where his first children were born. There, he probably met James I, crowned in 1603, after Queen Elizabeth's death. The two men had a common taste in theology that would forcefully shape Donne's later career. No country boy, Donne corresponded with endless dissatisfaction. He went abroad with Sir Walter Chute early in 1605, then returned and settled with his family in Mitcham, where he became research assistant to Thomas Morton, a rising Anglican churchman and theologian. For the coming few years, Donne's family steadily grew at Mitcham, while he ghosted a train of doctrinal pamphlets. He evaded all opportunities to enter the church.

This was a period of stagnation and impoverished life habits. A man as dramatic about his affairs as in the structure of his poems, Donne inscribed a letter to his wife recorded by Walton:

> Immediately after his dismission from his service, he sent a sad letter to his wife to acquaint her with it; and after the subscription of his name writ, "John Donne, Anne Donne, Undone,"—and God knows it proved too true.

His sudden sickness in prison, so reminiscent of his brother's death, and his steady infirmities thereafter, like the uncanny pun—Donne—undone—suggest a disposition to great hurt. Nor could the mood be sloughed off. When a friend lost his wife, Donne comforted him in kind, "If I should comfort you, it were an alms acceptable in no other title than when poor gives to poor, for I am more needy of it than you." His life was hard enough. His research was demanding and ill-paid, and against the Catholics who raised him. In 1607, Thomas Morton attempted to grant him his own benefice as a gracious friend and patron. Donne's reply, as recorded by Walton, is revealing of this stage in his life:

> My most worthy and most dear friend . . . I may not accept of your offer. But, Sir, my refusal is not for that I think myself too good for that calling for which kings, if they think so, are not good enough; nor for that my education and learning, though not eminent, may not, being assisted with God's grace and humility, render me in some measure fit for it. But I dare make so dear a friend as you are my confessor; some irregularities of my life have been so visible to some men that though I have, I thank God, made my peace with Him by penitential resolutions against them and by the assistance of His grace banished them by affections, yet this, which God knows to be so, is not so visible to man as to free me from their censures and it may be that sacred calling from a dishonour. And besides, whereas it is determined by the best of casuists that God's glory should be the first end and a maintenance the second motive to embrace that calling, and though each man may propose to himself both together; yet the

first may not be put last without a violation of conscience, which he that searches the heart will judge. And truly my present condition is such that if I ask my own conscience whether it be reconcilable to that rule, it is at this time so perplexed about it that I can neither give myself nor you an answer. You know, Sir, who says, "Happy is that man whose conscience doth not accuse him for that thing which he does." To these I might add other reasons that dissuade me; but I crave your favor that I may forbear to express them and thankfully decline your offer.

Far from a simple evasion, the passage begins confessing "some irregularities of my life." But they bar him only by repute; unto God he had already made his peace. What then is the barrier he later mentions, "my present condition?" "Condition" suggests something more elemental than secular ambition, the weight of some deep need for penance. Here also we remark *Biathanatos*, the unpublished defense of suicide Donne wrote at this time. We can only tap our way along a wall, remarking his readiness to confess his malaise, his extraordinary penitential labor, his rooting out of his religious origins, his futile trips, his poverty, his evasion of any Anglican career until just before his wife died.

In considering the somber stagnation of Donne's middle years, we must argue as finally trivial Sir George's savage attack, destructive as it was to his career. That late in his life, his disposition would not have been so depressed unless already inclined that way. Indeed, his extraordinarily inept handling of it suggests he in some way invited it. There is a fine Hamlet-like resonance in his father's sudden, early death and his mother's speedy remarriage; but the echo is too neat and tidy, and without any direct evidence in Donne's own writing. The absence of his father betrays itself in Donne's life, as in his poetry, not as a personality to make peace with, but a great emptiness he is unable to structure, in the lack of any secure government. He floundered between religions as between careers. So his poetry floundered among suspect cosmologies, outmoded paths of truth. Indeed, his years of wallowing during his marriage give us some clue to his need for penance. His initial career and marriage were a great, self-willed shaping, without a father as model, and under a mother who could destroy him. No wonder the secular libido in "The Extasie" projects an independent man, shaping his own private destiny. But the attempt proved premature, abortive. Obscurely, the disaster in his marriage betrayed it. For years, he now stood penance, and ceased to move, a participant in a marriage pointed nowhere.

In 1607, Mrs. Magdalen Herbert, mother of Lord Herbert of Cherbury and George Herbert, both poets of Donne's school, received a sequence of seven sonnets; "La Corona," Donne's first religious poetry. He also wrote for her Elegy IX, "The Autumnall." Some emotional engagement, however easy, must have been present here. Mrs. Herbert was a widow, and open to men younger than herself; in 1608, she married a knight half her age; Donne was only seven years her junior. "The Autumnall" has a suave, intimate detachment appropriate for such a relationship.

So Lady Huntingdon, the daughter of Sir Thomas Egerton's third wife, helped Donne in his debts. Perhaps through her, he met her cousin, Lucy Russell, Countess of Bedford, who received several of Donne's verse letters and inspired "Twicknam Garden," if not "A Nocturnall upon S. Lucies Day." Donne wrote elegies on her friends and relatives, and in 1608 named a daughter after her. So "Twicknam Garden" suggests a relationship less charged with an aura of personal engagement than "The Autumnall," more simply one of large, gentle acceptance.

Such emotional alliances must have been exceedingly important to Donne. The tone of the feminine in his early poetry, as in his early life, is too fraught with sudden clumsiness, arbitrary thrusts, and demonic figures, not to have been badly injured by the results of his marriage. His late love poems to these women are the titillation of a married man on a last fling of pale romance before his ordination, a man with a large old wound in his being, being healed by a steady wash of regard. The divinities of these poems are benign, not malignant.

Donne's illnesses were increasing at this time; raging fevers, continuous stomach ailments that eventually become cancerous. He wrote to a friend:

Everything refreshes, and I wither, and I grow older and not better, my strength diminishes and my load grows.

To another, he wrote:

I have contracted a sickness, which I cannot name nor describe. For it hath so much of a continual cramp, that it wrests the sinews . . . my pain hath drawn my head so much awry and holds it so, that mine eye cannot follow my hand.

In 1608, Donne applied to become his Majesty's secretary in Ireland, then to be Secretary of Virginia; but old rumors of scandal blocked the appointments. In 1608, Sir George More released Anne's considerable dowry of 80 pounds a year. Their life eased, as their health improved. Donne dressed more elegantly for London. In 1610, he published *Pseudo-Martyr*, depicting the English Jesuit martyrs, some his near relatives, as engaged in a martyr complex—lusting after suffering and self-destruction. In 1611, he published *Ignatius His Conclave*, a brisk satire, several times reprinted, depicting Loyola with Lucifer, and mocking the heliocentric universe. He acquired a wealthy patron in Sir Robert Drury, whom he accompanied abroad, and a brick house on Drury Lane he occupied from 1611 to 1621 for a nominal rent. Donne never met Drury's daughter, Elizabeth, who died before her fourteenth birthday, but wrote two *Anniversaries* in her memory, reflecting on crumbling ideas of order and popular notions of world decay.

His periodic trips away from home, as tutor, companion, or to solicit employment, both during the early marital period, and after his conditions somewhat eased, must have been somber. Sometimes Anne was pregnant, and fretted at his absence. In one trip to Paris in 1612, Donne had a clairvoyant nightmare of Anne and his newborn baby, both dead. By Walton's record, at the time of the dream, his wife had a miscarriage.

The four valediction poems and the song, "Sweetest love, I do not goe," were probably all to his wife. In them, we feel a balance of deep feeling and courteous self-control that gathered to an epiphany of concern and love in "A Valediction: of Weeping," then again in "A nocturnall upon S. Lucies Day," also, in a sense, a valediction. Here, he first permitted himself a Dionysian abandon of surrender and release, as the female figure is again dislodged and rises to a more benign divinity.

Donne continued his futile attempts at employment; but the king had already settled his fate:

> The King gave a positive denial to all requests and, having a discerning spirit, replied, "I know Mr. Donne is a learned man, has the abilities of a learned divine, and will prove a powerful preacher. And my desire is to prefer him that way, and in that way I will deny you nothing for him.

In January, 1615, Donne was ordained by the Bishop of London. On August 8, 1617, worn-out by her life, Anne died of a childbed fever at thirty-three, delivering her twelfth child, a still-born infant, leaving seven surviving children to be cared for. Her oldest daughter, Constance, took over the household.

Donne preached his first sermon at Greenwich, April 30, 1615. In 1616, he was elected Reader in Divinity in Lincoln's Inn, preaching about fifty sermons a year to a demanding audience. In 1617, he began to preach at Paul's Cross. There, masses of people gathered before the most renowned preacher in England. On November 19, 1621, he was elected Dean of St. Paul's, and first preached there on Christmas Day. Donne labored and prospered in his new vocation. James I arranged for him to accompany Viscount Doncaster to Germany, when he wrote, "A Hymne to Christ, at the Authors Last Going into Germany." There he renewed acquaintance with the Elector Palatine at Heidelberg, then visited the larger German cities, earning a gold medal in The Hague for a sermon there. At St. Paul's, he now preached about once a week, and visited the country parishes. He declined further money from his father-in-law, and invested in the Virginia Company. He moved his aging mother, still Roman Catholic, into the deanery with him. Aging himself, he grew peremptory in the chapel, rebuked his audience for indecorum, and had one man jailed for not kneeling on request.

Always of uncertain health, Donne nearly died of a fever in 1623. He then wrote *Devotions*, a series of meditations on sickness of body and soul. While he was ill, his oldest daughter, Constance, married Edward Alleyn, a stage manager older than her father, who once starred in *Tamburlaine.* Donne and his son-in-law quarreled over the dowry.

In 1625 James I died. Donne preached the first sermon for the newly crowned king. He now devoted his life to his sermons, spending an entire week in a single preparation, then fasting the day of its delivery. During the great plague of 1626, when thousands died each month, he sought refuge with the former Magdalen Herbert, her young husband, Sir John Dennin, and her son, George Herbert, soon to embark on his clerical career.

Donne himself now lived in the shadow of his coming death. A daughter, Lucy, died at eighteen; a son, George, fell prisoner in the Huguenot wars. His old friend, Ben Jonson, was bedridden after a paralytic stroke. A sick, aging man, Donne became easier with money, loaning large sums to friends, helping prisoners and poor scholars with their needs. His old chronic indigestion was now unmistakably a cancer of the stomach. On December 13, 1630, he drew up his will, then posed for a last portrait—naked inside his shroud—a portrait he kept by his bedside. On March 31, 1631, he died murmuring over and over, "Thy kingdom come, Thy will be done."

Donne's life is remarkable for its stages of unfolding. Straight-forward causation seems minor here. At any time, Donne could have been ordained; but only an inner flicker would move his spirit. All his outer preparation came to naught. Threads of insecurity disintegrated whatever he embraced. Entrenched in his world, he felt a death come, a war, a marriage, a king's word; and he was elsewhere, as an orbiting electron has a total, irreversible shift from ring to ring, its transitions invisible to the eye. He changed by a process of inner baking, not by strategies of situation. Such movements may seem odd to us; but religious history records a long tradition of such flounderings, evasions, and periodic inactivity, then a crystallization in a new being.

We grope for the binding thread in these evasive shifts. Donne's lyrics, fitful, skeptical, beleaguered as they are, suggest that thread in the gradual washing away of superficial excitements from the being of the speaker, in preparation for an utter engagement. Donne's love experience must neither be exaggerated nor minimized. His early, idle teases, flirtatious advances and withdrawals, are less simple promiscuity poems than tentative explorations of selfhood, qualified engagements, and role-playing, as the young aristocrat idly, enigmatically confronts his world. Their "I" arrives at logical propositions and social pratfalls; their "she" hangs insecurely at the fringes of his attention.

His engagement and marriage brought a brief, secular definition of selfhood. "I" was now the Elizabethan aristocrat, husband, and lover, "the other" his betrothed, their world the establishment of England. But an evanescent insubstantiality pervades lines like the following:

> I wonder by my troth, what thou, and I
> Did, till we lov'd? were we not wean'd till then?
> But suck'd on countrey pleasures, childishly?
> Or snorted we in the seven sleepers den?
> T'was so . . .
>
> ("The Good-Morrow," ll. 1–5)

Donne's lyrics work not by firm continuities, but by the shock and marvel of present engagements. Far from a Proust, he offers fragments of experience, not tapestries of unfolding life. And even in the experience, his beloved is too silent, passive, and automatic to rise as his "psychic other." "The Sunne Rising" is that rare love poem, where she could be sound asleep during its entire delivery. This is not yet the knot of a psychic engagement.

His father-in-law's rejection shattered his disposition, and hurtled him onto the world. Donne then underwent a sea change. He held back, studied, shifted about in shadows, clung to futile dreams and ambitions. The social fabric was no longer his garment. In small, nit-picky steps, he unthreaded each ambition until it all gave.

Before we examine his religious epiphany, we must withdraw from that characterization of Donne as intellectual—cold, aloof. The charge might apply to a secular young man, sowing his wild oats in the city, but not to Donne's wayward, intuitive spirit, his radical skepticism, his tentative gestures of exploration. The love poems are not the program of an apprentice Don Juan, but sketches of autonomy of a beleaguered aristocrat. Donne sought in them not to enjoy love, but to establish a viable equilibrium with the world. During years of drama, humor, and sardonic wit, he tasted and savored situations, steadily defining himself. But astute as he was, experience tore apart his love-marriage as the mirage of an innocent buffoon. For him then again to purge his spirit amid charity and scorn, and rise to a fresh union with God, bespeaks an aloof decision and austere courage without parallel in our literature.

Donne's religious epiphany began in "Goodfriday, 1613. Riding Westward," as he again took the role of solitary traveler, but now himself, in his life, not a mythic warrior, as in the early love lyrics. He rides west on Goodfriday, as all his life has been an evasive withdrawal of spirit, the landscape blank around him, a wasteland, where nothing registers. Like Jonah, he flees God's presence, which is not to be fled. Indeed, as in the old Westerns, the hero slouches out of town, evading a boss hinted at, felt, here, there, at odd moments, but always hidden. Even riding away as hero, he can feel him around the corner on Main Street, but coming closer. In a moment will come the moment of truth. So Dürer's solitary knights rode across a wilderness. But in Donne, the confrontation stays inward; his back turned, he finally rides away. The moment expresses the consummate irony of the human condition; yet somehow, it now does not matter. The very randomness of his fate is his source of healing. His back is turned in penance, to prepare for their ultimate meeting. Indeed, he rides westward as Christ hung on the cross, enduring accident and misfortune for the supreme gesture of grace. So, when they meet, it will be like Dante at the close of the *Paradiso*, as in a mirror, two identities becoming one:

> Restore thine Image, so much, by thy grace,
> That thou may'st know mee, and I'll turne my face.

Donne's masculine presence is strong in "Goodfriday, 1613. Riding Westward," but feminine aspects are now strongly there. In the Holy Sonnets he already struggled to be patient, trusting, and abide God's presence. His ego died hard there, in a tortured wrestling, his homosexual imagery and gestures little more than a desperate shudder at any image, any posture, any mode of expression that might attain God's manifest presence. To subdue his will, he took the role of a solicitous, serenely patient lover.

His God encountered at last, Donne rose to the epiphany of his last two hymns. Ever the Gothic poet, his flesh more subdued than ever, he stylizes the parts of his body, abstracts them into symbols; as he moves in skinny flashes toward earth, heaven, oblivion, God's spirit. His earlier comparisons with the world in "The Good-Morrow," "The Sunne Rising," are for rivalry and rejection. In "Hymne to God My God, in My Sicknesse," he enacts its destiny in himself. Lying in bed, he hymns the earth, his body, preparing to become God's music, His newfound instrument.

Donne's portrait in his shroud is an arresting emblem. Are we too far astray, seeing it as Donne in a bridal veil, dressed at once for his grave and his wedding? After a life-long pilgrimage, his fragmentations and withdrawals are over. His tight lips, bony, tormented face, and closed meditative eyes are fixed on the substance of eternity.

Donne's lyrics are occasionally slighted as expressing only fragments of selfhood, never a large wholeness. This follows when they are taken in isolation. Together, they build an airy Gothic structure, lofty, difficult of access—not a single, large hall—but winding alleys of thought, ponderous, with sudden shifts, blank walls, and unexpected deliveries; yet everywhere they allow masterly vistas of spirit; and everywhere their structure holds firm. Donne's own testimony at the close of his life as recorded by Walton, suggests the totality of engagement of Donne's spirit:

> . . . he replied, with a countenance so full of cheerful gravity as gave testimony of an inward tranquility of mind and of a soul willing to take a farewell of this world, and said—
>
> "I am not sad, but most of the night past I have entertained myself with many thoughts of several friends that have left me here, and are gone to that place from which they shall not return; and that within a few days I also shall go hence, and be no more

seen. And my preparation for this change is become my nightly meditation upon my bed, which my infirmities have now made restless to me. But at this present time I was in serious contemplation of the providence and goodness of God to me; to me, who am less than the least of His mercies; and looking back upon my life past, I now plainly see it was His hand that prevented me from all temporal employment; and that it was His will I should never settle nor thrive till I entered into the ministry; in which I have now lived almost twenty years—I hope to His glory—and by which, I most humbly thank him. I have been enabled to requite most of those friends which showed me kindness when my fortune was very low, as God knows it was; and—as it hath occasioned the expression of my gratitude—I thank God most of them have stood in need of my requital. I have lived to be useful and comfortably to my good father-in-law, Sir George More, whose patience God hath been pleased to exercise with many temporal crosses; I have maintained my own mother, whom it hath pleased God, after a plentiful fortune in her younger days, to bring to great decay in her very old age. I have quieted the consciences of many that have groaned under the burden of a wounded spirit, whose prayers I hope are available for me. I cannot plead innocency of life, especially of my youth; but I am to be judged by a merciful God, who is not willing to see what I have done amiss. And though of myself I have nothing to present to Him but sins and misery, yet I know He looks not upon me now as I am of myself, but as I am in my Saviour, and hath given me, even at this present time, some testimonies by His Holy Spirit, that I am of the number of His elect: I am therfore full of inexpressible joy, and shall die in peace."

# *Part* II

# *The Early Poems*

# 3

# The Promiscuity Poems

Donne's promiscuity poems—not simply seduction poems, but general defenses of promiscuity, "Goe, and Catche a Falling Starre," "Womans Constancy," "The Indifferent," "Loves Usury," "Communitie," "Confined Love," and "Loves Diet" —are curiously anemic exercises, with much rhetoric and little dramatic immediacy. "Communitie" may have trenchant implications; but its nouns are prim as a Sunday School tract:

> Good wee must love, and must hate ill,
> For ill is ill, and good good still,
> But there are things indifferent,
> Which wee may neither hate, nor love,
> But one, and then another prove,
> As wee shall find our fancy bent.
>
> (ll. 1–6)

So "Womans Constancy" trudges along on its polysyllables, "antedate . . . reverentiall . . . forsweare . . . purpos'd . . . lunatique . . ." These poems do not establish a setting, then advance an argument in context, as does a lyric like "The Extasie." Rhetorical throughout, they advance promiscuity as a position, with no grasp of the experience. Sliding behind his argument with schoolboy primness, the speaker sniffs at formulae, sketching in a position.

The relationship of the man and the woman in these poems curiously reverses the accepted social pattern, in that the woman is characteristically set in her ways, at times imperious, her path of promiscuity determined, the man a fresh, brash boy, a green hand at love, masking his inexperience behind arguments, images, and arch positions. Indeed, the speaker is so aloof, evasive, problematical, stylized, as to obscure his motivation. Thus he may be arguing her promiscuity to rationalize his own, using his sense of her unfaithfulness as a springboard to explore the ways of the world. These poems, then, are the fumblings of a rhetorical virtuoso, who stabs at truths, formulates gauzy judgments, insults, hides his hand, and pretends the mastery of a veteran as he learns his first lessons in love.

Their best, "Goe, and Catche," is also their mildest. It defends promiscuity late in the poem and only by inference, after much magic, exploration, and travel. Its first two stanzas are a zestful expansion of human experience in the dew of youth, touching the quicksilver unknown. Even the balancing melancholy closing each stanza, of hapless fortune, dreams of a true woman, has the imperious absolute of youth, the catch of an urgent, ardent voice, without the least taint of sexual involvement apparent. Even at the end of Stanza 2, the truth in question is not yet inescapably her continence. Only at the close of Stanza 3, as though by an unpredictable discovery, is her promiscuity insisted on; and yet the speaker, by the dazzle of song, knew from the first she would be "False, ere I come, to two, or three."

The poem does not defend promiscuity; on the contrary, the speaker, impishly lyrical and disillusioned as an apprentice Ecclesiastes, would himself pursue its opposite—"Such a Pilgrimage were sweet." And yet, this most modest promiscuity poem is the most persuasive, by its easy language, its casual openness. By comparison, "Womans Constancy" is too freighted with polysyllables; "The Indifferent" is a constricted gesture. Indeed, its easy tone itself hides an argument. It answers the objection to promiscuity from conventional morality by turning with honesty of mind to worldly advancement. Baldly, life in this world requires dishonesty. So, implicitly, if you are alive, you must be promiscuous.

A second, unuttered uneasiness—that promiscuous love

makes its adherents closed and secretive—it disarms by its open tone, affirming promiscuity in spontaneous experience and colloquial language. Only one word comes to three syllables, "Pilgrimage" (l. 20), suggesting an old-fashioned, unreal, tri-syllabic world of loyal women; but the easy, open world of one and two syllables is sudden and capricious, a brave new world, not the domain of sluggish libertines, where an innocent "borne to strange sights," who can ride "ten thousand dayes and nights" to report "all strange wonders" will witness universal promiscuity. Furthermore, the idea is only stumbled on, as the speaker is surprised and seduced by the world. The argument, "If everyone does it, why can't I?" is the more persuasive for remaining unuttered. Indeed, the speaker is a disarming marvel of contradiction, so sluggish he wants a guarantee to go next door, so inexperienced he consults friends about the world, so young he hangs in an atmosphere of boyish magic, a green and lyrical schoolboy, baldly asserting universal promiscuity, so worldly wise, the familiar wash of experience easily rinses through him. Fascinated, we supply his unuttered conclusion ourselves.

The manifest characters of "Goe, and Catche" are the perplexed lover and his companion explorer. By this reading, the speaker would seem very immature, dazzled by experience he has never had. Stanza 1 begins with covert references to sexual behavior; but on mentioning an actual woman, the language muffles to inert generalities, ". . . a woman true, and faire," and "False . . . to two, or three." And even these early references are marvelously distant. Thus, to catch a falling star precedes getting with child a mandrake root, a muffled allusion to intercourse and pregnancy. But a falling star is extraordinarily high, distant, and unfamiliar; a mother or exalted superior. A mandrake root, a vegetable metaphor for a woman's sexual organs, is replete with witchcraft. To cleave the devil's foot again suggests intercourse, but with a female devil, endowed with dangerous powers. "Mermaides singing" fascinated sailors till they drowned. This is not yet a specific woman—when she arrives, his language grows muffled, inert; but a womanly atmosphere hangs about and encloses his world, as a fifteen-year-old first intuits a changed world all about him, its character not yet defined. So her settled behavior suggests his relative inexperience. Her ways are set; he is still at the crossroads, wanting a "Pilgrimage sweet" to a true woman, but acknowledging a new, female universe of falling stars, mandrake roots, cleft devils, and mermaids for his groundwork of living.

Other elements suggest a gauzy child's world, its sheer choreography, with falling stars, primeval forests, the graveyard of time, the devil, the ocean of singing mermaids, all horizons explored, with speed to catch a star, endurance to ride until white with age. But then the poem ends with a pratfall, a plunge into exploration to discover the beauty next door is not to be bothered with, all dash and movement leading to a homebody resigned to sluggish inactivity. So marvel spinning beyond marvel ends in a thud of local realities. The next door sweetie is a tart. Fold your hands at home, boy; all else is futile.

So the syntax slows from impetuous lunges to a stationary thud. Stanza 1, for all its "goe . . . catche . . . get . . . tell . . . teach . . . finde . . ." slows from two imperatives in the first line to one in the second, one in the next two, another in two, the last in three lines. Indicatives capture the subordinate clauses, infinitives, participles. The imperatives ease from action, "goe . . . catche . . . get with child," to education, "tell . . . teach," to private learning, "finde . . ." The second stanza imperative, "ride," comes in line 3 and conditionally; and its last sentence has only an indicative, "will tear . . . swear . . ." The last stanza moves from a conditionally passive to a negative, to a subjunctive, the future of the verb *to be*, establishing what will never be. So a forceful opening action closes in a woman's falsifications, repeated again, and again, and again.

Each stanza is structured by an opposition between exploratory trip and inward moral truth; as a brave voyage exploring all space, cosmology, geography, alchemy, "all strange wonders," without a taint of Faustian evil, shattering limits in a secular "Pilgrimage," ends in a thud of inertia, the dew of youth in a realization that moral knowledge is useless, honest intelligence has no sure reward, there is no fair and true woman. So, stanza by stanza, the speaker thrashes about, affirming himself yet mistrustful at the core, beset with pessimism, promiscuity, misogyny, yet lyrically singing. He hangs, very young, above the untrustworthy world, carefully arranging perspectives, but never moving. Yet we are mistrustful. He is too young, too pat, too green for so large a judgment, finally to remain in his mother's parlor. We suspect a rationalization, a sluggish precocity, handsomely justifying its doing nothing.

This poem, then, would seem a good-natured pratfall, a nickel's worth of cynical information, justifying inertia in a world beset by marvels; yet the song has too lofty an ease, too suave a music for such cynical immaturity. In each stanza, four tetrameter lines begin and end with an accent in a rocking-horse rhythm of easy momentum, suggesting a child's marvelous explorations. The double catch of two two-syllable lines closes in a flat tetrameter line, bringing the rollicking canter to a truncated close. Then one added syllable at the end of lines 5 and 6 ease the rocking-horse opening to a tetrameter trochee. Then this is no green boy, struggling with his inexperience, but the sweet balance of a world thoroughly grasped and rendered in song. The close has not a flicker of bitterness, but offers a long-known truth with flat finality. Some composed suavity is here, not a green fifteen-year-old, consulting his comrade, but a man-of-the-world, striking a pose. But before whom?

We suggested in our introduction the two male figures are the same person, Donne, the apprentice lover, consulting Donne, the young metaphysician, about the girl next door. Such a conference suggests a late boyish stage, one heterosexual consulting another about the world; but the poem has an urbane ease more appropriate to a man talking out loud to be overheard by the girl next door. By this reading, the poem becomes a suave seduction poem, its theme of promiscuity a ploy, establishing romantic psychologies for himself and the girl in the coming affair, its speaker no precocious fifteen-year-old, but an elite nineteen-year-old, whose crowd cracks the mysteries of nature, travels for adventure. Establishing his credentials is part of the elegant, stylized ritual of courtship.

With elegant disdain, he speaks to himself out loud, not directly to the girl. Women are beneath his notice, a common pot of promiscuity. He needn't lift a finger to meet one. Ignored, they come abegging.

Yet for all his disdain, he insults with enormous flattery. Stanza 2, line 9, is slightly ambiguous—a fair woman cannot be true; but a drab lackluster would make her peace with fidelity for lack of a suitor. And the girl next door?

> Though at next doore we might meet,
> Though she were true, when you met her,
> And last, till you write your letter,
> Yet shee
> Will bee
> False, ere I come, to two, or three.

Other fair women are untrue; but she (whom he seemingly has not met) is false in twos and threes. Disdainful, he considers her peerless, and available. Indeed, their meeting is inevitable. The subjunctives "might meet" and "were" in lines 22, 23, become the indicatives "will be," "come" in lines 26, 27. The stage is set. Their encounter will soon take place.

His apparent ambivalence becomes in context his instructions in behavior. By calling all women promiscuous, he indicates their romance will remain ephemeral and sexual—the decent fellow tells her how he keeps score in love, and also establishes paradoxical respect. Since all women are loose, she is the more choice for being taken. By respecting conventional morality—"Such a Pilgrimage were sweet"—he becomes a decent seducer, thoroughly docile, not—heaven forbid!—a lecher. But for all their elegance, his lines betray his youth. They never hasten; never lose grace. Suave, circumspect, they never grab, explode inside, use sensual language; a fine boy, but short of manhood, his seduction is more artistic than confident. It closes with no sniff of coming triumph.

This reading seems viable, but is too dramatic for the music. "Goe, and Catche" is a serene song, too easy and lilting for a seduction speech. It never gallops, pants, or chokes up. Its radiance suggests Ariel, not Troilus, an amplitude of spirit, touching all truths, social, alchemical, far and near, but pursuing none relentlessly. Its largesse belongs neither to a fifteen-year-old apprentice, nor a nineteen-year-old seducer, but a mellow twenty-five-year-old, still radiant with childhood, romantic, flirtatious, yet with an equilibrium of maturity, one who knows everything, believes in nothing, and is at peace. His song is freighted with old innocence and present pleasures; he still talks to men and women, but essentially to himself, climbing through life with casual elegance.

By this reading, each stanza addresses a stage in the speaker's life. In Stanza 1, the ardent student spars with confidence in his grasp of mysteries, yet despairs of his career. The hapless "honest mind" will develop itself——knowledge is easy and attainable; yet advancement remains an unattainable mystery. In Stanza 2, studies are over, the voyages under way. Born to strange sights, he will ride ten thousand days and nights, seeking adventure; but as after Stanza 1, here too he grows hopeless of any womanly ideal on earth. Stanza 3 stands beyond all seeking. Society condenses to the antiquated custom of pilgrimage. The speaker has the tranquility of a cynic, all his fabrics spotted under the glare of noon.

This reading engulfs the poem, but is too open-armed for its teasing frivolity. The poem is only a song, not a miniature *Divine Comedy* in twenty-seven lines, a spoof of falling stars, shimmering society, white-haired travelers, singing mermaids, and a loose girl next door. Its adventures are a ploy, its skepticism an easy cliché. Who ever had intercourse with a mandrake root? By this reading, the speaker is an aristocrat, plucking his lute to add zest to our beer, not a word to be given a passing thought.

We find then, a homebody and explorer, a lover and sluggish cynic, a Renaissance man and a melodious playboy. What elusive presence do these figures veil? Why haven't we Wordsworth's tangible persona? Granted the dramatic mode presumes a withdrawn, mysterious author, yet Donne seems somehow too elusive. The hero with a thousand faces shimmers before us, his selfhood undefined. Mysterious as Donne remains, "Goe, and Catche" is a lyric *Apologia pro Vita Sua*, singing a coming of age: tranquil immobility, innocent wisdom. The speaker stands transparent, yet utterly withdrawn. His life fills his poem; yet the poem is larger than his life, expressing so much and no more, elegant, craftsmanly, singing experienced ignorance, programmatic looseness, skeptical enamorment, a primer of promiscuity in a wise and lyrical despair, offered by a libertine gentle as a snowflake.

Indeed, this shimmer of music washes beyond its speaker onto layers of his culture. The finest Elizabethan writers sensed the vast sea-change toward modernity. The "thou" here is, among other things, Donne's embattled culture, each stanza expressing a stage in its growth. In Stanza 1, a medieval spirit offers magic and enveloping spirits, with alchemy to explore heaven, hell, mermaids, devils, mandrake roots, no infinite universe, but a bagful of past years and a burden of falling stars. By Stanza 2, boundaries fall away; alchemy yields to travel and adventure, devils and mermaids to overseas wonders; Renaissance riders, white with age, sniff after adventures. By Stanza 3, the mystery is threadbare. To change neighborhoods is a meaningless tedium—people are the same everywhere. Under the sun, there is only ennui. The speaker sinks to a sluggish, disbelieving boy; his faces flare and subside in the Elizabethan suburbs.

Our discussion shows Donne as a craftsman, not an evangelist. He shapes a poem; he does not send a message. The evangelist can achieve magnificent poetry—Blake, Wordsworth, D. H. Lawrence leap to mind—but the craftsman remains intimate, yet self-contained. A single reverberating voice does not come to focus, addressing us. The poems do their own singing; various, even opposing voices harmonize in a manifold song. We remain in part eavesdroppers.

Indeed, Donne's reticence suggests his élite Catholic family, its sons exiles and martyrs. So Donne was simultaneously a refugee and of the native aristocracy, a potential prime minister and religious martyr, with deep masks in his poetry. This is no constant, airy, artful dancer; the washes of feeling that engulf this poet are too turbulent to let him stand before us, naked. Yet he rises as a craftsman dancer, his hand outstretched, always in a role, a gesture, a situation. Schooled from infancy to twilight, his lyric plots mask and invest his feelings on paper casually as an airy song, an invitation to a dance of love.

So Donne fragmented his persona; yet it is a bit neat to settle for these fragments. That shadowy flesh-and-blood, the secretive exhibitionist, ambitious saint and ardent skeptic, Jack Donne, was no chamber-orchestra conductor, waving his baton over his poetry. What we call separate voices are, more elementally, raw hunks of a fissured consciousness, male, female, idealistic, lustful, hieratic, insipid, welling forth and slapped into shape. Even Donne's bloodless pronouns in Stanza 3, "one . . . mee . . . I . . . wee . . . shee . . . you . . . hee . . . you . . . your . . . shee . . . I," are real as the barnacled nouns of Stanza 1, "falling starres . . . mandrake root . . . Divels . . . Mermaides." Both stanzas are psychic states welling into form. Stanza 3 is no more cerebral than Stanza 1. It expresses not a logical response, but a clap of inner emptiness, the systole and diastole of Donne's spirit.

This process of self-expression in Donne might be compared with Keats and Yeats, two other masterly lyric craftsmen. "Ode to a Grecian Urn" does not demand we change our school system, as Blake demands we change our morals. Keats felt he wrote only lyric poetry, despite the surviving fragment, "This Living Hand," but his terms, lyric and dramatic, are deceptive. Keats always wrote dramatic poetry—there is no other kind. He absorbs the nightingale's song, the Grecian urn, but in a symbiotic drama. "This Living Hand," the fragment engaging his ego, is evangelical, conveying a particular message to a particular person. A master craftsman, the man Keats breathed through all his poems, but not all of him; his ardor, not his personal situation; his radiance, not his rages and complexes; his rhapsodic arrivals, not the strategies of his life. Keats himself chafed at this, calling his poems "lyrical," not "dramatic." The fragment, "This Living Hand," with its shudder of awareness of pinched immediacy, its here and now of a meager spark of life, looms raw and magnificent; yet is engulfed by the evangelical impulse. But here, Donne is always the master craftsman. Clumsy, unresolved, yet his evasive selfhood was the more massively there, his raw inner material shaped into poems as it blobbed up.

Yeats overstepped Keats' lyric mode. His "Saint and Hunchback" projects two human warps in a symbiotic relationship; yet both share the complex scaffolding of a single, large view of history. Yeats articulated a collective consciousness more than a personal and private one. We tremble for western Europe, for Leda and the swan, not for Yeats or any human girl friend. Yeats' scaffolding was various and complex enough to offer his most wayward impulses a "local habitation and a name." The scaffolding always held. Donne's temperament enjoyed no such framework; indeed, he shook and mistrusted them. Most shadowy and open of poets, all masks, though he slighted masks, his craftsmanly detachment protected him as he spewed out the raw, irregular hunks of his nature on paper. He has occasional female speakers; they do not matter. What was there, came out. He pretended no order, hid no embarrassing material. Yeats' poems express a complex mosaic dome, Donne's a Hamlet with no Claudius to grapple with.

We grope here for Donne's controls, shaping the half-formed hunks of his consciousness as they blobbed up in his lyrics. Here a number of equilibria suggest themselves that give his lyrics a taut balance. There is the balance between dramatic and public modes of speech, lines addressed to a particular person in the poem, and lines addressed to the reader of the poem. His best lyrics project a particular situation, but one loose enough to be an exemplar, or ignored altogether. So "Goe, and Catche" involved two friends, but also challenges the reader to step lively and pay attention. Indeed, the dramatic and public modes reinforce each other. The dramatic relaxes the reader, not bullying him directly; the public includes him in the action. Their balance, our very inability to fit the poem finally into either, makes it neither speech nor play, but a rounded entity; a *Ding-an-sich*. Too dramatic, it would read as lopped-off dialogue; too public, it would lose empathy and suspense. Hovering between them, it remains open, closed, a shadowed object that speaks our inner voice. Less successful by these standards, "Womans Constancy" begins:

> Now thou hast lov'd me one whole day,
> To morrow when thou leav'st, what wilt thou say?
> (ll. 1–2)

From the start, we are outside this action, eavesdropping on a broken conversation. It intrigues us, but as a stranger's voice, not our own.

Another equilibrium is between private feelings and public sentiments. The unspoken promise of lyric poetry is to express our deepest impulses without betraying us. A lyric poem is a halfway house, a platform in the public domain that shares our personal, private voice. Too public, the poem becomes a pedagogic exercise; too personal, it denies us openness. Great lyric poetry offers an exhilaration as by Freud's theory of humor. Inhibition suddenly proves unnecessary. Out there, in public, that poem expresses our locked inhibitions and finds welcome. Embarrassed, we relax our guard and exult. Too private, the poem misses the open thoroughfare; too public, it sits out there, a road sign or advertisement.

Another equilibrium is between casualness and structure. Thus Donne's arguments are not formal presentations, but begin *in medias res*, opening worlds of experience we presumed shut off, yet with a hard-edge logical structure. The random opening makes inhibitions an unnecessary encumbrance. A world of experience makes the conclusion seem inescapable. So "Goe, and Catche" sweeps about making discoveries, to conclude no woman can be trusted. The speaker argues not to us directly, but to a friend in earshot, and therefore more intimately to us, the readers.

So Donne's language balances slang and archaisms, cliché-ridden phrases and a freight of loving anxiety. His casual, formalized clichés come from nursery, Sunday School, and law court, not out of Donne's crucible of imagination; they are the deposit of elemental human experience, blurred remains of multitudinous experience, "Get with child . . . Mermaides singing . . . envies stinging . . . to advance an honest mind." Yet unexpected gestures open loaded cellars of feeling like a trigger; as imperatives pulse through them, "goe . . . catche . . . get . . . tell." They finger aged pockets of experience to start a truth.

Thus, in "Goe, and Catche," promiscuity is suggested as a coy tease, the speaker protesting his innocence. His poem is no clearing of ground for a seduction, but background music for a flirtation, its exuberant music counterbalancing its lethargic speaker, a nice adolescent, slightly intimidated, but with a fine style, hopefully beginning an anxious, ardent love life. His gauzy nouns suggest a virgin. The girl next door listens, curious; but he stays at home, content with his song.

No other promiscuity poem works as well. "Womans Constancy" is locked in its situation. After a day of sexual license, the speaker warns the woman against fabricating reasons for leaving him, absolving himself of responsibility, with just a ring of self-righteousness as he leaves her. A committed lecher would not have bothered. If he is rationalizing, his arguments suggest an adolescent need to look honest, even dishonestly. Yet the poem may be a sudden, straightforward discovery of female psychology, the apprentice lover wildly, sullenly guessing her irrationality, her fabricated excuses, her lack of loyalty, and warning her, matching irrationality for irrationality, rejection for rejection.

This speaker seems a notch older than in "Goe, and Catche," uttering a first song of experience against a last, poignant song of innocence. The speaker is no coward; but his barrage of driven logic and harassed irrelevance has a pathetic ring. Insecure, he falls back on school brilliance, shadowboxing in logic, commanding no blunt truth. His use of logic, metaphysics, and law are from his situation, fearing legal consequences, confronting the irrational, his grasp of reality torn apart in the heat of sexual love. Dramatically—and this poem is narrowly dramatic—he gropes for her thoughts after hours of intimacy, and feels, with a snarl of discovery, that he knows nothing, has no security. A wave of ignorance washes across his eyes. He stands before a strange ocean, with no map or guide.

The speaker shows masculine force. Beset and insecure, he matches rejection for rejection. Ignorant, he will not be trampled on. Yet this strong self-assertion may be all a bluff. Nervous, hasty, brilliant, adolescent, he washes his hands. The poem finishes with a mousy perhaps—"I may thinke so too." He does not betray his intentions, only his clay feet. So the woman is aloof, enigmatic, autonomous, he bewildered, secretive, defiant. This is no formal courtly love poem, like others by Donne, but a slice-of-life of a speaker whose temperament leans to courtly love. It would seem that Donne leaned to courtly love poetry because he found its uneasy dynamic congenial to his temperament. The poems of emotional marriage and the analysis of love may erase this; but this speaker is on the run, not just on the move.

The verse is clumsy throughout. After a truncated tetrameter opening line, it lurched forward on pentameter lines, with occasional two- and three-line interruptions, tumbling out six questions with no apparent coherence, all ending on the line stop, piled in a seriatim drone to a one-sentence disengagement. This series of urgent questions parallels the imperatives of "Goe, and Catche," but woodenly, with no ordered development. Yet this congested music is dramatically effective. Wallowing in the wake of sex, his harassed questions attest to his insecurity, the thin logic of a befuddled anxiety. Only by a *quid pro quo* does he claim promiscuity too. This is no brave new world, but an open, choppy sea.

"Womans Constancy" might allow a female speaker; but its tone is against such a reading. The power of decision here is in the hands of the person addressed; the speaker only responds in kind. Yet such power is characteristically in the hands of the woman, in such dramatic lyrics, as "Goe, and Catche," "The Apparition," "The Legacie," "Loves Exchange," "The Message," "The Flea," "The Baite," and "The Prohibition." Furthermore, the conclusion of the poem seems to call for a male speaker:

> Vaine lunatique, against these scapes I could
> Dispute, and conquer, if I would,
> Which I abstaine to doe,
> For by to morrow, I may thinke so too.
>
> (ll. 14–17)

As a graduate student (female) succinctly put it, "A woman might think this; but she would never say it."

"The Indifferent" is saucy and public, with a pointed finger:

> I can love her, and her, and you and you,
> I can love any, so she be not true.
>
> (ll. 8–9)

In a yard, at a party, a naughty male is naughty out loud to a group of females, some listening, some not. His tone is spotty. Some lines have intriguing overtones; others fall flat with juvenile banality—"Her whom the country forms, and whom the town." The naughty cliché reversal of "dangerous constancy" suit a boys' club more than two lovers. Venus, the *deus ex machina* in Stanza 3, will set all to rights, not as a classical god evoked with adult seriousness, but as a little faïry godmother. Each stanza closes with a neatly trimmed aphorism:

> I can love any, so she be not true.
> (l. 9)
>
> Grow your fixt subject, because you are true?
> (l. 18)
>
> You shall be true to them, who'are false to you.
> (l. 27)

This seems too bare-faced a public preachment; but Donne is not to be trusted on a Sunday School lesson on love with Venus as his godmother. His juvenile acquiescence sets the scene for a jouncy seduction. The questions in Stanza 2 betray him as posturing throughout, a pontifical twelve-year-old serving as stalking horse for a suave, shadowy grown-up.

"Communitie" has an equally narrow tone, arriving at promiscuity through simplified abstractions more suited to theology than love. Where "The Indifferent" suggests a school situation, "Communitie" suggests a seminar, its terms too rarified for ethics. Yet it affirms a neutral, indifferent world, ruled by taste, even for promiscuity. The speaker's juvenalia betrays him in the last stanza; the extended metaphor of devouring fruit, eating a kernel and discarding its shell, is an extended oral metaphor. The patient, piecemeal logic is everywhere correct, but thin. Both "The Indifferent" and "Communitie" preach promiscuity in a brazen defiance of conventional ethics, beating a boyish drum of logic. Self-consciously waving a proposition, the speaker treads gingerly forward. Sinking his whole weight, he might go through.

"Confined Love" is equally remote, shifting closer through the solar system, the animal kingdom, travel, the establishment of a home. Except for one abstract reference to "womankind"

(l. 4), no woman intrudes on the poem. Yet for all his circumspection, his perverse logic is pugnacious, and would make a home of devoted people a locked vault of greed. A happy, generous, loving family presumes promiscuity. The conclusion is neat, but blandly absurd. The poem is a logical exercise.

"Loves Usury" advocates promiscuity, but under pressure of circumstance. The love god has been sniffed from afar. A strong temperament, trembling before the engagement of courtly love, he undertakes a harassed bluff. This poem is no coy evocation of Venus, but the assessment of a practiced lover, who sniffs the god of love coming, and bargains for time. There is an awful sense of playing for sanity in a dangerous game. The resilient music hasn't the variety of "Goe, and Catche," but an immediate bravura, and lusty force. Each stanza has six pentameter lines; but the two-foot second and last lines allow a catch of breath, as in close bargaining. So, high-styled, the speaker levels a broadside of verbs at love:

> Till then, Love, let my body raigne, and let
> Me travell, sojourne, snatch, plot, have, forget . . .
>
> (ll. 5–6)

The verbs suggest a harassed shifting about. So the shift from Anglo-Saxon to Latinate, then altogether to French:

> From country grasse, to comfitures of Court,
> Or cities quelque choses . . .
>
> (ll. 14–15)

indicates insecurity and baffled irritation, a loss of native familiarity. So, his heavy, truncated rhyme, "let report/My minde transport." His rhetoric ripples with the variety of a jury presentation. Belaboring his opponent as "usurious," he snatches what he can before love levels him.

The poem plunges *in medias res;* but the subjunctive, "thinke that yet/We'had never met" (l. 7–8), betrays that love has already brushed him. Still in shock, he gropes for terms before a second encounter. This is no inverse love poem. Under threat, the speaker surveys his resources; but his weakness is apparent throughout. His offer of twenty-to-one has a sporting bravado, but is a loser's gesture, snatching at any terms, as is his offer of self-degradation in Stanza 2. His plea, "thinke that yet/We'had never met," is pathetic wish-fulfilment. The coming life he foresees under Love, after flailing and thrashing about, is one of the passive victim, obedient "fruit of love" over whom Love can "doe thy will." *La belle dame sans merci* already has her victim. Despite his fine style, his closing couplet betrays him:

> Spare mee till then, I'll beare it, though shee bee
> One that loves mee.
>
> (ll. 23–24)

His final indignity is sex with a loving woman. The world of wholesome love is already repugnant.

Our last poem, "Loves Diet" has four stanzas, expressing a lethargic, anal-controlled temperament, that measures out sighs and tears, so much per day. The speaker here is not entirely clear. The common reading, calling for a male speaker throughout, is only possible if we take "my love" in line 2 as the subject addressed throughout the poem. But there is no other instance in Donne's lyrics where a male speaker bullies and controls some abstract entity, "my love." On the contrary, an independent "love" is characteristically a demonic force allied with the woman, not the man, and threatening to him. Indeed, this reading is particularly inappropriate among these oralities and physicalities, bordering on cannibalism. An abstract love could hardly keep its footing among such corpulences, diets, sighs, heats, tears, and drinks. Furthermore, a male addressing his love confuses the pronouns in Stanzas 2, 3, and 4. Does a male speaker complain of his own love:

> And if sometimes by stealth he got
> A she sigh from my mistresse heart,
> And though to feast on that, I let him see
> 'Twas neither very sound, nor meant to mee.
>
> (ll. 9–12)

Why has he a "mistresse heart?" Why is love a "he" at a time of 'she sighs' from a man? Who is the third person female in "If he suck'd hers" (l. 15)? Is a man jealous because his love is somehow nursing on a woman's tears? Exactly what is his jealousy?

The straightforward reading of the poem would give it a female speaker, a befuddled female slug, so involved in her body she can barely love outside herself. The opening polysyllables then become grotesquely literal and funny, a plodding female narcissist, who worries about weight-control in her bland, flat way:

> To what a cumbersome unwieldinesse
> And burdenous corpulence my love had growne,
> But that I did, to make it lesse,
> And keep it in proportion,
> Give it a diet, made it feed upon
> That which love worst endures, *discretion.*
>
> (ll. 1–6)

Given Donne's occasional vulgar ribaldry at this period, this reading stands even if we take the "cumbersome unwieldinesse" in Stanza 1 to refer to the man's penis, rather than to the woman's torso, which she refuses to stimulate beyond a certain point. By Stanzas 2 and 3, the sighs and tears rule out this reading; yet an opening ribaldry eminently suits the tone here. Yet even as an opening allusion, the reference is more appropriate to a female speaker than a male, who would most oddly refer to his organ as "my love."

Our calorie counter trims her stanza to 5, 5, 4, 4, 5, 5 feet per line, tightening its waist to tetrameters. Not very bright, and out of touch with reality, her love is a vague extension of her calorie-counting. Stanza 1 says flatly her choice is a decent diet of ardent love—let that hungry young fellow control himself. Her diet only allows so much per day. Italicizing "discretion" elevates it to a patron god. Other women worship Aphrodite; she worships *discretion*, her caloric golden mean.

Stanza 2 elaborates her anal-sadistic relationship with her hapless lover, apparently an ultimate masochistic lamebrain, compulsively trying to extract things from her, an extra tear from her "mistresse heart," or a sigh—she "let him see/'Twas neither very sound . . ." Describing a sigh as not "sound" is an unpleasant pun. Perhaps he misunderstood a long belch.

But Stanza 3 betrays a rival—our speaker is unsure of her supposedly mousy lover, now sucking her rival's tears, another unpleasant eating of body wastes. She assures him her rival weeps in all directions—her tears are but counterfeit sweat. Her one-a-day quota is more trustworthy. She derides her rival's counterfeit "meat," yet suspects they make love. The concern grows, promoting the rival from line 3 in Stanza 3 to line 2 in Stanza 4. Evidently taking over, the rival sends her reassuring letters.

The last stanza we read as a shift to the male speaker. This is somewhat clumsy without directions, like Marvell's in his dialogues, but not an irremediable objection. An artful balance of stage directions in a lyric poem—"He . . . ; she . . ."—would not be congenial to Donne; and the alternative, a male speaker throughout the poem, makes bewildering the pronouns and the frame of discourse. A handsome advantage in reading the poem as a shift to a male speaker in the last stanza is the balance of vegetable soul in Stanzas 1 to 4, with diet, corpulence, retention, etc., and the animal soul in Stanza 5, with a violent, jagged hunt.

In the last stanza, then, the man sloughs off her "buzzard" love. Enough carrion and body wastes! After four ponderous, bottled-up stanzas, feeding on sighs and tears, he is ready for love meat:

> I spring a mistresse, sweare, write, sigh, and weep;
> And the game kill'd, or lost, goe talke, and sleepe.
> (ll. 29–30)

But we mistrust this explosion of vitality from a man so long subservient to this plodding, self-indulgent narcissist. He rings less like a master lover, than as a harassed boy with delusions of grandeur, continuously extracting things from her body. Indeed, as in "Womans Constancy," a withdrawn woman domineers a harassed, but proud battler; and despite the farcical exaggeration, both poems resemble slice-of-life drama too much to be dismissed as lyrical exercises. This male deference and weakness recalls such courtly love poems as "Loves Exchange," a bent in the speaker's disposition rectified in "The Extasie."

Considered as a group, the promiscuity poems project no De Sade, isolating segments of the body, but a boy of high, theoretical daring, for all his chaste, windy bravura, waving his boyish sword in all directions as he treads gingerly forward. Only the doctrine of intercourse is suggested, the exhilaration of chasing women, not the experience that follows catching them. Indeed, as an actual woman approaches, his temperament grows muffled. The poems suggest lively play, but not sensuous experience, or the flow of vegetable passions. Even "Womans Constancy," which most simply renders a sexual experience, projects an embattled, insecure man. These are not robust, adult celebrations of promiscuity.

Indeed, despite their subject, most of them keep narrowly masculine, at arm's length from an actual woman. Courting, their speaker engages in high-blown student arguments, a sort of courtship dance, establishing his credentials. Indeed, his doctrinal exuberance, combined with extreme ignorance, suggests an ironic discrepancy between posture and social reality. The speaker in "Goe, and Catche" is delighted in, ironic perhaps, yet so charming, we ignore his possible next stage.

Donne worked, then, with a strong thread of negative capability. Like Shakespeare, he sank shafts into his unconscious, drew out strange psychic forms, and spread them on paper, yet was embattled and tumultuous, withdrawn, tangled in his own ego, without Shakespeare's large patience. A secretive Gothic craftsman, he flung out words, hid behind them, subtly belittled them. Keats labored to freight every vein with ore; Donne built thinner, harder verbal structures, tortuous constructs, like the wayward productions of a brilliant boy engineer. Yet his craftsmanly gesture sketched in the contours of his spirit, monumentally changing. Nothing snagged him, not fleshly fulfilment, nor doctrinal security. Nothing was quite sure. His pen was afloat, as was his spirit.

# 4

# The Misogyny Poems

Donne wrote five misogyny poems, "Loves Alchymie," "The Curse," "The Apparition," "Farewell to Love," and "Selfe Love." Harsh, ribald, cumbersome, grotesque, they discharge undigested experience in coarse language, their extreme episodes suggesting a deeper love experience than the promiscuity poems; yet they remain violent gestures of sudden disengagement.

"Loves Alchymie" expresses a thumping sour-grapes exasperation at women and love. It debunks a traditional presentation, mocks marriage, and defines women in an appalled black humor; like a grotesque medieval masque, it uses mummies, pregnant pots, hoarse minstrels, futile alchemists, and a chasing after bubbles. Its two stanzas ramble interminably, with a loose rhyme scheme and length of line, that somehow holds together, an imbecilic gluing together of lines that calls itself a stanza.

In Stanza 1, Edenic alchemists try to distill the elixir, lovers the essence of love; but line 1 grossly puns on the first person possessive, "Myne." Digging in "loves Myne" establishes property. The phrase is so concentrated as to suggest an oxymoron; surely if it is love, it is not mine. So in line 3, "I have lov'd, and got," a getting that follows hard on a love experience. As the alchemist cooks obscure ingredients to refine "th'Elixar"; so the lover seeks to possess the elixir of love. Yet all is in vain—the hidden mystery escapes him; only the alchemist's pot is soon pregnant, and so the woman, vulgarly her lover's pot. So, digging in obscure mines for love produces pregnant mistresses, squawling babies, and a tedious household bustle.

The lover's mind is as ridiculous as his way of life. The alchemist, a chemical drudge, the mythic elixir dangling before his nose, glories in his occasional accidental perfumes and medicines by which, presumably, he supports himself (ll. 8–10). Once he celebrated the search for "th'Elixar"; now he "glorifies his pregnant pot" (l. 8), a form of alchemical idolatry. So the dedicated lover digs his mines for the essence of love. But in lines this grotesque, digging in love's mine strongly suggests sexual intercourse, the "centrique happinesse" of love, as it were, dangling before his nose while he horses in bed. Moreover, mines suggest graves and cemeteries. So our idealistic lover, refining the essence of love, ends self-deluded in a symbolic grave, glorifying his pot, multiplying babies, and possessed by a mummy.

The work of the poem is a simultaneous clearing and maculation, a clearing of inert ideas and a smearing with contempt all pretense in love, indeed all pomposity and pretended order whatever, an explosion of exasperation at all unreal modes of grasping reality. An instinct is expressed here, more than an idea, a hunger without a name, an undefined fanatical challenge and confrontation that turns sour every taste in his brain. The speaker is after plain reality, if he can ever attain it. Sour, exasperated, he treats alchemy like stage witchcraft, with gross exaggeration and vividness to register disbelief. Its principles are not denied as such. Its vocabulary still possesses his language, "centrique happinesse . . . hidden mysterie . . . chymique . . . th'Elixar . . . pregnant pot," but its pursuit is "imposture all," the search impossible, the alchemist a ludicrous failure.

The speaker is after something intangible. There is a sense of a huge collapsing structure, of love, cosmological ideas, techniques for self-fulfilment. The freight of ideas still holds, but only because no one has blown hard at it. So the poem is expressing an attitude of mind more than it is saying something. It is testing its tendons in disbelief, flexing and shifting about to discover how far order can be undermined. As it moves, flaws crack across astronomy, morals, economics, love, magic, the social hierarchy; yet the poem has no horror, as do *Measure for Measure* or *Troilus and Cressida*. Its lines are rather the snort of a fledgling battlehorse. Its mastery of speaker over material is maintained to the end. Revelation piles on revelation; yet the poem closes with sage advice: "Hope not for minds in women." In the floodtide of collapsing structure, the speaker reveals the ways of the world in old, tired truths. So, exasperated, sarcastic, furious at his entrapment, he rails at his own condition, his metaphysical shudder only loosely focused on romantic love, as a snag, a prime example. Only the closing couplet, summarizing the implications of the analogies, hints at a more humanistic perspective:

> So, lovers dreame a rich and long delight,
> But get a winter-seeming summers night.
>
> (ll. 11–12)

The stanzas struggle forward clumsily; but the stanza break is clear. Stanza 2 comes with a measure of disengagement; as we shift from love to marriage, in metaphysics from alchemy to cosmology. The humanistic attitude closing Stanza 1 is itemized at the beginning of Stanza 2, in a tension with false ideals of cosmology or love. It is clearly one or the other:

> Our ease, our thrift, our honor, and our day,
> Shall we, for this vaine Bubles shadow pay?
>
> (ll. 13–14)

One ends up not so much an animal, as grossly imperceptive and uncivilized. Not only are such ideas vain; but their activity dulls the tongue, blurs discernment, deadens one to the truth, and produces a ridiculous buffoon. Alchemy, cosmology, and idealized love blot out "ease . . . thrift . . . honor . . . day." The word is not to be trusted of a man who:

> Would sweare as justly, that he heares,
> In that dayes rude hoarse minstralsey, the spheares.
>
> (ll. 21–22)

So ignorant ideals deaden us to reality and make it ridiculous.

"Vaine Bubles shadows" (l. 14) could refer to the boiling of bubbles in the alchemist's pot; but line 22 refers to the cosmic spheres. In place of stable medieval spheres, moving with harmonious music under their guardian angel, only "vaine Bubles" cast their empty shadows. Comparing changing cosmological ideas to changing attitudes in love could be regarded as a metaphysical conceit, to be compared with, say, early Eighteenth Century conceits; but the word "conceit" is inadequate to the frame of mind rendering the comparison, not being intuitive enough to the relationship here of his temperament to his subject matter. Donne is not rendering vivid a truth about love by a truth about cosmology. His poem is less an utterance, than a snort or exhalation of mind. It expresses not a thought, but a habit of thought. It does not actually go at truth, so much as it flexes its muscles to go at truth. The comparison is not a conceit, but an articulation of a possible conceit. In a rage of maculation, of catabolism, the speaker establishes the musculature of his mind over the musculature of the cosmos, his instincts of rectitude over the ethic of idealistic love. The world may say no; his mind does not bow or say amen.

So, in a glancing swipe, he questions the value of social hierarchy. The groom who believes in a love marriage is ignorant, unstable, and tasteless. Like a latter-day medieval believer, he would find his bride a sphere of love, with whose guardian angel his mind will presumably produce a harmony like the music of the spheres. But women have no straightforward minds. Their best arts are ornamental, "Sweetnesse and wit" (l. 24), physical grace and charm of speech. The reality of the relationship is "rude hoarse minstralsey" (l. 22), a Breugel celebration beneath social hierarchy. Thinking he is participating in the music of the spheres, he will engage in simpering polite gossip, sing "Greensleeves" after supper in two-part harmony. So, a man-servant can outdo his master in sexual pleasure, more easily stomaching "the short scorne of a bridegroomes play" (l. 17).

But the sardonic tearing-apart rises to another pitch at the close:

> . . . at their best
> Sweetnesse and wit, they'are but *Mummy*, possest.
> (ll. 23–24)

A woman is an antique pagan corpse, a dehydrated mummy with no rational soul. By the more conservative view of this period, living human bodies were earth shapes, possessed of a soul. Then, by a whimsical extension, women are artificial constructs, with no human soul; they are only possessed. But the word "possess't" has a straightforward commercial meaning, reinforcing "myne" and "get" in Stanza 1, as a piece of property. Helen Gardner refers to the superstitious use of Egyptian mummies at this time; but this only adds sardonic laughter to his frustrated exasperation, suggesting a double element of commercialism and the supernatural, possession of a property bond, and a seizure in spirit by a ghost or a devil. And this is marriage; thinking you are joining a living human being, you make a murky property arrangement for a clay figure possessed by uncanny forces that will soon possess you.

But "Mummy" has a straightforward, outrageously colloquial meaning. One's mother is affectionately called, "mummy," with unforced, reverberating Oedipal implications. In marriage, one may seek to break with home; but mummy possesses the bride, and, in turn, the groom. Indeed, the very adolescent search for idealized angels and "centrique happinesse" leads to Oedipal enslavement. The pun is the more significant in view of the characteristic stance of the speaker in the promiscuity poems as an apprentice lover, vis-à-vis a woman more settled in her ways than he. So here, the pun on "mummy" suggests an unresolved thread of juvenalia, an apprentice boy who keeps seeing his sexual object as somehow older, more settled, even with a touch of maternal warmth. These poems have a ring of early work.

The poem suggests two classes of possessing spirits, the supposed guardian angels, whose pursuit is a delusive enslavement, and those unnamed intruders that transform women into mummies. Milton, Hobbes, and others pursued an alternative monism; but Donne is no monist, settling accounts with material reality, but a fixed, embattled dualist, with an absolute commitment to autonomous spirit, one that gradually grew stronger, and finally gravitated to an utter commitment to God, as he shrugged off one plane and embraced the other entirely. At this early, secular stage, he is exasperated by a dualism impossible to structure and impossible to abandon. The speaker at the end has discharged his ribald outrage. He is disengaged from this or that particular girl; but disengagement from love or spirit is nowhere hinted at.

A poem so brief, yet so far-reaching, making farcical the search for truth, confessing the irrelevance of his own pursuits, breaking down all hierarchy, social, personal, or cosmological, is, if anything, about too much. The poem expresses some misogyny, disdainfully placing women below men in the hierarchy of existence; but this is absorbed into an annoyed impatience at the physicality of sex, a revulsion at the "diggers," the "mynes," the "chemyques," the "odoriferous things," a chafing of perplexed irritation at the discrepancy between physical intercourse and ideal essences of love. Its props belong in a barbaric Bavarian mummer's play at the grotesquerie of intercourse.

> Ends love in this, that my man,
> Can be as happy'as I can . . .
>
> (ll. 15–16)

The lugubrious aristocrat cries, the iron rungs of hierarchy wobbling under his feet. This is no settled attitude, but a twitch of wayward revulsion. It testifies to Donne's fecund openness, his freedom to slam out any momentary impulse, give it a garment of imagery and ideology. So each poem must be viewed as a gesture, not merely as a statement, poem placed alongside poem in the mosaic of Donne's spirit.

The gesture here is a very large one; but its tone of aggressive self-assertion would seem contradicted by its pathetic truths. So the sloughing off of the idealization of women extends to all idealization. The poem is finally a broad arrival at young adulthood, a settling of accounts with adolescent idealism and unreality, a hosing out of dead ideas, collapsed metaphysical structures, techniques useless to solve problems, even obsessions about property and society. Hence, as is rare in

Donne, the complete absence of any specific listener. Donne is his own listener, referring in an exasperation of impatience to alchemy, cosmology, love, sex, marriage, property, society, all the tangle of trouble that stand in his personal way. He is clearing ground to establish the groundwork of his life, with a shudder at the insecurity of it all. Love is the most important component involved; but the subject here is the stripping away of bad mental machinery for the business of living.

Donne expresses much doubt here and elsewhere about spheres and essences—indeed, his "First Anniversary" has put him in the vanguard of metaphysical speculation among Seventeenth Century poets:

> And new philosophy calls all in doubt,
> The element of fire is quite put out.
>
> (ll. 205–206)

Yet nowhere in his poetry does he make a gesture toward grasping a more viable cosmology. He has simply a revulsion of skepticism at existing structures in a habit of mind of radical doubt, sloughing off ideas, showing hallowed structures as forced and artificial. So the poem expresses simultaneously the coming of age of a tough mind, and a shock of revulsion at the lack of stable security anywhere, in an aesthetic gesture of stark paradox and dialectic.

The closing line is a piling of shock on shock, matter emptied of its angelic spirits, then demonically invested, Oedipal horror piled on metaphysical dismay. The raw totality of the breakdown transcends his immediate subject; its spirit is a graveyard of metaphysical relics that arouses exasperation, farcical fury, the raw reality of the psyche its only touchstone of truth. So Donne shifts, questions, and maneuvers; with a quick, ambivalent reversal, he throws into doubt in the last line the very securities his poem has painfully arrived at.

The elemental revulsion at clichés, metaphysical, moral, and psychological, recalls Shakespeare's *Troilus and Cressida*, a play also gripped by a general revulsion, aside from the personal motivations of the people in it. The entire play expresses an aesthetic of centrifugal violence, testing what can hold against the playwright's assault, thrashing about, testing, and flinging about securities and frames of reference. So Donne here works on an aesthetic of centrifugal violence, brushing away heaped relics and coming upon fresh bewilderments. His poems of emotional marriage may celebrate a paean of union; but his orgiastic fulfilment here lies in a smash of furious disintegration, its catharsis familiar, mistrustful, even demonic. This aesthetic of catabolism is a dominant strand throughout his poetry. His Holy Sonnets have the same restless thrashing about; but the structure of the cosmos, in and of itself, was not his subject, as it clearly was at times in Shakespeare. Thus, he never questions his dualism, but ends on the level of spirit, the shock of intimate union with "Mummy possest."

But when all cosmological disengagement has been explicated in "Loves Alchymie," the relationship of alchemists and mummies, the poem remains an exercise of sheer energetic fun, role debunking, and boyish wickedness. The rhythm is heavy and pounding, with an irregular stagger forward, as a boy might imitate a drunken sailors' dance:

> Oh, 'tis imposture all:
> And as no chymique yet th'Elixar got,
> But glorified his pregnant pot,
> If by the way to him befall
> Some odoriferous thing, or medicinall . . .
> (ll. 6–10)

Indeed, the first person plural of, "Our ease, our thrift, our honor, and our day,/Shall we . . ." (ll. 13–14), suggests the set of apprentices, squires and clerks, rising in a body to bargain for blocks of life, crying out in solidarity what pots are worth putting up to boil. Indeed, the very looseness of subject matter here, its over-large, self-indulgent grasp is a late adolescent, shaggy wilfulness, refusing to be put down or to trim its lines. This boy is truculent. He knows nobody is keeping score.

"The Curse" is also a "fun" poem, a fine lyric exercise, like the exercises among the promiscuity poems, apparently related to some occasion. Its four stanzas in 32 lines grind out curses on whoever would identify the speaker's mistress. Kent, in *King Lear*, cursed with more righteous fury; Prince Hal and Falstaff exchanged diatribes with more gusto and hearty bravura. This speaker has less vivacity, and belabors his subject to exhaustion. "Madnesse his sorrow, gout his cramp" (l. 9) is brief, conventional, and dull; his concern is not the culprit's physical condition, but family humiliation and abased love. His anger is neither elemental, nor barbaric enough for ultimate curses.

This cursing is our manifest content; but an opening ambiguity teases us. The speaker's anger is at the presumption of betraying his mistress; but beyond dispute, he has one. Then why the fury? Surely young aristocrats have had mistresses before. Why the uncontrolled rant? The immature pique seems appropriate to a giddy boy who cannot tolerate rumors of his love involvement; or else the unnamed woman may be above him in station or married altogether, entailing dangers of scandal. But then the closing couplet betrays him:

> For if it be a shee
> Nature before hand hath out-cursed mee.
> (ll. 31–32)

Afraid to be specific, he curses all women. But a boy with a mistress, who rants about the universal curse of womankind, is a charm of immaturity. Piqued, exasperated, he dresses down the wall. We trust his girl friend at the time never came upon his poem.

The poem rings as a dramatic episode—we trust his discretion in the matter—but the speaker is having too good a time, ranting about treason, family estate, tyranny, public schedules. We dare say Donne the man would have cursed more elementally, and more concretely. This is no exterminating angel, but a piqued boy, in a good-natured cursing exercise.

"The Curse" bristles with pique at a possible rejection; "The Apparition" grows incandescent at the event itself. The poem expresses a thin thread of revulsion, sliding through seventeen lines without a period, a stanza break, any rhyme scheme, or pattern of feet per line. With an extraordinarily hollow fixity of intent, the poem strips away to the event itself. No argument is developed, no story told, no episode embellished with motives or recrimination. There is only her gesture of rejection, and his narrow, pitched response, concentrated like a laser beam on her coming moment of self-discovery, a moment to which the entire poem is fixed in a catatonic fury. The poem deals with elemental existences, not washes of feeling and complex situations. Indeed, the speaker has such preternatural concentration, he is already a ghost in anticipation, forcing the future into shape, fixing its content, participating in its arrival. Indeed, as elsewhere Donne projects a female god of courtly love, and a female possessing spirit, so "The Apparition" is the confession of a warlock at the moment when he comes into being and ceases to be a living man.

Of all major English poets, Donne wrote most radically in the present tense, sharply articulating the very gesture of living, in all its bewildering, unexpected risk. But the present tense is most risky. The location of a poem in the present tense can also entail its loss for an emptiness of non-life, a random rattling of human pieces, tumbling into the grave. The tone here resembles Eliot's "The Hollow Men"; but Eliot only offers stylized intimations of experience, as he projects surrealistic figures with somber stagecraft, "headpiece filled with straw." Donne kept his grasp on reality. His episode here is literally real, however murky its atmosphere.

In articulating the import of a poet, we should not translate his words into another terminology too systematically, but keep as close as possible to his own expression, however bleak, rendering cosmology as cosmology, insanity as insanity, moral abstractions as moral abstractions. Such lyrics as "The Apparition" suggest time is no natural flow or bond, underlying all events, but simply the pace of the solitary psyche, the course of one's spark of life, with whatever jumps or interludes. Such an extreme position may have become difficult to advance seriously after Newton; but in this twilight period of the early Seventeenth Century, Donne could grasp a man feeling his libido snuffed out, his life force drained of nerve. Call it anti-time, limbo, what you will; but the spirit of this speaker is hard, dry, on the event, not the moody, emotional death-in-life of the Victorian poet, but the snapped chain of life and death.

Hence the ambiguity of the first line, "When by thy scorne,

O murdresse, I am dead." Lines 2 and 3 tell us with a wrench, he means a literal death to come, but line 1 uses the present tense without qualifying the word "murdresse." A murder has been committed, an inner death finished before its physical consummation. The man is a walking corpse. The poem has only two events, the speaker's present condition, emptied of occasion, setting, or content of any kind, like the damned in Dante's hell, who see the future, but not their present moment, and the coming moment, lived in anticipation, when she will grasp her own condition. His very ghostly condition is insubstantial. The comparative, "veryer" (l. 13), is an uncanny paradox. "Very" refers to real existence, and should be a matter of either-or, not of degree. Yet here her ghost is veryer; even his ghost has its existence only relative to hers, being a male possessing spirit. The speaker has slipped outside of time, the pace of events, and become a parasitic shadow waiting for its substance in her spirit. Hence, the present moment is beclouded, the future moment graphically depicted: her company, her physical condition, her very "cold quicksilver sweat"; as she realizes her thread of life is torn, loose, irrelevant.

Two phrases sketch in their former relationship. "Fain'd vestall" (l. 5) suggests a false pretender of some virginal dedication, so her anticipated rejoicing to be free "From all solicitation from mee" (l. 3). The relationship would seem to have been rather bitter, of an importunate solicitor and a diffident girl, who sloughs him off, pretending purity and dedication. But can we trust his testimony? Rejected, he judges her a pleasure-seeker, to be possessed by bored men (l. 7). His furious sincerity is appalling; but sober judgment suggests otherwise. He never had a firm grip on reality; his traumatic rejection would only snap it.

However, this piecing together of the story is too secular, too clinical, beside the point to the poem. This poem narrates a possession, not a social situation. Its gesture is the snapping of the thread of life in a man divorced from life, his adoption of a new vocation. At its end, he is become an apparition, a walking corpse, waiting to die and take possession in her weakness. This is beyond vengeance—even vengeance has overtones of passion; but he says bluntly, "my love is spent" (l. 15). Passion is over; he is in another order of existence, a damned shade, hanging in wait to possess her spirit.

He refuses to reveal what he will say (l. 14). We suspect not a moral judgment—the poem suggests she is altogether innocent. But given his knotted strength and adolescent weakness, his intensity and lack of grasp, his pleas for acceptance and defiant possession, at the least, he will tell her that neither of them will be lonely again. So radically estranged, cut off from her intimacy, he would slide into an apparition. When he possesses her, the two will be like two damned spirits, locked inside walls of ice in the lower reaches of Dante's hell, out of touch with reality, abandoned inside one another.

"The Apparition" is exceedingly dramatic, carved and projected as a warlock's resolution. By its plot and the stance of its speaker, we take it to be part of Donne's first great period of lyric writing. Here there is a thrashing about in insecure experience with nothing trusted and nothing decisively rejected. All its gestures are tentative, dramatized, projected. These poems are a clutter of inherited material, ghosts, demons, and warlocks. "Loves Alchymie" may flush out a framework of thought; but the poem ends in a fresh dilemma. The decisive flushing-out will not come until "The Extasie."

"Farewell to Love" records in four stanzas a rueful shift from reverend idealization to sour disinterest. Its rhyme scheme and length of line are a graceless complexity of ten-line stanzas, with a one-foot sag in line 7. At the start, the speaker revered some deity of love; but the transitory flit of society, the brevity of sexual pleasure, subsequent sorrow, the pressure of producing children, have all chilled his ardor. He will avoid women now, not to damage himself (l. 34), or just discharge his sexual heat (ll. 39–40). Again accepted hierarchies are debunked, clichés reduced to their raw physical substratum; but the speaker lacks the tumultuous authenticity of "Loves Alchymie." His lyric is a lively, grumbling refrain.

We suspect Grierson closes his edition of the *Songs and Sonnets* with our last poem, "Selfe Love," because it is the runt of the litter. Helen Gardner doubts Donne wrote it altogether. Words are missing in lines 15 and 16. The tetrameter line sometimes begins with an accent (ll. 1, 3, 5), sometimes not (ll. 7, 11, 17), in clumsy fashion. The poem should be a ballad, yet no stanzas are indicated; and the thoughts slide from four-line to two-line units. It is an improvisation, a patch of thought. The speaker rejects an interminable series of loves, some cogently, some on mere excuses. One senses a stoic self-sufficiency here, not a haunting fear of life. The concluding couplet suggests final security only in self-regard:

> I will vent that humour then
> In mine own selfe love.
>
> (ll. 23–24)

So the poet lightly stakes out a security in self-love, yet with no more finality here than elsewhere. In the Holy Sonnets, he rejected self-love, as he did aught else.

Donne's misogyny poems, it would seem, are not a revulsion against women. His doctrine of their inferiority to men was common in the Seventeenth Century. His revulsion is rather against the act and ideal of loving, using an earthy directness after the high-blown presumptions of idealized love, a closer grasp of the physicality of love, its insecurity, its dishonesty, its pretense of lofty idealism. Intoxicated by the movement of the world, Donne is dumbfounded by its slippery unsureness. Everywhere he fights for anchors; everywhere he smells fishmongers. A foul and pestilent congregation of vapors sticks to his firmament. His attempts at catharsis roll by as eccentric episodes. On earth, he has no out. Yet despite his restless, spreading disbelief, these poems express a soaring masculine power, a confidence in his knife-like purpose, a healthy clearing of ground, grappling with accepted assumptions. They are Donne's most rendered poems, objective, hardheaded, sculptured, most easily detached from the personality that wrote them. His hand had strength to disregard the thoughts gesturing them.

## 5

# The Rejection Poems

Casual love entails rejections as well as involvements. So four rejection poems, "The Legacie," "Loves Exchange," "Loves Deitie," and "The Message," balance Donne's promiscuity poems. Though rueful with chagrin, even enslavement, they express no genuine tragic loss. "The Legacie" shows only a murky befuddlement. "The Message," more robust and exhilarated, finds a heart or two eyes no great price for freedom. "Loves Exchange," the most painful and fully articulated, is caught up in demonism and barbaric godhead of the love god. "Loves Deitie," a suave courtly love poem, suggests implications the opposite of its manifest meaning.

The first poem, "The Legacie," suggests a song in its opening tetrameter couplet, then slows somewhat clumsily to a more meditative stanza, adding a foot in line 4. These two rhymes are repeated in lines 5 and 6, with a foot again added in line 6. The stanza then finishes with a heroic couplet. Befuddled as is its music, the speaker insults the girl with rather tart rhetoric; but a certain hanky-panky of blurred identity in death and resurrection obscures the insult. He writes:

When I dyed last, and Deare, I dye
As often as from thee I goe . . .

(ll. 1–2)

But death by a time schedule cannot be so fatal. So his easy language mocks his identity as a truly dedicated lover—Shakespeare's Cleopatra was more persuasive:

> Though it be but an houre agoe,
> And Lovers houres be full eternity.
>
> (ll. 3–4)

Rejected, with questionable grounds for self-respect, the speaker is forever dying and being reborn, disappearing and popping up. He is himself; but by Stanza 2 he is also her. So, in lines 7 and 8, he is a self-examining suicide, at once his executor and also himself his legacy, the subject of his will. For all his presumption of urbanity, this speaker's identity has been badly shaken.

Stanza 2 expresses, quite simply, an enormous masochistic response to rejection. Being symbolically killed, he would send her his heart, piling generosity on cruelty in response to her rejection. But the masochism keeps becoming its sadistic counterpart in a bewildered hanky-panky. So his stylized, exaggerated devotion suggests a pose; as on the level of music, the opening easy, lilting music keeps getting its lines too long. By the close of Stanza 2, he finally articulates his deeper impulse for revenge:

> It kill'd mee againe, that I who still was true,
> In life, in my last Will should cozen you.
>
> (ll. 15–16)

Ignorant of himself, he works at cross-purposes, cozening her as he attempts to enrich her, mocking her as he flatters her.

Finally, in Stanza 3, he ruefully meditates her makeshift heart, a promiscuous heart of imitation leather. "Colours" has an overtone of dishonest rhetoric; "corners" violates the circle, an emblem of perfection, and makes it an imperfect, untrustworthy heart. The closing insult would seem languidly unpleasant, a masochistic thrashing gradually easing into a more honest and spiteful rejection. But their identities have been so confused in line 10, "my selfe, (that is you, not I,)" that the closing point, "for twas thine," does not entirely rule him out. A rueful dullard, he ends with no more than a rhetorical pout. He makes a show of pique, having no better face to show.

The detailed image of the heart seems surrealistic, but lacks the eerie conviction of true surrealism. Its introduction in Stanza 2 is evasive, mannerist, and coy, a slouch playing with a surrealistic image. Its use is internally consistent, with the barest veil of conviction to mask the speaker's naked banality. Here, Donne adds a mannerist emblem to his repertoire of gestures of maculation, on every level defusing sacred emblems, mistrusting traditional cosmology, overturning social mores. In these poems, Donne tears at truths, mistrusts them, chews them, tosses them from side to side. Just as his promiscuity poems empty and deny the doctrine of continence; so his image of the heart as a misused leather purse mocks the cliché of the heart as a vessel of love.

"The Legacie" does have one odd distinction. Its line "It was not good, it was not bad" (l. 19) is perhaps the most banal Donne ever wrote. Dramatically, it suits the self-indulgent pout of its speaker flawlessly.

The opposition suggested in "Womans Constancy" and "Loves Diet," of a controlling, detached woman and a harassed, defiant lover is pushed and objectified in "Loves Exchange" to a full-blown depiction of the courtly love drama. Here are its harsh lines, its mysterious, shrouded areas, the demonic confrontations and self-assertive fury of a Dürer engraving. Its bitterness is extreme, its destruction massive; its love deity is the most rampant in all Donne's lyrics, its speaker and victim a strong warrior. Save for one oblique reference to "she" (l. 20) as his rejecting sweetheart, he confronts, not her, but the god of courtly love. A veteran warrior, the speaker shows a colloquial familiarity with the experience of love in the opening couplet:

> *Love*, any devill else but you,
> Would for a given Soule give something too.

The couplet at once established love as a demonic god, literally the devil, and the speaker's easy familiarity with him. This is no green boy, but a man of affairs, tested and proudly confident. So the odd stanzaic music, a rhyme scheme of two couplets and a triplet, that alternate four- and five-foot lines, suggests at once a powerful habit of discipline and an inability to make it stick. This is the music of a speaker attempting tight couplets with military control, but staggering along, not managing ground under his feet, as he somehow makes a stanza.

In Stanza 1, his impatience with the god of love is imperative enough to hide his inner condition. This is a traditional British attitude of irritated compliance to courtly love, by contrast to a more continental acquiescence. So, in Stanza 1, a downright honest warrior remembers when he saw no sense in love, taking it as a variation of "Riming, Huntsmanship, or Play" (l. 4), but those more public court activities offered a poem, a trophy, a prize; in love, the participant gives more and gets nothing. It simply makes no sense. But the last line, that he is "alas, by being lowly, lower," hints of a condition more desperate than he has yet suggested, that he has been snagged, hurt, entangled, how badly we do not yet know.

Stanza 2 marches irregularly forward; as he evasively bargains with nothing to bargain with, his true condition remaining shrouded in mystery. The speaker is bluntly honest about courtly love behavior; he is no giddy enthusiast who would falsify a driven tear, or sigh, or vow, then live with its make-believe, its gauzy lies and emotional delirium. Though courtly love is an arbitrary falsification of human nature and a wholesome life, its devotees, self-infatuated slaves, would sue for "a *non obstante*" to the laws of nature. They are wedded to their path, minions of the god of love; but our bluff English warrior cannot so giddily falsify himself.

He continues uselessly evading, bargaining, through Stanza 3; but the bargaining grows more desperate, the pressure increasing. He is unable to surrender his native sanity; and yet, contemptible and false as is courtly love, he begs for it, begs weakness, blindness, imbecility. As he talks, he begins to think about his present condition, how childish he is, how lowly, the subject of common gossip, an embarrassment to his acquaintances, a joke to his beloved.

By Stanza 4, the bargaining breaks down, its rhetoric useless. The speaker acknowledges the justice of his attaining nothing, the absolute propriety of the tyrranical god of love, his betrayal not submitting to its "first motions" (l. 23). Then, in the middle of the stanza, the first extended image of a captured town unfolds; and the poem changes its character.

Blind rhetoric and evasion give way to a contemplation of his own condition. The strident presence of the god of love becomes increasingly manifest, as the metaphor unfolds. The speaker, hidden behind his warrior dignity, becomes manifest as utterly ruined:

> Small townes which stand stiffe, till great shot
> Enforce them, by warres law *condition* not.
> Such in loves warfare is my case . . .
>
> (ll. 24–26)

The language grows denser, from rhetorical counters to a choked experience. Whole domains of involvement, law, war, religion, pile and densely blur on one another. "Condition" in line 25 suggests at once legal negotiations and the elemental human condition, all prostrate before the laws of war. "Case" in line 26 refers to law and warfare. "Article" in line 27 suggests legal articles, also the articles of war.

But now, over this crosshatch of references, slides the word "grace." Both war and law suggest an absence of grace; but basically grace is the grace of God. But here we begin to intuit a black reversal of figure and ground, systematic as in a photographic negative. The god whose grace operates here is the devil, the god of love. Our bluff, hearty English warrior is in a black landscape, one fundamentally counter to all natural order, all its moral controls reversed; and he is submitting to the diabolism of courtly love, suing for its anti-grace; yet even that is denied him. Uneasily, we sense that the diabolism that invests the entire poem was temporarily masked by the honest fortitude of our solitary warrior; but his soul is already lost, his future, his career, with nothing left but his manly style. Dürer's visions of pilgrimage spring to mind, of strong warriors crossing the realm of the devil. So, in cool, prosaic allusions, line 27 loosely suggests the black grace of abasement, the absorption by the devil of the forces of nature, the suspension of its laws, black dispensations.

And now his anti-grace has been summoned, this terrible god shows his face in implacable denial. Whether classical or Biblical, a Medusa or Jehovah, the naked face has overwhelming power. The very phrase, "this," is repeated as a pounding ceremonial drum, ending Stanza 4, opening Stanza 5, then again in line 31, demoralizing, destroying all it confronts. The master manipulator of all idolatry (l. 30), the supreme reverse king of kings, this elemental divinity can empty monasteries, resurrect the dead, melt the earth, make the desert teem with cities. Diplomacy, law, and warfare fade away as paltry metaphors. The god of love makes "Mynes" and "Quarries," the Seventeenth Century concept of the work of the devil. Our warrior stands before it, stalwart, but a broken sinner, depraved by love, one of the sturdy damned of the earth.

So the closing stanza projects his future in diabolical reversal of "The Canonization," stone still, rigid of body, fixed in place, in an utter helpless passivity. Fixed by a Medusa godhead of love, we finally have a breathing corpse, still sparring for dignity. In "The Canonization," special pressures force a canonization for love; here, rejected by love, he would be an emblem and anatomy for future rebels, like a traitor's body, drawn, quartered, and exposed on a city wall. The closing couplet suggests what he would exemplify as part of love's service. He warns against torture, lest he not be a satisfactory anatomy that teaches how a body loves. This would be pointless in causing people to abandon love altogether. Dead, he would be a demonstration model of how to love. Broken and enslaved, he still bargains not to be destroyed altogether.

Such is the manifest content of the poem; yet the poem stands as a magnificent piece of craftsmanship, a dramatic tour-de-force of extraordinary vividness and dramatic shape, not as the articulation of some man's condition, as in the later poems. This poet knows himself a virtuoso. The heavy, irregular march forward of the music, the diabolical camaraderie, the even balance of three stanzas of rhetoric against three of self-exposure, the confrontation of warrior and all-powerful idol, all express strongly-etched, magnificent control. Donne is arriving at the voice of courtly love in his culture. Its personal strands are strong; but they are blended into a large public tapestry, an experience rendered with apparently utter objectivity. We do not fish for the poet gliding behind it. Yet this full rendering detaches the poet, keeps Donne out of his poem. Thereafter, the immediacy and grip of Donne's personal self gradually takes over his poems. The "I" of "Goodfriday, 1613. Riding Westward" is more monumentally personal than the "I" of "Loves Exchange." The equilibrium here is wholly public. In Donne's own day, witches were burned at the stake. Donne's own temper had a medieval and reformation cast of fanaticism. In "Loves Usury," he bargains with the god of love; in "The Apparition," a depraved man becomes an appalling demonic spirit. So here, a warrior undergoes enslavement in earnest.

There is a curious ambivalence in the repeated phrase, "This face," that echoes the pun on "Mummy possest" in "Loves Alchymie." When the speaker cries, "Having put Love as last to show this face" (l. 28), it is not entirely clear if the face belongs to the god of love, or is of the imperious woman whom he adores. Indeed, the repeated, "this face," one following hard on the other, suggests a tone of surrealistic horror, face behind face, head behind head looming ever larger, the god the woman writ large, the woman the god in concentrated immediacy. So woman blends with demon, as in "Mummy possest," where the overtones of motherly dominance blend with possessing demons.

The repeated overtone helps define more precisely the tonality of woman in Donne's poetry at this time. The image of Donne as an early libertine has been questioned by Eliot and others, who would suggest a more circumspect behavior. This has value in correcting our biographical data, but is beside the point to the creative consciousness of the poet, the dynamic his poetry structures. Libertines, actual or sublimated, can be various as saints in their temperaments. Whatever his social experience, several aspects of the female image are characteristic in Donne's consciousness as he shaped his lyrics, whether they expressed anxiety or euphoria, realism or mythic projection.

Firstly, far from being smaller, more unsure and dependent than the man, the woman is characteristically reserved, stronger, more decisive, in some sense older or more settled in her ways. The man characteristically woos; the woman characteristically decides. This is too various to be simply a formal convention of courtly love. Thus, in "Womans Constancy," a slice-of-life monologue, the woman decides, while the man bravely prepares to dispute her; she would seem older, in experience, if not in age. So, in "Goe, and Catche a Falling Starre," the woman is set in her ways, while the man is wistful about his impossible pilgrimage. In "The Apparition," the woman terminates the relationship. In "Loves Diet," the man breaks away, but only after an appalling dependency, and with a self-assertion too strenuous and harassed altogether to be believed. So the man argues, courts, defines, with broadsides of rhetoric, an overgrown apprentice and schoolboy lover. In a suave balance in "The Flea," the man is suitor, the woman the creature of decision. He talks; she draws blood. We do not suggest any abject demeaning on the speaker's part. On the contrary, his rhetoric has a winning overtone of bravado, his solicitation a cheery presumption; yet he seems constantly on the move. His is not the decision.

The woman also characteristically comes as a given, a thing apart, outside the structure of order and accepted values. There is a masculine domain, broadly the expanses of civilization, country marvel and foreign adventure in "Goe, and Catche," a web of moral arguments in "Womans Constancy," but no comparable woman's world of experience, not even a hint as to its contents, in education, clothes, family structure, entertainment, to be joined to the man's. Except for her seduction, an opaque veil surrounds the woman's world. At its best, the repeated shock of discovery that the woman is different from the man constitutes a wholesome growth into adulthood. Growth out of adolescence always entails some stripping away of boyish clichés. So, in "Loves Alchymie," the experience of the discovery of love triggers off a complex flushing out of decayed ideas. The clean rectitude of such an emotional growth gives the lyrics an immediate validity in the strenuous growth into adult life. But this inevitably entails a sense of risk. The speaker is too frequently at bay, mobilizing a burgeoning sense of manhood, harassed and frantic in "Womans Constancy," dull and rationalizing in "The Legacie," driven to an uncanny fixation in "The Apparition." We do not as yet find a reassuring love relationship, a "mummy" who simply mothers her boy. Indeed, this sense of threat and clarification, of having to measure up in love to an older, more settled female figure, suggests the alienation between John Donne and Elizabeth Donne, his actual mother, with whatever overtones of rejection and alienation this entails. This would account for the repeatedly older, more sure and decisive female figure.

Indeed, this reinforces another curious junction in these poems, of the woman with some god or demonic figure. Thus, "Mummy possest" suggests "mummy" as in some sense demonic. So, in "Loves Exchange," a face looms behind a face, demon and woman echoing one another. So, in "Loves Usury," the god of love comes into view as actual love is first felt. Indeed, the convention of courtly love that would make the god of love a fresh, alien usurper is wholly in accord with Donne's view at this time. The steady rediscovery of alien, dangerous, uncanny power in women may or may not be related to Donne's own mother; but the flow back and forth from woman to cosmic principle, which here is threatening, returns in a wholly fresh guise in the last love poems and the *Anniversaries*, marking the close of a period in Donne's poetic experience.

"Loves Deitie" has vastly more urbane charm. Its god of love is as arbitrary and unnatural, but by now is a familiar burden, not a sudden, shocking tyrant. Indeed, its opening couplet is Donne's most relaxed, mellow, witty, and poised, its dreamy music reminiscent of Yeats:

> I long to talke with some old lovers ghost,
> Who dyed before the god of Love was borne:

Musically, its easy regularity has one slight catch. Its rhyme scheme joins a quatrain to a triplet; but six pentameter lines close on a tetrameter, suggesting a tightening at the close, a prudent reserve. The lines are limpidly smooth, simply end-stopped or simply ongoing, except for line 12, where an unaccented period is followed by a five-syllable word in the next line:

> Actives to passives. Correspondencie
> Only his subject was . . .
>
> (ll. 12–13)

This irregularity has a naughty charm. "Correspondencie" is a difficult and clumsy equilibrium, and barely fits in the stanza, continuing onto the word "only," with its accent on the wrong syllable. Its predicate comes before the subject and verb; yet it somehow manages. "Correspondencie" is clearly difficult to come by.

By speculating of lovers before the god of love was born, Donne implies with urbane aplomb that the god of love is a late imposition, in contrast to nature and idealized love. His first three stanzas grumble with easy dissatisfaction over a false idealization, and project three stages in the history of love. In Stanza 1, the old, true lover, who loves reciprocally and with quiet dignity, is contrasted with the speaker himself, a rejected lover. With unabashed ebullience, the speaker confesses himself:

> Sunke so low, as to love one which did scorne.
>
> (1. 4)

Stanza 2 develops stage 2 of the god of love, its first arrival, when at a moment of great arousal, love is deified; this heightens and eases the experience, making sexual union a gesture of divine service. The god of love, a young, apprentice divinity, had a modest practice, to catch any glimmerings of mutual love, and ease the surrender to sexual love. An independent, he frees the act of love from other divinities, makes it easy and immediate, not a botch of experience.

Stanza 3 belongs to the third stage of love. Hierarchy is upset. Love keeps no order on Olympus. Its proper function was the vegetable impulse of "correspondencie," the fitting of "actives to passives"; but it extends authority over the animal, vegetable, and rational soul, the tyrannical god of courtly love:

> To rage, to lust, to write to, to commend.
>
> (1. 17)

In mock exuberance, this urbane slave proclaims a battle cry of pure wish fulfilment, for a spontaneous revolt against the tyrant:

> Oh were we wakn'ed by this Tyrannie
> To ungod this child againe, it could not bee
> I should love her, who loves not mee.
>
> (ll. 19–21)

But having proclaimed his freedom in Stanza 4, the speaker embraces his neurosis with a loud confessional. Proclaiming himself "Rebell and Atheist," he accepts the civil and religious rule of love, trembling with easy panic before its hidden power. But the evasive urbanity of the music of Stanza 4 precludes genuine terror. The speaker fusses over too many things, darkly suggesting what he leaves unnamed. He fears love could make him stop loving—presumably he has been seduced by love. But this is too witless, loving an unresponding woman, with no deep emotional involvement apparent in his words. Or love could make her love him, an offensive idea, since she has loved before. What delicacy of honor! What stout fraternity spirit! The speaker is reduced to courting emotional virgins, who have never given their hearts. But calling a loving woman a "deeper plague" (l. 25) on moral grounds suggests dissimulation. One's skin has a plague, not one's conscience; plague is a biological affront, not a moral horror. So the closing couplet is Sunday School simple, cliché-ridden, and proper, finishing with complacent finality:

> Falsehood is worse than hate; and that must bee,
> If shee whom I love, should love mee.
>
> (ll. 27–28)

This bland, conventional ending, compared with the suave, allusive opening lines, indeed, its depressed self-denial against the vivacious ebullience of the music, suggests the poem is a dramatic put-on from first to last. Indeed, his dropping the last foot of every stanza suggests such a holding back. The word "love" is a simple euphemism for sexual relations. So melodiously sterile an acquiescence suggests not the fulfilment of masochism, but a secret manipulator who has exactly what he wants, a perfect excuse for promiscuity in a society of dissolute masochists, all servants of the god of love. Indeed, a recurring theme throughout the promiscuity poems is making-do in an acquiescent tit-for-tat—if she can, why can't I? Donne here applies it to the tyranny of the god of courtly love. Charming, urbane, reticent, where others will suffer commitment and denial, he will eat his cake and have it.

Our last rejection poem, "The Message," is the happiest. Radiantly defiant, the rejected lover anticipates a reversal and equalization in her coming rejection. The poem soars forward with dramatic ebullience, a simple tetrameter couplet, then another tetrameter line, then is tangled and interrupted by four choppy lines, a four-syllable trochaic couplet, another lopping off the last unaccented syllable, cutting, squeezing, and finally relaxing in a last iambic tetrameter line. So the temperament of the irrepressible speaker, a robust singer and happy warrior, has jounced along in a life of simple tetrameters. Squeezed by the forced circumstance of artificial love, pinched, rejected, he skids along, then breaks into his previous exuberant independence.

This split music expresses the splitting of his life. Thus lines 3 and 8 make a single couplet, expressing simple honesty of spirit:

> Yet since there they have learn'd such ill,
> Fit for no good fight, keep them still.

But the word "forc'd" forces apart the even couplet of his life:

> Such forc'd fashions,
> And false passions,

another tetrameter line, chopped into two dimeter lines, its accents reversed, and rammed into his easy tetrameter couplet and life.

Yet his masculine simplicity and ardor are irresistible. With a casual reversal in Stanza 3, he asks back his eyes and heart, that he might "laugh and joy" (l. 19), when she is rejected in turn. Bother the conventions of courtly love—the impulse to revenge is too strong; his nature cannot be denied. Here, as in Donne's promiscuity poems, he is harassed by a stronger woman, with hints of magical power; but he demands equalization. Spurning courtly love, he thrashes for equality, never mind how it is put together.

# 6

# The Compromises of Love

Between promiscuity and solitude, flirtation and rejection, lies a gray zone, where a careful budget of adjustments to love and sexuality makes possible the complex rhythms of ordinary living. In "Breake of Day" and "A Lecture upon the Shadow," simple scheduling is determinant. In "The Baite," "The Flea," and "The Prohibition," unexplored personal tensions make love alien, shallow, or oddly whimsical.

"Breake of Day" has lines too limp to hold attention. Comparing this speaker to the female speaker of "Loves Diet," so involved in the productions of her body, we speculate that Donne may have liked women, but he didn't like them articulate. Hardin Craig, in *The Enchanted Glass*, discusses the Elizabethan convention of docile, aquiescent women, rather like Desdemona. In "The Extasie," the woman responds with shadowy aquiescence. So here, the woman chafes a bit, but accepts her lot. Her mind is a special one. She has evidently amassed second-hand a vocabulary of clichés she parades with a learned smack, that light and darkness have significance, that rising is the opposite of lying down, a technique of neat opposition of phrases she paddles through with gusto. The thoughts pile on one another in feeble clichés, antitheses that neatly lean together though they make almost no sense:

> Why should we rise, because 'tis light?
> Did we lie downe, because 'twas night?

The inescapable answer to such questions rises like a lover's "amen."

Indeed, the neat inadequacy of the questions leads one to question if the woman has an intellect at all, a concern the Seventeenth Century did not take lightly, also if she has any capacity for passion. The artificial, strained, mechanical series of postures suggests not a passionate grasp of an immediate situation, but a vague, huffy discomfort, borrowing words and ideas, because no native ones are there to be generated. Here is a vegetable soul, in whom rejection produces a constrained irritation, without passion or intellectual grasp, only a pat opposition of stances:

> Love which in spight of darknesse brought us hether,
> Should in despight of light keepe us together.
>
> (ll. 5–6)

Each stanza consists of two rhyming tetrameter couplets and a pentameter couplet. Musically, this is most jarring. Rhyming couplets chop up a stanza into staccatto two-line units, that string one after another. They do not build and interweave to link a stanza. And the sentences are as clumsily put together as the stanzas. Stanza 1 piles four end-stopped questions to a puffy moralism with a feminine ending. Stanza 2 consists of a single long sentence, its halting minor clauses so interwoven that the verbs scarcely support their limp nouns. Indeed, Stanza 2 is a piling and weaving of clichés, their syntax loosely hooked together. Clearly, this woman has only a superficial rapport with words; and no passion to stir their loose, well-mannered formulations. Appetites scarcely surge across her words, only an easy, self-righteous jar, and an acquiescent emptiness.

Stanza 3 begins with a purple one-line flourish:

> Must businesse thee from hence remove?
>
> (l. 13)

The solitary meditative acceptance of fate that follows suggests her lover departed on hearing line 13. We salute his good taste. At the close, she grasps her situation—treated like a married man's mistress—but utters no protest. So, finally, she frets, but she acknowledges the truth, and that is her measure of catharsis.

"A Lecture upon the Shadow" is tight musically, as is its situation, with no chinks showing. It stirs emotional reverberations; yet the lack of affect seems dull and leaden, too stiff for empty air. The first line is abruptly dramatic, with a flat imperative, "Stand still." We then follow this hushed presence with geometrical precision through an insubstantial wasteland of sunlight and shadow. The closest analogies to its seriousness, its surrealistic silence, its hollow, geometrical exterior, are some de Chirico paintings, where serious, earnest human mechanisms move in austere silence across stylized eternities.

The music has a muffled reverberation too taut to be sung. It is more architectonic than rhythmic, with the finality of formal, abstract sculpture. It has two long, slightly irregular stanzas, each alternated with a detached heroic couplet. Each of its long stanzas has 4, 5, 4, 4, 5, 5, 3, 5, 4, 4, 5 feet per line, all iambic except lines 3 and 4, which begin on the accent. The rhyme scheme is a, a, b, b, c, d, d, c, e, e, e. Each stanza thus begins with a rhymed couplet, completely end-stopped, just as a detached couplet replies to and rounds out each stanza with a moral aphorism. It then attempts, as it were, another couplet; but a bouncing irregularity intervenes, a jogging tetrameter couplet, just unpredictable enough to get the stanza under way, again tautly rhymed:

> These three houres that we have spent,
> Walking here, Two shadowes went . . .
>
> (ll. 3–4)

The couplet then runs on, in meter and thought, into "along with us." A closed quatrain then follows, irregular, indented in the middle, but again impeccably end-stopped. A tight, formal triplet then closes the stanza. Lest this seem a chance reading, we might note that the punctuation of Stanza 2 is virtually identical with Stanza 1, with the same architectural formality.

An element of surrealism enters with the capitalized "Love" in line 2. Is the speaker addressing some specific woman, affectionately called "Love?" But such intimate address violates the tight formality here. Furthermore, she is not invoked again even once in the remainder of the poem, a ghostly, unfelt presence, not a woman. Or is he addressing an abstract being "Love," perhaps even some stylized equivalent of the god of love? The woman is so pallid only her shadow is palpable; and the ambiguity in the word "Love" echoes the ambiguity in "this face" in "Loves Exchange." There are apparently inexplicable forces in the speaker's universe, demons and seizures, blendings of person and cosmic force, presences one addresses, as it were, at an angle, but not head-on. So the poem is gripped by a stylized quiet, where people meet no more than their bodies.

Indeed, even the present tense of this poem is blurred, frozen, blocked out of fresh participation. The speaker is not breaking into a fresh thought. His reading of an old philosophy lecture rather suggests an eternal reenactment, abstracted, repetitive, impersonal as a mathematical formula, just as "The Extasie" suggests a ritualized enactment. This fragility of the present tense, its vulnerability, its petrified occasions, its "inscape," again links Donne and Shakespeare. His poem is, as it were, so in the present tense, intuitive to the texture of time, it winces with every shift and sinking of spirit. So the speaker hops across a checkerboard of time, unable to anchor himself or relate to anything, hopping with small verbs and stations of time, "Stand still . . . these three houres . . . but, now the Sunne is . . . We doe . . . did grow . . . but, now 'tis not so . . . morning shadowes . . . loves day is short." Yet even the lunar detachment of these formal motions is contrasted to the more formal and abstract moral of the closing heroic couplet, defining love by its mathematical analogy in day and night.

The poem has a reality of mathematics, not of flesh and earth. Light and shadow define themselves in mathematical terms. Motion is thin, uncompromising, geometrical. The first gesture glides toward love, the second away, each gesture steady, inevitable, sharp-lined as a circling planet. The first stanza rises to "the high'st degree" (l. 12), the second declines in a high abstraction of maladjusted lovers, posturing, deceit, weakness. But then, the speaker clips off the metaphor as not working:

> Love is a growing, or full constant light;
> And his first minute, after noone, is night.
>
> (ll. 25–26)

The surrealistic glaze can suggest a dramatic situation, or simply offer a tone of experience. If there is a situation, it must be ferreted out beneath its flawless texture, by a nuance, an intuition of the unsaid. Thus the closing couplet expresses an absolute ideal of love, that accepts nothing but its perfection. The closing sentence, "And his first minute, after noone, is night," is not factual, analyzing the nature of love, but moral, expressing the commitment of the speaker to reject any falling away.

So punctilious a moralist is a love fanatic. Indeed, taking the speaker as a person, he demands such perfection, his clipped, shadowy abstractions are unnerving. Barely in touch with sensuous reality, he is the polar opposite of the speaker of "Loves Alchymie," waist-deep in pots, mines, and chemicals. Indeed, his fanaticism, under the grip of an abstracted, mathematical mentality, suggests some insanity. A lunar lover, he adjusts his love to mathematical time, yet represses all gross physical compromises of habit and body. Even his abstract closing statement of the abrupt disappearance of love relates to their situation. In the oblique, abstracted manner of a tight stylist, obsessive about sullying himself, he is explaining why they must abruptly part. Indeed, more dramatically, the entire poem may be a formalized farewell speech, laying down the abstract grounds for a parting. And for all his disengagement, his proprieties have a formal courtesy that is rather winning. He suggests not a hint of personal impatience or recrimination, only the inevitable shift of events.

The poem thus allows a dramatic reading; but such an episode is kept so thin, the poem can be read simply as the wash of a transitory mood, a sense of eerie unreality at the waning of love, a catch of lifelessness, a mathematical Olympus, where bloodless, eternal truths enact a less than human destiny. By either reading, the hard dilemma is posed how absolute love can be compromised with the flow of fractional experience. Unreal, helpless to shape his situation, the speaker finished the poem in a tight futility. To him, love compromises are impossible.

"The Baite" is the first of three poems exploring, with whimsical, muted reverence, the fumbling ignorance and limitations of human nature before any ideal of love. The discrepancy between the ideal and the real, established with lugubrious discovery in "Loves Alchymie," is here treated with much more knowing and bemused accommodation as the way of the world. The wrenched ideal, its painful lack of dignity, the impossibility of a Garden of Eden, are fully acknowledged; yet the speaker accepts this game of love. He bows before half-comprehended passions, and embraces the painful servitude they entail. His masochism rests in easy equilibrium—it reads as fun. His gestures are trammeled in artful music; they are not locked mechanisms of perverse, repetitive behavior. The reader is enamored of the incantatory music, touched by the pity of it all; yet the music is so delicious he can hardly take it seriously, at once a parody of Marlowe and an opulent experience. Here, a flawless craftsmanship slaps together flawed, uncraftsmanly emotions.

Donne's reply to Marlowe's "The Passionate Shepherd to His Love," "The Baite" is a mannerist reply of experience to a pastoral song of innocence. Its character as a reply multiplies its facets of meaning and allows it a slack richness of address, never wholly in focus. Thus, the speaker at once addresses his love and addresses Marlowe over her shoulder, seduces her companionship and offers a demonstration model of the implications of pastoral innocence. Marlowe's Eden had a wholly natural garb, beds of roses, coats of flowers, gowns of wool, "which from our pretty lambs we pull." The upholstery of Donne's Eden is wholly artificial:

> Of golden sands, and christall brookes,
> With silken lines, and silver hookes.
>
> (ll. 3–4)

Indeed, the stylized, decorative machinery of "golden sands and christall brookes . . . silken lines and silver hookes," recalls the theatrical artifice of Elizabethan masques, itself a stylized cry of innocence, rendering pastoral courtship with sedate predictability. Donne might well be teasing Marlowe, calling his open, natural ardor another literary cliché, another stance of a masque among many such stances, each with its own stylized cry of discovery of new pleasures.

Even musically, as Donne imitates Marlowe's simple quatrain stanza of iambic tetrameter, he simplifies his balance of phrases to rock the verse with easy ennui, suggesting some simple-mindedness. Marlowe always slightly imbalanced his punctuation, keeping his lines discoveries of innocent surprise, impetuous rushes of words. He would never allow the rocking-horse balance of:

> Of golden sands, and christall brookes,
> With silken lines, and silver hookes.
>
> (ll. 3–4)

Casual qualifications sprinkle "The Baite," that suffuse it with worlds of experience. The massive freight of an *Ecclesiastes* is rendered with Oscar Wilde's mannerist rhetoric and artificial ease. The substitution of "some" for "all" in line 2 is the qualification of experience in place of wondrous discovery. The speaker knows his pleasures, and will not bother any untested. No aspiration jars the delicious familiarities of his set ordeal of pain and pleasure. So the slight qualification and ambiguity of "Begging themselves they may betray" (l. 8). "Themselves" began as the object of "begging," and then is revealed as the object of "betray." So they begin begging themselves, and end ambiguously begging the woman. But this is the ambiguity of the passive masochist, who is never sure whom he is really talking to, and to what extent he perpetrates what he gladly endures. So the ambiguity of "Gladder to catch thee, than thou him" (l. 12). Do the eager fish solicit the swimmer by passively catching her attention, enamoring her with their delicious bodies in her vicinity; or do they actively catch her in their fishy jaws, trammel her in their net of bodies? The ambiguity rests unresolved; yet they end in her grasp.

The poem develops, not as a narrative of actual events, but as a succession of unfolding fantasies; as the speaker betrays his inner condition. Thus, Stanza 1 veers slightly, but steadily farther from Marlowe. Line 1, Donne only divides with a comma, substituting a slower, rocking-horse rhythm for Marlowe's ardent impetuosity. Line 2 substitutes "some" for "all," shifting from an eager discovery of the unknown to the pursuit of more familiar tastes. Line 3 substitutes "gold" and "christall" for "valleys, groves, hills, and fields," transposing courtly masques for rolling country, precious stones for natural fertility. And line 4, dwelling on implements of fishing, adds baiting, temptation, and helplessness. Silken lines and silver hooks also belong to female underwear, making them more the woman's property than the man's. The reversal is extreme. The normal metaphor is of a man fishing, the hook an emblem of his sexual organ. At best, we would think the lovers egalitarian fishermen; but we stir uneasily at the slack suggestion here. Who is fishing for whom; and what exactly is getting hooked?

Stanza 2 extends Stanza 1 in unfolding permissiveness. Her eyes, outshining the sun (1. 6), reverberate with soft perversion. The sun is kingly, a male emblem; but her eyes replace the sun as the moving force, the driving warmth of sexual attraction the new authority. There is again the blur of ambiguity at the particular flesh-and-blood woman and some cosmic force. It is unutterably attractive, yet unnatural, even dangerous, a usurpation he welcomes. So the wicked little fishes are enamored of their easy catch. They push around her, begging to be had. There is the same discrepancy in size, as in so many of these poems, she large as the sun, the male figures small as minnows.

Stanza 3 pushes Stanza 2 to an extreme height. The veiled allusion to sexual attraction, the warm, whispering river, comes stylized in depiction. Donne here approaches, not Dürer, but Tintoretto, in a glazed, mannerist enactment. Our Susanna swims nude, not to catch the elders on the shore—that image has faded from our attention—but to catch the life inside the river. We are in the swim of life, splashing about in tasteful, knowing sex with familiar security. In this wash of pleasurable competition, only winners are possible—to a happy masochist to lose is a contradiction in terms.

The mixture of lyric musical aplomb and somewhat jaded experience, of boyish wonder and a veteran knowledge of the experience of love echoes the mixture of "Goe, and Catche a Falling Starre," only here it is almost a stylized parody, pushed in sheer exuberance to almost any length. In a reiterated metaphor of the final clause, emphatic in Stanza 3 and heightened in Stanza 4, each party swims to the other's pleasure as their own:

> Each fish, which every channell hath,
> Will amorously to thee swimme,
> Gladder to catch thee, than thou him.
>
> (ll. 10–12)

Is this a Garden of Eden of generosity in love, a surge of agape, a giving of all of oneself in sacrifice and sexual love? But these are poor little fish, masochistic innocents, swimming to their doom. Does the stanza express wondrous euphoria or savage, farcical laughter? Is Donne mocking love or religion, saintliness or sexual indulgence? Nothing abashes the speaker, as he rushes on among the compromises of social congestion and self-indulgent pleasure in the shallow basin of love.

As the poem progresses, he grows smaller, and she enlarges. His "golden sands and christall brookes" contract to a school of minnows in the water. So in Stanza 2, she rivaled the sun; in Stanza 4, she is outside and controlling both sun and moon, darkening them at her pleasure. "Leave" in line 15 is a request for permission. The speaker is blind without her light, his final cause, controlling sun and moon at her caprice, giving him light for him to see by.

Again, as in "Loves Alchymie," the analogy of the pursuit of love to the pursuit of religion or cosmology casts doubt in both directions. Neither is strictly a metaphor for the other. Analogous domains are rather loosely sketched in a correspondence, to express a habit of mind, of metaphysical uneasiness and skepticism about love. But again, as in "Loves Alchymie," the mood is one of healthy growth and clean power, whatever the extent of the doubt. The speech is too firmly in command of its material, the music too imperturbably melodic. This is still a young man, mewing his mighty youth. We do not worry about the implications of his speech—he can rearrange his attitude tomorrow—but the poem exults in his imagination, the grasp and force of his intellect. So, in another speaker, the masochism would jar us as perverse, a Seventeenth Century Swinburne, seeking a flagellation. But this is clearly not the settled masochism of an adult, but the adolescent masochism of an unsure youth, gripped by the nostalgia of childhood, still overshadowed by a grown woman, yet too frolicsome to worry—all will yet be well; and if not, that is another chapter in another life.

The same openness applies to the mixture of listeners. The entire poem is Donne's reply to Marlowe's "Passionate Shepherd," his pleasurable ennui measured against Marlowe's pastoral innocence. His larder of old irritations yields a stylized smorgasbord of ardent love, stylized masques, courtship experience, and religious parody, all in a jaded landscape of happy enslavement. If "The Apparition" is the experience of a haunted warlock, "The Baite" is the luxurious self-expression of a minor courtly fish by Circe's island. So he ostensibly addresses his sweetheart, mimicking Marlowe, and rendering a Marlowe theme with variations, as though saying, "Do you give innocent ardor so radiant a prognosis, Marlowe? Life overlaps life and passion feeds on passion. Experience consists of old pleasures forever kicking to new life. Your innocent gallant will finish his innocence sliding about among all the lady's fishes; and he will love it."

The exposure steadily increases. Stanza 5 is so enamored of treachery and sudden death, it offers a tapestry of reeds, shells, weeds, snares, windowy nets, and slimy nests, to suggest lusty, perverse fascination. By normal usage the male figure is the fisherman, the sport of fishing his instinct to attack and capture his prey; but here the male figure is fished for by her hooks, her body and clothes the treacherous bait. Indeed, Stanza 6 brings the setting of Stanza 5 to a consummate masochistic orgy, with overtones of ravishment, manipulation, and solicited death. Lines 21 and 22 depict the event of ravishment, lines 23 and 24 the infatuation of the fishes with the idea, a seizure of intoxication reminiscent of courtly love, with the curious, traitorous fishermen, their "sleave-silk flies" wholly unnatural, in a forced experience. The poem reads as a masochistic *fin-de-siècle* nocturne, also as a boy's exuberant song of experience, also as Donne's reply to Marlowe—"Only a masochistic innocent would find delightful your pastoral Eden. The way of love is not rapturous discovery, but compromise."

If "The Baite" flounders in the glazed tropics of love, "The Flea" maintains a cautious, dancing equilibrium of courtship. On the surface, the couple are badly matched. His speeches hover near black humor, carrying on in gallant ardor after each unpleasant squelch; yet the poem finally suggests they may be perfectly matched, an aristocratic adolescent and his coarse girl friend, who doesn't mind squeezing a flea to death with her fingernail. The music, of three rhyming couplets and a trimeter, each jogging along with a tetrameter line and a pentameter, maintains a halting trot, darting too far, then equalizing itself.

We have already discussed the structure of "The Flea," its dialogue of his speeches and her gestures; but equally remarkable is the peculiar blend of emotion in courtship, its compromises with various strands of personal need. As "The Baite" gradually exposed its masochistic speaker, who strives to be caught like a fish; so here, her gesture of killing the flea—and him by symbolic extension—shows a masochistic fascination. He is killed here as a flea; in "The Baite" he was killed in the guise of a fish. So, at the end, the speaker does not rise to a pitch of ardor or sink in despair, but makes yet another rhetorical point, maintaining equilibrium. This is not courtship in a seduction, but courtship for its own sake, the equilibrium of an adolescent dandy, who never loses face, but maintains his pace and style in a capricious, clumsy society.

"The Prohibition" unfolds with studied earnestness the playful implications of "The Baite" and "The Flea." No sadistic gesture is exhibited; but the speaker's awed ignorance of her bespeaks a blanket insecurity on his part. He warns her not of his possible revenge, but his possible death. No impulse of cruelty is in this speaker. He characterizes himself not as a complete masochist, as strongly suggested in "The Baite," but simply as weak, inert, with general passivity. There is just so much he can take. Too violent a passion will kill him. The closing lines reveal his motives for undertaking the compromise:

> Lest thou thy love and hate and mee undoe,
> *To let mee live, O love and hate mee too.*
>
> (ll. 23–24)

To lose her altogether would kill him, and too extreme a passion of love or hate. He therefore bargains his life against her self-control. Their love relationship will be a compromise with no extremes of feeling, and even a degree of self-abasement on his part:

> So shall I, live, thy Stage, not triumph bee.
>
> (l. 22)

With this compromise, they will get along.

So the voice of the poem speaks; his situation is undefined. But we noted similar bargaining in "Loves Exchange" and "Loves Usury," under the helpless enslavement of courtly love. This speaker is muffled, abstracted, his situation without vivacity, apparently another victim of *la belle dame sans merci*, sullenly making terms in a plodding acquiescence, under conditions of the most abject enslavement. The most he aspires is to "live, thy Stage, not triumph bee." From a free man, one would expect more soaring aspirations.

For all the variety in the poems of this group, some extraordinarily vivacious, some shallow and dull, we find throughout a limited, immature temperament, with even an overtone of masochism and femininity. Yet the power of growth seems clearly there. His groundwork is unsure, his inclination to argument a precious weakness; yet buried inside him is an obscure demand for utter intimacy of spirit. Its location has not as yet defined itself.

# *Part III*

## *The Poems of Marriage*

# 7

# The Structure of Love

After a long thrashing of pitched, dramatic voices, a floundering amid unstable flirtations in a social world of promiscuity, misogyny, and rejection, where a blur of spirit allowed a slippage into warlock or demon, a group of lyrics, "Negative Love," "The Extasie," "Aire and Angels," and "Loves Growth," build piecemeal a structure of love deeper than an emotional relationship. These poems suggest a fresh structuring to experience. The earlier poems suggested dangers, fresh modes of assault, surprising reversals of attitude. In poems like "Loves Exchange," the poem gradually lays bare the speaker's utterly desperate plight. By contrast, "The Extasie" and "Aire and Angels" carefully irradiate murky twists of impulse, so as to clarify their grounds, show how they shift, where the lovers are headed. New ground is here being cleared. Indeed, "Aire and Angels" would seem closely to follow "The Extasie," refining structures "The Extasie" hammered into place. Some veil has here fallen away. With a clarity of touch, the speaker fingers some new world in a marvel of discovery. We have here the careful precision of a steady, believable presence, not an odd or extreme dramatic projection. The voice, controlled, reserved, correct, is more interested in exploring its position than in dramatizing itself.

Somehow, this speaker has more continuity from poem to poem, and seems closer to the being of the poet. He seems allowing himself a greater margin of dispassionate openness.

Courtly love is not merely abandoned; the grounds of love are defined in neo-Platonic terms that preclude its theoretical possibility. Our sense is that only Donne's courtship and marriage seem decisive enough to allow so fundamental a shift in structure of spirit in the speaker.

"Negative Love," the most elusive of the four, has two stanzas of unobtrusive tetrameters, rhyming a, a, b, b, a, b, c, c, c. Rhyming tetrameters have the danger of suggesting a hobbyhorse rhythm of lilting march. The speaker avoids this with a comma interruption after the third foot in line 1, then going on into line 2, where commas after three successive syllables establish, by their hesitation, a meditative thought, or an easy correction. Yet the tight formal music cannot be disregarded, two couplets, then a recapitulation of each of their rhymes, finally to be released into a triplet of inescapable finality. The music is reticent, dignified, conventional, in flawless balance. Nothing is left dangling. Yet suggestions of easy social assurance gather to a closing line of such fatuous complacency, we must read the poem as gently hilarious satire.

A negative definition of love has deep religious overtones—traditional theologians have long so defined God. In even, reserved language, the speaker uses simple negatives in the first stanza, not to characterize love, but to show it as ineffable. Before long, we grasp uneasily that love to the speaker is not merely ineffable, but incomprehensible, beyond touch or feeling. Lines 1 and 2 eliminate physical attraction as its basis, lines 3 and 4 moral or intellectual gifts. He aspires then to some divine essence in love; yet the speaker keeps neatly conventional. He considers only social acceptance; he relates to no standard per se, only to its adherents, and his high place on some hierarchy of human excellence.

The reference to physical attraction is mousy, self-congratulatory:

> I never stoop'd so low, as they
> Which on an eye, cheeke, lip, can prey . . .
>
> (ll. 1–2)

To prey on facial features recalls "The Rape of the Lock." Usually "prey" calls for less aerial appetites. Indeed, in an ironic pun, common liberties "prey" on a lady's eye; the speaker "prays" to more negative attributes. There is even a veiled religious satire in the pun, a hint that the maladjusted "preyer" "prays." The very opening phrase, "I never stoop'd so low," calls for the Restoration reply, "But one stoops to conquer." Indeed, "stoop" suggests deference and humility as well as a strategy of conquest, reinforcing a pun on "prey." The closing word, "they," emphatic without an end stop, has a comic social ring, "I never stoop'd so low, as THEY . . ."

The second couplet is equally condescending:

> Seldome to them, which soare no higher
> Than virtue or the mind to 'admire . . .
>
> (ll. 3–4)

The verb "stoop'd" in line 1 carries over and balances against the verb "soare." Evidently, the speaker would be stooping to a level common men soar to. By line 4, this young man begins to charm us. The complacent superiority of a social butterfly belies his lofty sense of nobility. Is he a solitary? He seems ignorant of any relationship whatever. Surely aside from admiring a woman's mind, one can engage in pleasurable conversation; aside from preying on her face, one can simply enjoy her good looks, or aspire to a more loving relationship. But the speaker would deny himself even so dignified a self-indulgence. What then does this lover do with his time? The answer is simple—he relates to her negative capability.

The last five lines of Stanza 1 justify the grandiose superiority of his rarified approach:

> For sense, and understanding may
> Know, what gives fuell to their fire:
>
> (ll. 5–6)

Apparently, even the more elevated common lover, who admires such spiritual attributes as sense and understanding, is inadequate, because comprehension entails risk. If you know what you want, you will sense when it is missing. Our speaker uniquely loves her incomprehensible, intangible, and unutterable essence. In lines 7 to 10, he modestly allows that his love is "silly"; it even calls for real courage. But he finds justification in loving what is beyond circumstance, that cannot be grasped, craved, or missed.

The beginning of Stanza 2, with the teasing suspense of an "If" of doubt, is closest to outright religious satire. God is "perfectest," a superlative of perfection, a state which should allow no degrees of arrival. God can be expressed only by negatives. Indeed, in complacent satire of religious fanaticism, he barricades his mode of love behind a repeated "all," making his love a flat either-or to all other love:

> To All, which all love, I say no.
>
> (l. 13)

To the common loves of attractive appearance, virtue, sense, and understanding, he says no. Indeed, to a comprehension of the dynamics by which life moves, the knowledge of "what gives fuell to their fire," he says no. His love is a thing apart.

This mystical butterfly has his own counterpart to her numinous essence:

> If any who deciphers best,
> What we know not, our selves, can know,
> Let him teach mee that nothing . . .
>
> (ll. 14–16)

But his concluding self-congratulations makes this humility frivolous:

> This
> As yet my ease, and comfort is,
> Though I speed not, I cannot misse.
>
> (ll. 16–18)

The last line compresses an immobility of paradox. He cannot "speed," i.e., arrive at anything; but it doesn't matter. Her unutterable essence is beyond risk or chance, being beyond sense. Once acquired, the unknowable gift is presumably his forever. His final grace is secure loneliness.

The speaker here is still a projected voice; but the broad, gentle satire undermines his frame of reference as he projects it. Such a cleaning-out process as suggested in "Loves Alchymie" is here much farther along. "They" and "them" point with easy detachment to the social world. The speaker's blindness suggests a smug echo of a traditional view of love as divine. The satire is double-edged. The view expressed has boxed in its speaker, put him out-of-touch with any human experience. Courtly love is not called for here, but an encounter with reality stripped clean of clichés, a tumultuous anarchy of experience to produce a fresh grasp.

Yet the sense remains, so striking are the negative attributes, that the poem is veiled religious satire. We recall in "The Baite," the identification of the woman with the divine figure, a celestial essence who can darken sun and moon and control the light of reason. Also "Negative Love" has a first hint of a secular libido, further explored in "The Extasie," in the mystery of "what gives fuell to their fire." The satirical fun in "Negative Love" is more aggressive and detached. By this poem, like Spenser, Hooker, and the Elizabethan Protestants, Donne can reject the meditative way for broad, open human experience. The medieval Catholic approach is gently pooh-poohed. God in His ineffable negative attributes is a keystone for blind social complacency. This speaker wants a shock of encounter, not presumptions about essences. Donne is evidently easing out of his early Catholic attitudes, and bending toward a Protestant temperament.

"The Extasie," by our reading, is Donne's turning point from his previous poetic concerns. It has a strangely muted quality, experience distilled as in a crucible to its simplified essence, worked over, and studied for its process of change. We examine it, turn it about; it shrugs us off. Donne's fullest narrative in poetry, it is perhaps his least dramatic. We would tease the speaker of "Negative Love"; these ecstatics we would only emulate. Its episode has an enclosed, untouchable perfection, vividness, import, even magnificence, but not the grip of immediate experience. The speaker reveals what his gesture requires, his elemental physicality and muted passions, not his smack as a man, his color, weight, or irritability. The atmosphere is one of slowly awakening intuitions. Essential passions are barely heard.

A curious decorum distinguishes this from the accepted dialogues of love of the period, maintaining the poem in a subdued monochrome. The poem has forty instances of the first person plural; only once do we have the two separate pronouns, and then the woman is in the third person plural:

> Our soules, (which to advance their state,
> Were gone out,) hung 'twixt her, and mee.
> (ll. 15–16)

But if his partner is a "her," then whom does the repeated "we" address? And the woman, in word and gesture, remains in steady, reticent acquiescence to the man, like his shadow. The meeting hangs in the air, an encounter and no encounter, no "I" and "thou" in dialogue, but an awkward duet without direct address. This is no love story, with accidents, suspicions, and clarified intent, but a ritual enactment of a union, distilled, and rendered eternal. "We" are together throughout the poem.

"Negotiate" in line 17 is thus deceptive. The process is not negotiation, but harmonization, after a clumsy, distraught opening. "Cimented" (l. 5) expresses close, constricted hands, a chafing inability to move. Twisted and threaded eyebeams (ll. 7–8) recalls the contemporary doctrine of sight as emitted eye-beams, but more important is its expression of extreme physical discomfort, threaded eyes over cemented hands. This couple needs, not the commitment of trust, but the technique of intimacy, to shift from cramped closeness to ecstatic love. The development is closer to the *Kama Sutra* than to *Romeo and Juliet*.

Such a narrative we call an enactment, i.e., a locked series of activities, religious, secular, or even pornographic, whose forces work by some inner process to a catharsis, a blessing, a renewal of energy. Large, engulfing needs heavily define the characters, in a rather frozen setting. The magisterial "we" here sings no song of innocent fulfilment, as in Spenser's "Epithalamiom." It rehearses not the experience of ecstasy, but its proceedings, not an innocent flowering as it is enjoyed, but the stages by which innocence is arrived at.

At the start, a commitment to love has already been made. The couple sits on an open bank in cramped discomfort, holding hands and gazing at each other. But their environment seems out of focus, with strangely human attitudes, appropriate to the ritual of an enactment. Indeed, its stylized tone recalls *Pilgrim's Progress*. The pathetic fallacy has been suspended. Shaped like a pillow, the bank suggests they sleep together; like a pregnant belly, it suggests the consequences. The bank rises to "the violet's reclining head" as a momma's trunk to her infant, her belly to the male organ. The tone is one of hushed ease. The vegetable soul is in full ascendance, as though awakening from twilight sleep. Amid images of vegetable fulfilment, their own vegetable impulses for sexuality dumbly come awake. But they are blocked, without grace or movement, in a frustrated fulfilment, a choked sublimation:

> So to'entergraft our hands, as yet
> Was all the meanes to make us one,
> And pictures in our eyes to get
> Was all our propagation.
>
> (ll. 9–12)

The stalemate of the vegetable soul stirs awake their animal warrior souls; but these also block in a stalemate, "two equall Armies" between which "Fate suspends uncertaine victorie" (ll. 13–14). So, still blocked in frustrations, the shift continues, from the vegetable to the animal soul; and now the rational soul is finally awakened.

At first advance, their rational souls are wholly self-centered. They "to advance their state,/Were gone out" (ll. 15–16). The word "advance" is an extension on the level of the rational soul of "two equal armies" hanging in "uncertaine victorie," on the level of the animal soul. So, on the level of the vegetable soul, they blindly struggle for self-assertion in sex, to "entergraft our hands," "pictures in our eyes to get." The first advance in love is a clumsy, selfish pressure. But its antithesis is not agape or self-transcendant love. The poem in this sense is wholly pagan and secular. Their rational souls rather ascend out of the body onto some neo-Platonic hierarchy of existence to arrive at a harmonization. Indeed, the lines recall Plato's Myth of the Cave, where souls rise from the prison of the body to their proper abode in heaven:

And whil'st our soules negotiate there,
Wee like sepulchrall statues lay;
All day, the same our postures were,
And wee said nothing, all the day.
(ll. 17–20)

The suggestions of neo-Platonism here are strong, but should not be pushed too far. Donne was a dualist; but here his dualism is at its most tentative; and a more Lutheran theology of encounter is in the offing. In Plato's Myth of the Cave, the souls rise from a bodily prison to their proper abode for a harmony with the world of ideas, then to be forced back to their bodies. Donne's souls attain a harmony with one another amid no world of ideas, and return of themselves to their proper bodies. The stepladder movement from soul to soul, the ecstasy of insight of the rational soul, strike a neo-Platonic note; but Donne never envisaged a neo-Platonic easing of selfhood into the divine world soul. His souls achieve the ecstasy of intimacy with one another, not the illumination of eternal truth. Indeed, given his metaphysical shudder, his tainted cosmologies and suspect jargon, we must always question the use of any scaffolding of thought in Donne. Here, its use is for secure intimacy of spirit. After the controlling demons of the early poems, the slippery withdrawal of the women, the speaker clears a stepladder of firm structure, climbs it into the overworld, and engages in an encounter there as an independent being. To demand more of Donne than a scaffolding for his intimacy of spirit is illicit. With Donne the poet, we have only a gesture of spirit, shutting one door, and opening another.

But overlaying the secular and neo-Platonic scaffolding is a ponderous religious metaphor. Two bodies lie inert, as between Good Friday and Easter Sunday, their souls temporarily gone. Indeed, the phrase "sepulchrall statues" recalls lifesize Elizabethan sarcophagus figures in a posture of prayer, waiting for the resurrection. Westminster Abbey has several such husband-and-wife statues. Entwined with the neo-Platonic framework is a mystique of rebirth, anticipating the immortality in "The Good-Morrow." This is a muffled reverberation, an echo-chamber of religious experience behind a secular theme of utter arrival in love. Indeed, the posture, two bodies all day side by side in a field, rigid as statues, suggests not realism, but a ritual enactment. Their bodies are rigid, being trivial to the negotiation of souls. They are irrelevant to the enactment here.

The sleeping spirit awakens in lazy stages, pushed into wakefulness by a block in the soul below it, the vegetable soul into sexuality, the animal soul to power, the rational soul to self-advancement. And even in the rational soul, first the analytic or ratiocinative soul negotiates for self-advancement (l. 17), then the mystical or illuminated soul grasps the truth as a totality. This soul speaks its own language (l. 22). A man slowly rises to it, and catches the language of illumination under pressure of "good love" (l. 23), here secular, not sacred. As the higher soul comes awake under the power of love, ego boundaries dissolve, the embattlement of two psychic armies. The two lovers now echo one another (ll. 25–26). New concoctions become possible, fresh, unexpected mixtures of being, bringing a purification, the secular equivalent of the arrival of grace.

"This Extasie" (l. 29) then follows, before its implications are apparent, as an instant, luminous grasp of reality, not God's presence, nor the Platonic sun of truth, but the essence of utter intimacy with a woman. A fresh, Renaissance wind is stirring here. The human spirit is drifting toward secularization. Indeed, this is rapturous, mystical illumination as a particular love is born, with an inner personal light as in the *Mona Lisa*, utterly autonomous, within its own experience.

The first implication unfolded in illumination is crucial:

> Wee see by this, it was not sexe,
> Wee see, wee saw not what did move:
>
> (ll. 31–32)

This is the first reference in English to "sexe" as a mode of behavior, not simply the body sexual organs. Naming courtship by its organs of consummation establishes sex as an efficient and final cause in love relations, sidestepping the presence of God and mimicking the entire paraphernalia of the religious quest, the Edenic setting, the interaction of souls, the ladder of perfection, the language of illumination. The speaker consecrates a temple without an altar. But grasping the libidinous force of sex, Donne advances beyond the first vegetable impulse for self-expression in intercourse—"it was not sexe"—to the work of love (l. 35). No childhood and adolescent development is here suggested, nor the dynamic of family relations; yet the core of modern libido theory is projected here, love (and here "love" means sexual love) as energizing and unifying human behavior, binding human beings intimately to one another, i.e., as an efficient and final cause of human behavior:

> When love, with one another so
> Interinanimates two soules,
> That abler soule, which thence doth flow,
> Defects of lonelinesse controules.
>
> (ll. 41–44)

The easy secularization and blur of divinity and romantic love toyed with in "The Baite" and "Negative Love" here come to a head.

The metaphor of the violet transplant (ll. 37–44) acts as a corrective to the earlier reference to the "violet's reclining head" (l. 3). There, a vegetable metaphor suggests sexuality, parenthood, but no intimacy, nor real growth. Here, the bountiful, growing violet transplant intimates that intimacy in love multiplies love and beauty. Hence also the earlier stalemate is corrected, of two armies blocked by the limited, static amount of available goods; so that the advance of one automatically diminishes the other. Here, under love, all parts multiply and strengthen by their participation. Harmony is then possible in union.

The ecstasy itself is an illumination into the structure of being in love. It begins following the tripartite division of the vegetable, animal, and rational souls; yet the soul, illuminated by love, contains a "mixture of things" (l. 34), stressing its unpredictable mingling, the soul as plastic, various, unpredictable, with no regular ingredients:

> But as all severall soules containe
> Mixture of things, they know not what,

Love, these mixt soules, doth mixe againe,
And makes both one, each this and that.

(ll. 33–36)

Donne was evidently approaching a plastic sense of spirit, one he airily reconciles with the more traditional static soul in lines 45–48, as a sort of molecule with the separate souls as its atoms. This is again programmatically secular, the composition of a neo-Platonic, not a Christian soul. The ecstasy is an illumination that the essential man is not a sum of static parts, but the binding itself, "that subtile knot, which makes us man" (l. 64), an open, plastic fusion without a palpable godhead, strengthened with union. The old fear of a weakening in vegetable fulfilment is thus reassured. Fresh energy is projected, renewed strength in love.

Its block removed, the temperament now moves of itself toward sexual union:

But O alas, so long, so farre
Our bodies why doe wee forbeare?

(ll. 49–50)

The broken diction, the exclamation, the repetition of phrase, are only grammatically a question; essentially they are an articulate sigh for sexual union. But then the question is taken at face value (ll. 51–72), and answered in a second, abstract discussion of the relationship of body and soul that seems a falling off in the poem. Longer than the first, 21 to 17 lines, it is at the climax of the poem, where concentration is called for, and baldly presented, with no clear listener whom the lover is addressing.

Indeed, the two clarifications of the workings of the soul, ll. 33–48, and ll. 53–68, while complimenting each other, stand in contrast to one another. The first has the openness of a volatile, secular soul. "Mixture of things" (l. 34) suggests not some necessary proportion, but a more random individualism, as soul moves to soul in parley, body to body in spontaneous intuition. The second reestablishes its context of settled hierarchy:

They are ours, though they are not wee, Wee are
The intelligences, they the spheare.
(ll. 51–52)

A step-by-step order of influences thus expresses the old correspondences of a suspect astronomy:

On man heavens influence workes not so,
But that it first imprints the ayre,
Soe soule into the soule may flow,
Though it to body first repaire.
(ll. 57–60)

The earlier impulse is evidently shrouded, not rescinded:

Because such fingers need to knit
That subtile knot, which makes us man:
(ll. 63–64)

This knitting of the "mixture of things" is an unpredictable soul-making, but against a hierarchical structure.

Here, however, one must finally note that Donne remains a dualist. In the domain of spirit, his intuitions are open, skeptical, improvisatory, dynamic, presuming only the encounter itself, the "mixture of things" to allow a "subtile knot." In the second clarification, the body arrives at organized community, hierarchy, and mutual service, not true fusion:

To'our bodies turne wee then, that so
Weake men on love reveal'd may looke;
Loves mysteries in soules doe grow,
But yet the body is his booke.
(ll. 69–72)

And yet the formal detachment of the second clarification has an elegant propriety. "The Extasie" is structured not by logical development, but on waves of impulse, the desire for physical intimacy, blocked off and worked around. The first wave, a childish attraction, sitting by a bank among gentle allusions to a pillow, a pregnant bank, a reclining head, a propagation of the eyes, is then blocked by their jarring spirits, two armies, each attempting to dominate the other. The parley of their souls, working around it, leads to a more urgent impulse to sexual love, (ll. 49–50), and a succeeding, unidentified block, one that evokes old phobias about the body, that must be exorcised. A knotting of body and soul into one man is not attempted. The second clarification rather reestablishes a hierarchy of souls above bodies, in a proper courtesy to one another:

> We owe them thankes, because they thus,
> Did us, to us, at first convay,
> Yeelded their forces, sense, to us,
> Nor are drosse to us, but allay.
>
> ll. 53–56)

The poem moves then in two giant interludes, following two sexual impulses. The first, of simple animal sexuality, opens in clarification "the extasie," mingling their spirits in knowledge and total union; the second settles back in conservative hierarchy. The two clarifications form a rising and falling motion, a first rebellious thrust of spirit, affirming a fluid libido in a thrust of union and change. Unuttered bodily phobias then evoke a more familiar conservatism, easing the couple's fear of change "when we'are to bodies gone." The only shadow here is her shadowy echo of him. Donne here fully articulates himself; his "other" of spirit still has no independent presence.

Yet for a moment, in "The Extasie," Donne establishes a new mode of supreme excellence, an exalted radiance above the sepulchral statues of their bodies. His earlier excellence was one of strong independence and heroic spirit in a hostile situation, the happy warrior of "The Message," the embattled slave of "Loves Exchange." Even in a more youthful hero, as in "Goe, and Catche a Falling Starre," the excellence is of accomplished solitude and urbane aplomb. Here, the neo-Platonic framework, given the syncretism of the Elizabethan period, does not presume a neo-Platonic cosmology. The excellence is not one of stalwart masculinity on the plains of life, but exalted radiance above it, not masculine solitude, but a wedding of souls. Donne projects this setting of ecstasy only for clarification, not as his natural abode; but it soon invests "Aire and Angels" and "The Good-Morrow."

"Aire and Angels" is a slighter poem. Calm and meditative

throughout, it assumes the discoveries of "The Extasie." Thus, the ecstasy of insight arrived at after a struggle in line 29 is here the casual habit of the speaker, who communes with essences as he finds them about him. "Aire and Angels" has an uncertain equilibrium, but no deep, inner conflicts. An air of cleanliness overflows these lines, a fresh wind of radiant clarity. A fine-lined hierarchy of body and spirit extends up among the air and angels. The speaker moves up and down it with an exalted peace, touching a fabric here, defining a place there. There are no demonic tyrannies in this exalted, insubstantial Eden. "The Extasie" ends in a hard-won equilibrium; that equilibrium here is an elegant dance of love. The supreme arrival is here already become a radiant habit.

The hierarchical structure here is somewhat more Platonic. "The Extasie" projected a hierarchical climb from rung to rung toward a radiant illumination. "Aire and Angels" projects ideal essences in a more leisurely detached dualism. Romantically or seriously, occasional objects embody some ideal essence. This is, then, an aristocracy of occasional ideals; of universal partial participation, as Plato taught it, we have no hint. The speaker wanders about in a life of marvel, here and there apperceiving an embodiment of some essence. His radical innocence exceeds that in "The Extasie," with no depravity or guilt, not any cleansing process. There is no preliminary stage of negotiation of soul; he knew his beloved before he met her, as a form of perfection. A mind clear as a bell radiantly floats about, concerned only for minute adjustments of harmonious intimacy when stumbling on a perfect object. In "The Extasie," the weight of the body can be felt; here "limmes of flesh" are possessed by a soul as angels possess flames. The poem establishes clarity, not passion, a fine sureness on the scaffolding of love, an utterly secure intimacy. The speaker would focus his sight in an air so angelic his insecure eyes wobble slightly. His problem is a surer adjustment of parts, to control his wobble.

The poem recalls a strange tone struck occasionally in Seventeenth Century poetry, of a vision of radical innocence, not a simple wish-fantasy of paradise, but an embattled, fortress Eden, sequestered from the general blight of depravity. Given the severe theology of the time, the either-or of common depravity and selective grace, the poet projects an isle sequestered from the common curse. The speaker, as it were, offers an objective correlative for his twinge of radical innocence. Gaunt's speech in *Richard II* projects such an embattled little Eden:

> This royal throne of kings, this scept'red isle,
> This earth of majesty, this seat of Mars,
> This other Eden, demi-paradise,
> This fortress built by Nature for herself
> Against infection and the hand of war,
> This happy breed of men, this little world,
> This precious stone set in the silver sea,
> Which serves it in the office of a wall,
> Or as a moat defensive to a house,
> Against the envy of less happier lands;
> This blessed plot, this earth, this realm, this England.
>
> (II. i. ll. 40–50)

"Peace" by Henry Vaughan has striking parallels:

> My soul, there is a country
> Far beyond the stars,
> Where stands a wingëd sentry
> All skillful in the wars;
> There, above noise and danger
> Sweet Peace sits crowned with smiles . . .
>
> (ll. 1–6)

For all the gap of half a century, the shift in genre and degree of social involvement, both passages express the same simplification of innocence, its concentration into one region. Both Edens are under armed guard against an embattled world. Both passages express at once a sense of freedom from the constant jostle of depravity, and also a sense of pathos. Neither passage is suffused with a sense of oceanic fulfilment in an innocent world. An embattled Eden, under arms, is almost a contradiction in terms. Indeed, there is a subdued sense of the price to be paid for the innocence there, to save its assertion from being an act of hubris. In Gaunt's passage, Edenic England is already just a memory, having been rendered depraved by Richard's sin. In Vaughan's passage, Eden is a haven attained after death. He will pay with his life for that "country far beyond the stars."

In "Aire and Angels," the sense of poignance is more evanescent. It projects just such a sequestered Eden; yet the speaker is so innocent, he scarcely knows a world exists outside it. It registers only by an uneasy sense of omission. The poem is too caught up in a radiantly aerial setting of shapeless flames and lovely glorious nothings. Adjusting ourselves to air and angels, we twinge uneasily for the plumbing under our feet. The speaker pieces out his Eden with no control of his hubris, as in Shakespeare and Vaughan. Newborn in love, in a dream trance of radical innocence, he registers perfect things by apperception, arranges his harmonies of love by the behavior of angels. The sequestration of the area of love grows sharper in "The Good-Morrow," then gradually increases until the harrowing assault on the Eden of love in "The Canonization." If "The Good-Morrow" reads like Donne's marriage poem, "Aire and Angels" reads like his poem of engagement.

The poem expresses the first dreamy arrival in love. The major verb in line 1 is past perfect, in line 5 is the simple past, in line 12 is the present tense. The poem takes place, as it were, at the moment of arrival, in a double focus of anticipation of love and its first recognition. But he knew her before he first saw her. So the world of ideas and the natural world overlap one another in a blur:

> Twice or thrice had I loved thee,
> Before I knew thy face or name;
> So in a voice, so in a shapeless flame,
> *Angells* affect us oft, and worship'd bee . . .
>
> (ll. 1–4)

In "Goodfriday, 1613. Riding Westward," Donne refers to the intelligence that moves a sphere; here he refers to an angel perceived in a voice or flame. The angels are probably, but not certainly, guardian angels, the same as the intelligences, but given a sensibility as custodians of natural objects. Indeed, Donne gives them substantial independence, angels possessing a flame as love might possess her body. The relationship is thus one of benign possession, an exorcism of the demonic possession of the earlier poems. The speaker would thus possess his newfound beloved, but does not know how. Everything about him is in double focus. He has just come awake to a new world; and there is a universal wobble, events in disfocus with their anticipation, an ideal essence with his substantial beloved. Nothing is ordinary or straitforward. Angels move on voices, perfection on her presence, all in a wobble of disfocus. But love is an efficient cause as well as an ideal spirit, impelling the soul, its child, to take a body. Stanza 1, then, is the gesture of establishing love. Its speaker has a fascinating selfishness. In the radiant gleam and disfocus of a wobbly reality, he wants to fix himself. Then, unbalanced, first finding his love, over-eager, he tries to make the knot too tight:

> Whilst thus to ballast love, I thought,
> And so more steddily to have gone,
> With wares which would sinke admiration,
> I saw, I had loves pinnace overfraught . . .
>
> (ll. 15–18)

He has a blurred disposition, body and spirit all unstable, all in a complex irregular motion. He searches a fit for his love, some object slightly below, that it can rest comfortably in, but not too far below, which would be forced. As an angel puts on air (ll. 23–24), so her love can bear his love—we suppose her body can bear his body, though he is too well-bred to articulate this. The sense of love here, as a fine fit, is aggressively secular and classical. Utterly suave, urbanely egotistical, finely self-effacing, he establishes the angel in his love. With disconcerting aplomb, our lover finally adjusts his wobble.

If "The Extasie" and "Aire and Angels" inhabit a halfway house of autonomous love in a hierarchical universe, "Loves Growth," also aggressively secular, plunges love into a wholly open universe, with no hierarchy whatever, only relentless, glorious fecundity. Its sense of the structure of love is too firm readily to allow a dating with the earlier poems. If read in the sequence of marital poems, it would come some while after they have been joined in love. Its metaphysics is also more advanced than in "The Extasie" or "Aire and Angels," substituting an uncontrolled fecundity for their neo-Platonic structure. It therefore suggests a writing a winter after they fell in love, in a detached, confident, plainspoken mood, that would allow so radical and unfettered a cosmology. The analogy to the sun, to the stars (l. 18), to a blossoming root (l. 20), and concentric circles in water (l. 21), establish love as a primal force, an independent first principle. Its universe is not static, but of ceaseless growth, its perfection not of purity (l. 1), but of immeasurable abundance, from which all abundance comes:

> Me thinkes I lyed all winter, when I swore,
> My love was infinite, if spring make'it more.
>
> (ll. 5–6)

The analogies to sunlight, blossoms on a bough, concentric circles in water (ll. 18–22), suggest a boundless universe, with no inbred principle of self-control, no impulse of gradation and place. The sun illuminates the entire heaven; boughs bear all the blossoms they can; ripples spread to the farthest shore. The suggestion is of uncontrolled fecundity in place of enlightened hierarchy. Love is no force for order, balance, stable equilibrium, or wisdom, but an impetuous overflow and fecundity, princely royal (l. 26), powerful as the sun (l. 18), indeed, so one-dimensional, impersonal, and blindly universal, the poem reads as a gesture of tearing loose the last web of structure and hierarchy.

These poems suggest a complex piecing out of a definition of love in a difficult universe, laden with phobias and old metaphysical machinery. They express an odd mixture of marvel and detached wisdom, wry, mystical elegance, a fine stepping into a dance with unsure rhythms. So "Aire and Angels" takes halting half-steps in a hierarchy too aerial to be grasped. "Negative Love" affirms with gentle irony an unreal devotion in abstraction. Its opposite, "Loves Growth," projects a romantic fecundity, stripped bare in fanatical devotion. As for "The Extasie," its conception of the libido, its flexible experience of self-definition, its fine, easy metaphysical hierarchy, its autonomy in love, give it a nobility and poise comparable to the *Mona Lisa* as imbued with the spirit of exalted discovery of the high Renaissance.

# 8

# The Marital Poems

The theme of awakening from sleep dominates Donne's marital poems. In "The Sunne Rising," he literally wakes up; "The Good-Morrow" presumes such an awakening. In "The Canonization," the couple will awaken to a higher new life, canonized in love. "The Dreame" hovers on wakefulness. This has an astute ring. To the psyche, each new stage in life feels like an awakening from sleep. Weakened or omitted, as in "The Anniversarie," "Loves Infiniteness," or "The Undertaking," the poem has less strength. The two most vivid, "The Sunne Rising" and "The Good-Morrow," express a direct, literal awakening.

Donne's usual structures of imagery show curious lacunae. He has a play of light and darkness, day and night, but not the seasons of the year or the shift from youth to age, the entire globe, its shape, size, and way of moving, but not the rolling countryside. "A Nocturnall upon S. Lucies Day" opens and closes, "Tis the yeares midnight, and it is the dayes;" but this is an ultimate midnight, not a season of fall and winter. So "Goodfriday, 1613. Riding Westward" registers the crucifixion, but not the country he traversed. Donne worked by vision, not the play of his surroundings; he registered crises, not the unfolding tapestry of life. "The Storme" and "The Calme" are vivid and particular, but their situation lacks the deepest human reverberations. They are finally just journal letters.

His are ego poems of stark immediacy, electric with situations to be mastered, not the largesse of nature, the rolling of the seasons. Abrupt to the brief staccato of day and night, light and darkness, they slough off any empathetic communion with nature. They remain consumingly dramatic, confronting himself, a woman, the presence of God, taking positions, stark, final gestures. God's earth is a trinket; the countryside is beside the point.

Hence the rare pleasure of "The Good-Morrow," where nature and he awaken together in the early morning. Experience is become transparent. He has just traversed the passage of the straits; as daylight washes across his bridal chamber. Waves of insight, layers of old experience overlap each other, and all visible. Indeed, the action of the poem is the settling of the crystal of his life in a new structure.

The music here has a massive solidity. An iambic pentameter quatrain is rounded out, not with a couplet, but a triplet with an Alexandrine close a, b, a, b, c, c, c. The entire man feels engaged here; as he did not in "The Extasie" or "Aire and Angels." The colloquial opening, "I wonder by my troth," bursts out of a puddle of sleepy bewilderment; not a controlled argument follows it, but a splash of pleasant memories. Its three stanzas express successive moments that glide spontaneously forward without felt steps. The burst of bewilderment, "I wonder by my troth," spills from the lips, not from the brain; yet its pun is central to his experience. "Troth" means "truth," but also "betrothal." But "troth" also registers a pledge. He has pledged his "troth"; and that is now his truth, his touchstone of commitment.

Each stanza divides into two parts, a sudden disposition in the quatrain, then a closing triplet that derives its implications and evokes the next stanza. Thus, four opening, hesitant questions express the befuddlement of suddenly awakening with his bride. The speaker has lost control over the chain of time. The anchor of the past is dissolving into childish memories. The triplet then registers a fresh plateau of being, using a series of variations on the verb "to be" to register a sudden, stark kick of reality. "T'was so" has the finality of "nothing else is" in "The Sunne Rising." So "But this, all pleasures fancies bee" is a final judgment on the reality of previous pleasures. The stanza close, "t'was but a dreame of thee," builds a firm wall between reality and the qualified wakefulness of his former life.

In this context, "fancies (l. 5)" and "dreame (l. 7)" express a gauzy, sham reality, registered by the abrupt clause, "T'was so." The passage must be taken as literally true. Donne's grasp of metaphysics was too firm to allow otherwise. He allowed only psychic reality, the domain of spirit; the physical universe was a shifting, insecure trough of events. This would support a rather Platonic dualism; but Donne's domain of spirit was vital, libidinous, with a strong thrust toward personal encounter and ego fulfilment, not a lofty universality absorbed in the contemplation of eternal ideas. Given his strong dualism, the more vital his psychic experience, the more firm its reality. We therefore take as literal such statements as "T'was so" and "But this, all pleasures fancies bee," literal also:

> If ever any beauty I did see,
> Which I desir'd, and got, t'was but a dreame of thee.
> (ll. 6–7)

He awakens, then, to a new domain of existence. He has staked out his chosen half acre of ground. He need slide no more. His marital experience will be his reality of spirit. As we have noted, all his life Donne surged toward immediate intimacy. Here he has surmounted gradations of wakefulness, and sings a hymn of joy, not only because he is now most happy but also most relieved. His metaphysical shudder, his uneasy sense of the drift of reality, is at last settling into a pattern. His inner being is stamping its reality on a blurry world.

Stanza 2 bids welcome to this new state of soul, one of radical openness and wakefulness. People normally watch with eyes, to mask and guard themselves, while hiding their souls; but these watch with their souls, not "out of feare" (l. 9), but to share their love more intimately. Love is here the master power, a prime source of controlling authority and force. This is, by implication, another religious rejection. The master love normally reserved for God is here invested in the libido of sexual love, "For love, all love of other sights controules" (l. 10). So the experience of love fixes reality in its location and makes that place infinite, "And makes one little roome, an every where" (l. 11), giving infinity a secular dimension.

Having established his sense of place and its controlling force of love in the quatrain, the speaker relates it in the triplet to the rival temptations of forces in the world around him. In this great age of English expansion after the Armada, he envisions love in opposition to Elizabethan adventure. All explorations, under Ralegh, Drake, or another, are to possess the world; but they, possessing one another, form a world unto themselves (ll. 13–14).

This poem has a dazzle of overlapping experiences, transparent to one another. The casual, colloquial speech, making a personal movement, parallels a public progression, as in "Goe, and Catche a Falling Starre," from a medieval to a Renaissance experience. Hence the manorial relaxation of Stanza 1, its "seven sleepers den" suggesting folk legend and superstition. So "wean'd" and "countrey pleasures" suggest old, traditional concerns. At the same time, breast-feeding and weaning suffuse the stanza with childish life and personal history. So the "seven sleepers den" suggests a literal mass of children, tumbling in a cot, by contrast with two adults, joined in sexual love.

As Stanza 1 is manorial, magical, and childish, Stanza 2 is adventuresome, exploratory, and adolescent, full of the map-making of sturdy boys, the experience of apprentice warriors in Elizabethan England, engaged in fighting, discovery, and the possession of new worlds. So the stanza bristles and darts about. Other discoverers tear across the seas to new worlds, pile map on map. The speaker himself would survey his home territory, establish its borders, make his "one little roome, an every where." He knows what constitutes real power.

If the first two stanzas parallel "Goe, and Catche a Falling Starre," the third stanza marks a fresh turn of spirit. Thus, "Goe, and Catche" finally arrives at a pratfall of disbelief, where "The Good-Morrow" finally achieves an adulthood of visionary amplitude. Line 14, the last line of Stanza 2, forms the bridge to Stanza 3. In Stanza 2, the speaker is, as it were, on the earth's surface, struggling for his own in an atmosphere of "controules," "discoverers," "possesse." By Stanza 3, the speaker is mysteriously above the earth. Indeed, in a visual puzzle reminiscent of medieval mystical maps, where a human body outlines the cosmos, his face or body forms half a globe turned on its other half, which is her face or body, their reflection in each other's eyes suggesting union and fertility. After the tempestuous seizures of property in Stanza 1, these lines offer tranquility and eternal calm:

> My face in thine eye, thine in mine appeares,
> And true plaine hearts doe in the faces rest.
>
> (ll. 15–16)

Together, they form a globe, eternal, being flawless, and at rest in contemplation of one another. Indeed, any motion would be futile, since motion is an endeavor; and they have arrived at perfection:

> Where can we finde two better hemispheares
> Without sharpe North, without declining West?
>
> (ll. 17–18)

So the suggestions of unchangeable perfection lift them above the sublunar earth, coeval with the celestial spheres, flawlessly attuned, and immortal (ll. 19–21). Thus, a casual, bewildered good-morrow to a new love becomes an awakening unto eternity.

There is a curious geometrical skew here from stanza to stanza. At the start, the couple, as it were, pops into view, two country pixies awakening in bed together, yet still tumbling among the legendary seven sleepers and nursing infants. By Stanza 2, they carve out their domain, "one little roome," already become a world. By Stanza 3, they have absorbed that world and are afloat in space, but undetermined in size; whereas by its close, their flawless hemispheres suggest the cosmic spheres, and they are immortal. This growth in size should be projected literally, as expressing a euphoria of utter fulfilment. Newly wedded, radiantly in love, exuberant beyond transport, they swell in their bed, thrust aside the world's experience, outgrow the earth, become equal to the universe, their love immortal.

"The Good-Morrow" soars with an Ariel clarity. From its opening of relaxed wonder, the speaker, absorbed in the love experience, rubs his eyes, then, looking about him, offers his bride radiant abstractions of spirit. Each stanza begins with a beautiful hesitation, in a fresh wash of experience assimilated in the triplet. "The Sunne Rising" stirs Plantagenet congestion. Its speaker inhabits a dense capital, not a spreading manor. It begins with an urgent trespass of sunlight. The speaker then reduces his rival monarch, the sun, to servile docility. The music responds to this dense atmosphere, offering a congestion of feet per line, 4, 2, 5, 5, 4, 4, 5, 5, 5, 5, a haphazard rhyme scheme a, b, b, a, c, d, c, d, e, e. Yet the stanza finally manages an equilibrium. Its rhymes settle to two quatrains and a couplet. Its length of line begins with jarred irregularity but finally settles to the pentameter line.

"The Good-Morrow" is a lyrical awakening of wedded love; "The Sunne Rising" establishes a young aristocrat, expressing with exuberant flamboyance what he allows in wedded love, and what he presumes. In "The Good-Morrow," two wedded equals are absorbed in perfect equilibrium: "My face in thine eye, thine in mine appeares" (l. 15) "two better hemispheares" (l. 17), "mix'd equally" (l. 19). "The Sunne Rising" puts them in a harmonious opposition, she as "India" (l. 17), he its "Kings" (l. 19), she his domain, he her monarch. So the end-line, "Myne," suggests possession, as in "Loves Alchymie." Enclosed by the same pronoun in a succession of rhymes, "mee," "Myne," "mee," the succession establishes her as his possession and rule. "She'is all States, and all Princes, I."

Personal reverberations multiply, when we date these poems with Donne's marriage. To date them two or three years later, upon his shattered career, would make them a grotesque gallows joke. Yet even our date has an awesome portent. The entire mentality of the Elizabethan period was too aware of hubris for Donne not to grasp its implications. So Shakespeare's Julius Caesar proclaimed, then was assassinated hours later:

Danger knows full well
That Caesar is more dangerous then he:
We are two lions litter'd in one day,
And I the elder and more terrible.
(II. ii. ll. 44–47)

So the speaker here proclaims to the sun:

Thine age askes ease, and since thy duties bee
To warme the world, that's done in warming us.
Shine here to us, and thou art every where;
This bed thy center is, these walls, thy spheare.
(ll. 27–30)

Indeed, we have already remarked the wistful pathos of "Aire and Angels," its reduced Eden, with an innocent unawareness of what is beneath its feet. So "The Good-Morrow" expresses an unabashed, simplistic expansion in size, until the world disappears under the speaker's feet. The entire decorum of Elizabethan statecraft forbade such megalomania; its drama again and again demonstrated with a heavy knell the price of such overreaching. For Donne, the scrupulous, ambitious private secretary of an Elizabethan statesman, such sentiments are simply incredible, especially considering the stature and temperament of his father-in-law. In his first lyric period, Donne projected special voices. Here at last, his own voice breaks out, and as a presence afloat in a dreamy wonder, his moral Eden miles above the arena of human depravity, steadily swelling in an innocent of rhapsodic hubris.

"The Sunne Rising" projects an aristocrat, not simply a lover, one who undertakes to establish a right relationship to the sun, not to his bride. Tough, exuberant, used to the highest competition, he quarrels with the sun over who will be king-of-the-hill. He opens his speech with a rhetorical bravura:

Busie old foole, unruly Sunne,
Why dost thou thus,
Through windowes, and through curtaines call on us?
(ll. 1–3)

This is shrewd schoolboy mockery, taunting the sun as a Polonius, a "Busie old foole," the attendant lord, hiding behind curtains, calling through windows, to do his attendant duty. The braggadocio of the speaker continues in Stanza 2 as the speaker stakes monarchy against monarchy, estate against estate, reaching around the world. This vividly extends the vignettes of boyish life in Stanza 1, the schoolboys, apprentices, and court huntsmen, rushing about their schedules. So the speaker, disturbed by the sun, who presumes he is boss, promptly lunges forward to match him, India for India, and mine for mine.

The competition with the sun has larger vibrations. As "The Good-Morrow" expands in size, so "The Sunne Rising" engages in a flip-flop of geometrical exuberance. The sun in Donne's day was being established as center of the universe. By our date, the telescope would be invented in less than a decade; but there was already a stir of cosmological unease, nor was the Copernican hypothesis ever entirely silenced. A newly married young aristocrat, abreast with current astronomical gossip, would playfully taunt the sun, a possible replacement of the earth as center of the universe, as a shuffling servant. By a geometrical flip-flop, he would make his marital bed the center of the universe, the sun his satellite.

But psychologically, a more elemental factor is involved. The poem begins as a third figure, the sun, enters the bedroom in the morning, so it holds three, the speaker, his bride, and the sun. But given the system of correspondences, the sun would represent the father, the king, the ruler of the universe. In this context, of entering the bridal bed and giving the young groom orders, the dominant correspondence would be that of the father, the boss of the establishment. The action of the poem, at its core, is the dethronement of the father. So the newly self-crowned king proclaims, "Thine age askes ease" (l. 27) to his predecessor, like a latter-day Jupiter to his father Kronos.

Indeed, the articulation of the king metaphor over the father metaphor at the end of Stanza 2 and in Stanza 3 reinforces our sense of the structure of Donne's psyche. His own father, dead when he was four, was a subdued factor in Donne's poems. The dominant female figure looms strongly throughout his life; but the dominant male element was shifted to the state. So here, it is the king he would replace as head of his own household. Indeed, by our dating, this poem coincides with the date of Essex's imprisonment in Sir Thomas Egerton's custody, and his subsequent execution. But Essex was Donne's comrade and commander in the sacking of Cadiz, and the subsequent unfortunate trip to the West Indies; and Essex was also trying to replace an older monarch. So the line "Thine age askes ease" addressed to a monarch has a contemporary ring of identity with Essex.

Yet for all its hubris, its manic, boyish exuberance, its utterly self-centered speaker, we exult in his euphoria. How else should an alert, lusty young aristocrat feel, newly married and commandeering his world? For the poem rings as wholesome, sharply focusing on reality with a clarity and radiant poise. We are not shut off in a dream chamber, but enjoy the transparencies of "The Good-Morrow." Thus we see schoolboys, sour apprentices, and lusty court huntsmen. There is no either-or of experience; we overlook the globe, preside over kings, taste the wealth of India—and all this without once getting out of bed! Yet our speaker is no green, virginal innocent, gliding through a euphoric self-indulgence, but a young civil servant, shaping a career in statecraft in which his bride will have a hearty part. Even Stanza 2 expresses her as majestic, not Edenic. "India of spice and Myne" alludes to an empire, not simple sensuous love. The speaker is establishing his home-base in bed, but will range around the globe with euphoric self-assertion: this India, this spice, this mine—it's mine! In the poem he not only acquires a bride, but also his first servant, the sun.

But for all his euphoria, the speaker has an alert grasp of the metaphysics of love. The flat, four-syllable line, "Nothing else is" (l. 22), affirms with verbal audacity the reality of psychic force over its material underpinning. Given Donne's web of spirits, human and divine, one might call this pan-solipsism, the intuition that, fundamentally, existence contains only a web of spirits. Hence, Donne could play at cosmologies, indulge in correspondences and their denial; they didn't concern him that much, being all insubstantial alongside the world of spirit. "Nothing else is" dismisses the state, the earth itself:

Love, all alike, no season knowes, nor clyme,
Nor houres, dayes, moneths, which are the rags of time.
(ll. 9–10)

He steadily establishes the contrast of real and make-believe. Love is the body of time; calendars and schedules are but its rags. So the play of princes, the "mimique" of honor, the alchemy of wealth, all refer to the gauze of the financial and social world; under that gauze are the vivacities of love.

Indeed, egocentric or not, by the end, the speaker breathes his full commitment to love. "This bed thy center is" (l. 30) establishes not intercourse, but sexual love, his intimate, libidinous bond to his sweetheart as the center of his reality. The function of the sun is to "warme the world" (l. 28). So she is his earth, a presence so elemental, his reticence at warming her earth reads only as aristocratic reserve.

"The Sunne Rising" parallels "The Good-Morrow" in expressing successive ages, though their range is narrower here. Thus, Stanza 1 projects an early adolescent period, the gang-stage of "late schoole boyes and sowre prentices." Indeed, it opens as the sun, his sergeant-at-arms, bursts into his bedroom, yelling and firing orders, to which he blusters back a double insult, "sawcy, pedantique wretch," calling him middle-aged, ill-mannered, and a schoolteacher. In Stanza 2, he first stabs at manhood, still competing, plunging about in travel and adventure. In Stanza 3, the competition relaxes; his urgency to travel eases; and he settles into an adult object of love.

The dazzled air of "The Good-Morrow," its sheer transparency, is heightened in "The Sunne Rising." If the more usual texture of Donne's lyrics recalls a Dürer engraving; here, a vivid, precise egg tempera washes worlds of discourse across one another. The glare of sunlight slaps the speaker awake. Indulgently, he insults the sun with a patronizing clock of schoolboy schedules, "the rags of time," the turbulent inadequacy of boyish experience. Stanza 2 washes across another universe, of monarchy and empire, Stanza 3 another of astronomy and the cosmic expanse. And love rises to every occasion.

Indeed, the speaker's loving, marvelous gall never pooh-poohs his ardent exuberance, never shrinks before his increasingly vehement self-assertion, and is always light of foot, shifting with dazzling precision. Indeed, this light-footed mastery of love is the final myth of love, that the commitment of love brings freedom and mastery; the lover, embracing his sweetheart, can range at will. Sprawled in bed after a night of love, he puts India in its place, overshadows kings, smacks together spice and mine, and gives its orders to the unruly sun. A bedroom Tamburlaine, a Faustian apprentice imp, a passionate, career-minded Ariel, he is an elemental, utterly free, utterly in love. Donne's exuberant dream of a magnificently limned impossibility marks him a Renaissance Apollo of a giddy aristocrat, unbound, serenely majestic, madly in love. By our dating, shortly after writing this poem, Donne wrote his letter to Sir George More, informing him of his marriage to his daughter.

In "The Anniversarie," something has cracked. "The Sunne Rising" expressed a vivacious exuberance; "The Anniversarie" is more subdued, more mature and majestic. Indeed, one level on which "The Good-Morrow," "The Sunne Rising," "The Anniversarie," and "The Canonization" constitute a loose series is the curious way each begins at an age level a notch higher than its predecessor. Thus, "The Sunne Rising" finishes as the speaker enthrones himself, having overthrown the rule of the sun. "The Anniversarie" begins with a tone of majestic young manhood, a condition comparable to "All Kings."

The music is majestic as in a grand ballroom. Three couplets gradually lengthen step, from four to five feet per line. Then, as though joined by an opposite column, they double to four rhymed lines, a tetrameter, and two pentameters finishing on a stately Alexandrine. The self-contained couplets open on one another, making the entire stanza a single sentence of interlocking music. Its very items are envisioned in a majestic march, kings, court favorites, the aristocracy. "The sun it self, which makes times" (l. 3), recalls the sun of "The Sunne Rising," ordering the rags of time. There, the sun competes for final authority; here, it accepts a divided monarchy. But this court march is a dance of death: "All other things, to their destruction draw" (l. 6). Only the lovers stand apart, untouchable by time:

> Only our love hath no decay;
> This, no to morrow hath, nor yesterday,
> Running it never runs from us away,
> But truly keepes his first, last, everlasting day.
> (ll. 7–10)

Majestic as is Stanza 1, its vivacity is attenuated. Modes of experience, as in the first two marriage poems, no longer wash across one another. The measured ballroom march lacks fresh air, the catch of colloquial speech. Its hubris has too dignified a sonority; its eternity is affirmed in long, loose lines, not sparkling with geometrical exuberance. The lines have muffled, stereotypic, status-laden nouns: kings, favorites, glory, the sun. No handy, surprising objects or vivid individuals leap into view. Indeed, the very location of the two lovers outside the double march, in an island apart, has the melancholy of isolation, for all its marching dignity. The rolling ball of earth has contracted to a single organized social march; and they are outside of it. In the earlier poems, they were in the center of things, in their bedchamber, in the tumultuous midst of life, yet above it.

More ominous is Stanza 2. Its dwelling on the grave makes a hollow reassurance of the immortality completing Stanza 1. Radiant believers, whose "love hath no decay," but always keep a "first, last, everlasting day," do not dwell on the experience of the grave. To this speaker, the experience of dying is not trivial. Indeed, this poem has too formal an equilibrium for spontaneous celebration. The glorious march of state of Stanza 1 is balanced by its eventual destruction. Organized society is balanced by the wedded lovers. Stanza 1, expressing the dance of life, is balanced by Stanza 2, expressing the settlements of the grave.

Stanza 2 affirms eternal love in lines of dignity, but no strength. Its grammar is everywhere impeded by parenthetical phrases, inverse word order, the separation of subject from verb from object, exclamations, qualifications, complex minor clauses. Baldly, the speaker of this poem has lost his nerve. Stanza 2 has nouns as stereotypic as Stanza 1. Their burial is described as a species of hiding (l. 11), their death as their divorce (l. 12). The speaker affirms an eternity of love, dwelling on corpses, divorce, walls, tears, graves. He would still have them as monarchs:

> Alas, as well as other Princes, wee,
> (Who Prince enough in one another bee,)
>
> (ll. 13–14)

But the qualification, "enough," settles for pathetically little; and in this context, princes are a hollow comparison. There is an alienation of love from the normal thoughts of life, as well as from normal social contacts: "But soules where nothing dwells but love/ (All other thoughts being inmates) . . ." (ll. 17–18).

Such a tone befits Donne's first wedding anniversary. The blow has fallen—he is unemployed, under arrest; but its finality has not yet registered. A chance connection, a sudden turn of fate, and all might yet be well. Muffled, Donne shifts about, shadow-boxes, affirms his faith, but all with a hollow softness, an extraordinarily painful dignity. He had just extended his horns, in a gesture of hubris. Battered, his ego is back in hiding.

Dead, he shall be "throughly blest," enjoy genuine equality (l. 21). Lines 23–24 affirm their supreme monarchy; but they sound hollow after the qualifications in line 14. Even the question, "Who is so safe as wee" (l. 25) is charged with uneasiness. Surely more orgiastic values than safety can be found to celebrate an anniversary. Yet, dwelling on the grave, the speaker ends confident in their loyalty to one another and affirming a life of dignity for them. Muffled as he is, he has not yet given up his way.

By "The Canonization," the blow had registered. In "The Sunne Rising," short, congested lines eased into pentameters; in "The Canonization," the pentameters gradually shorten and grow staccato, its feet per line 5, 4, 5, 5, 4, 4, 5, 4, 3. So too, its rhyme scheme, a, b, b, a, c, c, c, d, d, speeds up from a quatrain to a triplet to an unbalanced, foreshortened couplet.

"The Sunne Rising" begins successfully mastering an outside interference; "The Canonization" grows increasingly embattled and harassed. The speaker breathes faster, swinging from side to side. Indeed, the most effective reading would refer each "you" in Stanza 1 to a different person. Tied to a stake like a baited bear, the speaker swings about at his assaulting dogs, his well-meaning friends, cajoling, ordering him about, commiserating. To them all, he cries, "Take you a course, get you a place" (l. 5), frantic, indignant, his plight increasingly desperate. Indeed, Helen Gardner's date, after the crowning of James I, from the line "Or the Kings reall, or his stamped face" (l. 7) accords with this sequence. A date after James' coronation in 1603 would suit Donne's unfolding temperament, increasingly harassed, with short stumbling steps, all to no end; as the very grounds of government change, the march of society rushes forward.

The cumulative phrases of Stanzas 1 and 3, as well as the piled questions in Stanza 2, all bespeak an explosive onrush of speech. The first and last line of each stanza end with the word "love," a pistolshot refrain of a poet grappling for security while staggering for support. The opening colloquial phrase, "For Godsake hold your tongue," has a casual precision, like that of "The Good-Morrow." He curses, "For Godsake," at once hiding in and defending holy sacraments. Forced outside the social fabric by his marriage, he falls back on God. Even his palsy, gout, and few gray hairs have a petulant ring, as though he is now denying his hubris. An Apollo might have merited such a destruction, being precious perfect; but he is palsied, gouty, and aging. Let him then endure an ordinary fate.

Stanza 2 increases his frantic harassment. His rhetorical questions seem begging for a justification. The second person pronoun, the insistant "you" of Stanza 1, altogether disappears. Uneven phrases speed up to end-stopped questions. Attention shifts from attainable goods to phobias of what the speaker's love might do. No external situation is any longer discernible, only a frantic speaker, blindly casting about, evading, answering, justifying, addressing no one.

By Stanza 3, his frantic speech eases; his imagination begins again to associate. He acknowledges he seems ridiculous, "call us what you will" (l. 19), then tumbles out a series of associations—the "flye," the "Taper," "the 'Eagle and the Dove," "the Phoenix." "Taper" reads better as a taper-moth than as a candle, beginning a series of winged creatures, each slightly larger and more mythic than the last. He is now rolling with his staccato accusations, absorbing them, rising to a reply. Touching the Phoenix myth, he claims a rebirth in love, the creation of a new self:

> So to one neutrall thing both sexes fit,
> We dye and rise the same, and prove
> Mysterious by this love.
>
> (ll. 25–27)

The poem here eliminates any common ground on the fringes of the area of love, as the earlier poems suggested. So, in "The Good-Morrow," the lovers, self-contained and indifferent, remained in this world; in "The Sunne Rising," they are again self-contained. Here, no dignified middle ground is allowed.

Stanza 4 is most poignant. Donne might literally have aspired to a "half-acre tombe," like the princely Elizabethan tombs, but surrendered it for a "well wrought urne." So, he might literally have been registered in the English chronicles as a statesman, but will now settle for his "pretty roomes" in his own sonnets.

The separation becomes final in Stanza 5. Forced out of this world, he will find fulfilment, canonized in the next. Once the new celestial monarch, his spirit is now a hermitage. He is a contradiction to life, his love a rage. Even the emblem of fertility, seeing each other mirrored in each other's eyes, is constricted to a drive by force, not to embody new worlds, but to spy upon old ones. It is unclear if the last line and a half, "Beg from above/ A patterne of your love!" is included in the invocation beginning, "You whom reverend love" (l. 37), or is the reply of the lovers to those who invoke them. If the latter, then the reply is one of lofty, defiant self-affirmation; if the former, then the lovers are pathetic outcasts, summoned to seek above for a pattern that nothing on earth can fit. The simultaneous possibility of both readings expresses a terrifying ambiguity and irresolution, a catharsis at once of bewilderment, defiance, and lofty self-affirmation. Yet for all the ambiguity, one thing is settled. In "The Anniversarie," he still hung in the balance. By "The Canonization," in this world, his case is closed.

"The Dreame" is so muted an episode, so casual a flicker of feeling, the openness and intimacy gives us some rule-of-thumb for the dating. But there is also the echo of "Aire and Angels." As there, he loved her before he knew her, fumbling between ideal images, and the blur of fleshly reality, so here, he dreams realities about her, and experiences her reality as an idealized dream. So the lines glide in muted half-notes, its arguments tangled in conceits, dreams on the fringes of reality, realities in future dreams. As in "Aire and Angels," Donne is again flirting with Plato's world of ideas in a mood-piece of poignant wistfulness, angel in a tangled blur with flesh, insecurity in the deepest trust, an impressionistic rendering of Donne's own wavering spirit, to whom her validity is the only touchstone of truth. Yet Donne's spirit is losing its wayward elusiveness. We here touch the pool of his mind, full of presences, fears, ideas of angels and of women, rough-grained, flickering, reverberating. This is a poem of the deepest love. How intimate he is, murmuring to her as to himself, the mask dissolved between them. And for all his starts of fear, he would be "all spirit, pure, and brave" (l. 25).

The same unease governs "Loves Infiniteness," and spoils its effect. The poem hangs on no occasion, but is triggered into being by a semantic difficulty. She may have given all of herself in love, but changed, or misunderstood the terms. The logical resolution offered is that love is not a static, but a growing thing; but semantic resolutions seldom allay emotional insecurities. The assertion, "Wee will have a way" (l. 31), has not yet found the present tense. We wish the speaker luck.

"The Undertaking" is a bit more spare, less ardently lyrical, yet with the lilting ballad meter and secure emotion of a song. It begins, repeating with complete satisfaction the theme of "Negative Love." The man with inner beauty loathes its superficial forms:

> But he who lovelinesse within
> Hath found, all outward loathes,
> For he who colour loves, and skinne,
> Loves but their oldest clothes.
>
> (ll. 13–16)

The dualism is still here; this love is in some way sacred and apart from "prophane men" (l. 22). Total union is impossible, to "forget the Hee and Shee" (l. 20). Yet exaggerated as is the mood, it is direct and open. The speaker extols her precious being, not her attributes; but he is singing a song. In a love song, hyperbole is the sweetest truth.

# 9

# Poems of Parting

After his marriage, Donne traveled about both in England and abroad to earn money, maintain connections, and reestablish his career. Between Anne's repeated pregnancies and failing health, and his own failings and insecure floundering, their partings must have been taxing. His poems of parting attempt to ease her feelings and part with a dignified, calm farewell. So we would read four of these poems, "Sweetest Love, I do not goe," "A Valediction: Forbidding Mourning," "A Valediction: of My Name in the Window," discussed elsewhere, and "A Valediction: of Weeping." "The Expiration," which Helen Gardner dates earlier, seems to follow a night of more casual love. We therefore discuss it here only for comparison.

The poems are rhetorical, to establish tranquility during a formal farewell. Their characteristic tension is between structure, expressed in the ritual of parting, with its overtones of masculine command and formal security, and a breakdown of structure in raw mourning, and a need for comfort and closeness. This formalism grows denser under the pressure of mourning, until a deep tension develops over the very uses of civilization, as infantile insecurities embattle the ritual of farewell. Finally, civilization itself, never that securely established in Donne's consciousness, stands at stake in these poems.

Musically, they have an equilibrium, on the verge of breaking down, in stanzaic structure, rhetoric, and imagery, that somehow manages to reestablish itself. Thus, the false mastery beginning "A Valediction: of My Name in the Window" breaks down, despite his bravura; he articulates his fear and insecurity, then breathes a purged farewell. "Sweetest love, I do not goe" and "A Valediction: Forbidding Mourning" maintain an artful equilibrium of coaxing and self-control, truthfulness and distracting play, until a mood of peace is established. As for "A Valediction: of Weeping," from the first, its bursts of emotion are uncontrollable.

"Sweetest love, I do not goe" is a musical rarity in Donne, the first stanza differing metrically from the succeeding stanzas. The first four lines in each stanza swing open a conventional ballad form with a radiant lilt, the more ardent for dropping the opening, unaccented syllable of the first and third line. The fifth line has a catch of uneasiness, its two-foot line snagging on a "but," an expression of discomfort, a sense of impossibility. The first stanza then finishes in a calm resolution in three trimeter lines. The succeeding four stanzas use a more lilting tetrameter couplet, beginning and ending on the accent, then round out the stanza on a simple trimeter, rhyming with the awkward dimeter line. The withholding in the first stanza expresses a twinge of insecurity, trammeled and caught up in the music; but once established, the music has irresistible mastery.

The first stanza opens with a shallow reassurance he is not leaving her for another. Her deepest unconscious may have harbored such a thought; but to open the poem with such a reassurance distracts her from more obvious insecurities, that he is poor, and needs money and a job. The opening stance thus establishes the magic of make-believe and the distraction of unnecessary reassurances, giving the parting the illusion of secure play. Thus he closes Stanza 1, saying that parting practices the art of dying, another quibble to distract her from his serious departure. Yet meanwhile, he acknowledges the many small deaths that are the fabric of life; so that his departure is at once a species of dying and the texture of life.

Stanza 2, by a simple correspondence, makes him monarch of his situation. Like the sun, he is master of his affairs, the shaper of his trip. Yet there is ambivalence in the correspondence to the sun. The line, "He hath no desire nor sense" (l. 11), casually denying the sun any final cause, by implication presumes the solar system is insensate. But correspondence is beside the point, except as the basis of a compliment and a conceit. He is impervious, monarchial as the sun, with half the distance to travel, and with a will to return, having her as his final cause:

> Then feare not mee,
> But beleeve that I shall make
> Speedier journeyes, since I take
> More wings and spurres than hee.
>
> (ll. 13–16)

A slight foreshortening in line 12, "Then feare not mee," instead of "feare not for mee," leaves "mee" possibly the direct object of "feare." So he acknowledges her secret fear, that he can hurt her by an extended absence. But gentle as is the poem, this picks up the absurd reassurance in Stanza 1, "Sweetest love, I do not goe,/ For wearinesse of thee," that he may blame her for their insecure circumstances, even harboring thoughts of revenge. So he assures her he will return with more wings and spurs than the sun.

The lament at the passage of time that opens Stanza 3 would be lugubrious, were it not so lilting. The first quatrain of this stanza expresses man's helplessness before fate, the second masochistic self-destruction. Thus layer uncovers layer; as he broadens "Then feare not mee" to acknowledge their power to hurt each other. Yet for all the shocking helplessness he confesses, the lilting ease of the music belies it, mastering his confessions in song and transforming them into an entertainment.

Yet the scare will out. He began the song, assuring her he would not hurt her. By Stanza 4, he acknowledges her immense power to hurt him, and exposes his entire purpose, to control her mourning at his departure. He cautions her against too much overt mourning, lest her mourning destroy him. But given the delicate, yet radiant lilt of this song, each phrase, each qualification, each reassurance binds their identity more intimately together. By Stanza 4, we can no longer be sure which concern is a mask for which, whose vulnerability is uppermost in his mind, whose physical stamina is most at stake.

Stanza 4 thus opens with a strange duet of singing and sighing, a medley of Tin-Pan-Alley sentimentality, stylized clichés of feeling, and a wooing into wonder, fearing pain and concerned for his dignity. He coaxes her, suggesting her sighing is low class, a sentimental gesture. Mocking, imitating her, making his music ever denser, he pulls out all the stops, alliterates his "s"s and "w"s, banally identifies blood and tears:

> When thou sigh'st, thou sigh'st not winde,
> But sigh'st my soule away,
> When thou weep'st, unkindly kinde,
> My lifes blood doth decay.
>
> (ll. 25–28)

The rich, heavy music makes a strong rhythm of his anxiety. Exaggerating his own vulnerability, distracting her with hearts-and-flowers pleas that he be spared, he is begging her to protect herself and for his sake:

> It cannot bee
> That thou lov'st mee, as thou say'st,
> If in thine my life thou waste,
> Thou art the best of mee.
>
> (ll. 29–32)

Thus, given their close identity, his mock concern for himself masks a concern for her health, as her presence fills him. Thus, the line "Thou art the best of mee" is a sentimental extension of "Nothing else is" in "The Sunne Rising," retaining an overtone of literal signification.

Yet his mock concern for himself in Stanza 4 transforms to a real concern for himself in Stanza 5. Now he has successfully averted too strenuous a mourning, he can express his own fears and insecurities. But even this is directed to her, to shape her mind, instruct her against bad thoughts, and with an exaggerated flattery, that given their intimacy, even from afar, her thoughts can control his fate. So the mood lightens. His warning is couched in a superstition of thought control, that her mind can control destiny, a conceit to coax a good mood. And having eased every wrench of parting, he finally compares their parting to falling asleep in each other's arms. The source of each other's life, they cannot be parted at all.

"A Valediction: Forbidding Mourning" like "Sweetest love, I do not goe," seeks to ease excessive grief by the distraction of a play of ideas, suggesting that two lovers cannot be parted. These two are gesture poems, articulated courtesy cards, formalized gestures to a beloved. The critical debate as to how loving are Donne's love poems, indeed, the function of Donne's conceits comes to a nub in this poem, with its distant, celestial imagery, its dry music, its elaborate image of a compass, its complex structure of ideas. A recapitulation of some matters might help clarify our reading of this poem.

In general, Donne's early love poems—his promiscuity poems, his poems of misogyny and rejection—really express self-discovery in love. An elegant, evasive young aristocrat, sloughing off a secret religious code and family bond, he tests situations and attitudes in poem after poem, establishes consequences, explores his own mind and heart. Their reading as love poems, indeed, the affection they evoke in female readers, is a tribute to their underlying good sense, despite the adolescent insecurities here. Many a woman has turned with affection to a man of strong intelligence, floundering amid confusions to establish the truth of his life. Nevertheless, this early speaker is too evasive and self-involved to assess his capacity to love. His projection of voices, his masking himself in the cloak of his poems, his continual rhetorical elaborations, suggest at least exceeding reserve.

The marital poems and the poems on the structure of love more carefully define the grounds of love. Apollonian poems, whose freight of emotion bespeaks exuberant love, their radiant clarity is charged with more than a thinly intellectual involvement. If they seem limited, it is in the give-and-take between the two lovers. The women are a somewhat pallid, loving echo of the man, as he defines and celebrates his emotional marriage. We miss the spontaneous participation of a temperament that joyously shares in love, as in Shakespeare's Rosalind, Viola, and Cleopatra. Here, Donne's long muffling of self-development suggests a deeply loving, but aloof man, slow in development, who will give more than he shares, enjoy more than he participates, a husband and a father more than a companion in life. Donne's reticence throughout his life, his few, muffled references to Anne, all suggest such a quiet devotion.

Paradoxically enough, these late poems, of parting, love's death, and the mellow poignance of love, first express a Dionysiac release, poems such as "A Valediction: of Weeping" and "A Nocturnall upon S. Lucies Day." Here, Donne's capacity for feeling was enormous, however muffled his participation; yet "A Valediction: Forbidding Mourning," with its thin, dry texture, its stanzas of pinched music, opens on a stuffy death scene, and ends with a three-stanza comparison of his love to the motions of a compass. Its conventional tetrameter quatrain has too clipped a brevity to qualify as a song. The opening line has an awkward extra syllable, the second a comma break after the third foot; the third ends on five long, successive syllables; the fourth sets off its closing "no" with comma and colon. Such music wobbles on a dry, measured beat. In a straitforward love lyric, it would seem to express a dry, emotionless mind, its images overblown, its sentiments airy abstractions, offering a tidy security. Nevertheless, in a dramatic situation, the poem comes choked with emotional power.

The silences of a dramatic lyric must be strongly projected, with a play back and forth between word and attitude, stance and situation. The lines have meaning only in the context of their speaker. Thus, this speaker reads as a naturally reticent man, leaving his beloved in uncertainty and deep trouble, when his first concern must be for her health and peace of mind. Easy self-expression here would be self-indulgent, if not reprehensible. Our poem is thus a dialogue of statement and attitude, unrolling in a tight, constricted manner, with an equally awkward music, imagery, and thought. Its lines seem pinched and constrained to the taut borders of sanity. The lines express thoughts stretched above an intolerably bleak, austere reality. For all his careful dignity, we feel a heart is breaking here.

In Stanzas 1 and 2, a dignified deathbed scene is intended to exemplify their parting, the genteel dying man, "virtuous

. . . mildly . . . whisper," his friends quietly discussing if he is still breathing, all making the death chamber a model of civilized, decorous living. So Stanza 2 spells out that he wants a parting of tasteful sorrow, not a tear-flood and sigh-tempest that would end all civilized human contact. Yet Stanza 2 ends betraying their thin contact with humanity:

> T'were prophanation of our joyes
> To tell the layetie our love.
>
> (ll. 7–8)

Such sanctification on a plane apart from common society recalls "The Canonization," where their canonization was at least in part a shrinking from universal condemnation. For them now to adopt models of decorous behavior has a pathetic ring. So the freight of negatives and self-denial thickens, Stanza 1 ending in a "no," Stanza 2 building "no . . . no . . . nor," a loss of life balancing a profanation of joy.

Stanzas 3 to 6 compare their love to the spheres; but in making them heavenly, he thins them to pure, insubstantial worth, "Like gold to ayery thinnesse beate." The dry, sluggish music suggests a lack of spirit. The negatives woven into the cryptic lines do not suggest secure detachment, or absorption into one another. Earthquakes are harmful, but not celestial trepidations. "Dull, sublunary lovers" part when separated; they, a single soul, thin but are not separated. So Stanza 4 piles negatives on qualifications. Insignificant lovers "cannot admit/ Absence, because it doth remove." Stanza 5 thins out selfhood until "our selves know not what it is." Negatives engulf the limbs of the body, "Care lesse, eyes, lips, and hands to misse." Thinning among negations, they attain celestial insubstantiality, without blood, warm flesh, weeping, pain, or earthly substance, "an expansion,/ Like gold to ayery thinnesse beate."

The contrast to "The Good-Morrow" is most poignant. There, too, they form a celestial sphere, but with no sanctified exclusion from the secular world. On the contrary, the earth is spread before them, a busy ant-heap; as they steadily expand into a single flawless sphere, each in perfect attention to the other, flawless in love, sublimely immortal. In "A Valediction:

Forbidding Mourning," they thin and withdraw, so full of negatives, so proper in their decorum, they can encompass nothing.

And having elevated their love to the spheres simultaneous with a negation of substance, the speaker drags out an extended metaphor of a compass. But beginning creation in *Paradise Lost*, Christ measured out the heavens with a celestial compass; for the circle it draws is the emblem of perfection. So this compass has mystical overtones, appropriate to the celestial metaphor. Nevertheless, Donne's lines keep this a minor theme, and not the dominant meaning. Speaking mechanically of its appearance and way of moving, the speaker makes the compass their emblem, an instrument without blood, warm flesh, pain, or common earthly substance, two rigid metal posts, fixed together by the head to keep each other moving aright. For all its taut, cryptic lines, the image extends on the page with a pedestrian amplitude to make a point about mutual control. Indeed, the mathematics of the last stanza recalls "A Lecture upon the Shadow," that expressed another detached evasion of reality. We therefore read the compass metaphor neither as metaphysical exploration nor an arid exercise of imagination, but the terrifying strain of a mind choked with love, helpless, chained off from communication, yet somehow uttering comfort.

"A Valediction: of Weeping" is a farewell poem whose attempts at structure collapse in apparent failure. "The Flea" has a dialogue of word and gesture as two flirts spar with one another. Here, the dialogue is within the speaker, between his courteous gestures and emotional breakdown, his surges of feeling and evocations of word magic. The poem begins *in medias res*, just after a dignified farewell speech has broken down in tears. Stanza 1 then begins with the tears still streaming down his cheeks. Smiling slightly with an awkward gesture of apology, he attempts to make images of his tears even as he weeps them, somehow absorb them into social discourse.

By Stanza 2, the discourse has won. He has fabricated a complex image of a globe, and stands in momentary command; his voice rings crisp and dry, having successfully mastered his grief. Then a second breakdown closes Stanza 2, and a period without speech. Shrunk in silence until she stands over him, he raises his head for Stanza 3. All dignity is now gone, all masks, all solemn evasions. Without dignity or pretense at power, helplessly weeping behind a smashed wall of feeling, bereft of his one life anchor, he envisions, not the lurid, romantic death of a latter-day Tristan, but the drab drowning of a family man, strayed from home. Terrified, yet suddenly with dignity, he begs his beloved not to weep, not destroy them both. His hell has become an illumination.

The poem sprawls across the page, yet makes musical sense. Its stanza, spanning a two-foot opening and a seven-foot close, has a range equal to its emotions. Its choked, two-foot opening line attempts to control its flow of words. Three lines of expansive pentameter then cut to a two-foot couplet in a spasmodic attempt to right itself again. But an overly long triplet drags into a seven-foot closing line.

Stanza 1 is the most fussy. The speaker blusters without clarity. His words play significance against triviality, elevated images against trashy nothing, with a bitter irony. The references to money are suspect, reflecting the cause of his trip. His struggles for status, jobs, trusted connections, all reduce themselves to a need for money. He has abandoned the stable world to make her his medium of exchange; and now her tears flow about him, his new medium of exchange, and he remains impoverished, ashamed. His marriage, the buoyant either-or of "The Good-Morrow" is now a drab actuality. So embitterment wells up under the fabric of his farewell, shadowy misgivings and old revulsions, as images of tears and money shift back and forth. When he says, "by this Mintage they are something worth" (l. 4), the qualification, "something," undercuts their worth to a possible triviality. But tears are produced by the body, reinforcing an old identification of money with feces. The grief is oozing through the protective mask. Unwashed, he articulates his own repressions, and bids his beloved be easy with him gone.

But his beloved is not simply a new mode of value, but his monarch, whose face he celebrates, coin by coin, and gesture by gesture. He has even reduced himself to a woman, calling his tears "pregnant of thee" (l. 6), her follower and dependent, a pregnant sterility, weeping her tears. A catch of self-mockery reverberates here. Once he served the king himself with dignified reserve for honest coinage; now he is liege to a woman. But Donne's own marriage was a steady production of infants, many of whom died young, even by miscarriage. So, in bewildered mockery, leaving to get money for their support, desperately poor, Donne faces his bride, pregnancy for pregnancy, insubstantial tear for insubstantial child, producing his coinage, "Fruite of much griefe" (l. 7). Misgivings hammer at his tongue, the sense that all his force has collapsed, his masculinity, his role in society dissolved to a watery futility. Embarrassed, he confesses his confusion, mocks their relationship, apologizes for his discourtesy. All in a hanky-panky of blustering dignity, self-justification, and helpless resentment, he coins worthless tears in the sterile act of separation. And finally, the stanza ebbs in moody futility. His tears are literal nothings; as they will be separated by a body of water, weeping apart as they now weep together.

His froth of eager excitement brushed away, with all ugly overtones, he grapples with the pressures of parting, and civilizes his tears in an extended metaphor. In momentary civility, his language steadies through Stanza 2; as the tear rises from a suspect commercial metaphor to an enduring globe, an all, when openly defined, a nothing until painted over. So his detachment has momentarily hardened. In Stanza 1, he was helpless, weeping; in Stanza 2, he is a detached worker, building an objective world. A tidy structure stands high and dry—the globe! Look at it; nothing is hidden! So Stanza 2 moves in even, orchestrated solemnity, four lines building an "all" out of "nothing." Then, in a balancing movement, mocking the gesture of world-making, more tears rise, overflow, mingle together. His channels of feeling have enlarged before the ebb and flow of human experience. By the end of the stanza, the shattering grief ebbs in a release of feeling, the globe of a tear, his heaven, become a briny nothing, a huge round painted ball. Here we have a moody catharsis that might close the poem.

And then his perilous equilibrium collapses, silently, mysteriously, irretrievably. In Stanza 2, his murky, oceanic chaos withdrew. It now surges up again; as huge waves of emotion well up within him. Agonized, ineffectual, he gazes across the gulf between them. She is ambiguously "more then Moone" (l. 19), his ultimate female power, the force of the terrestrial globe and all material decay. Helplessly, he wallows in her insensate water, subject to the caprice of the currents of life. She seems quiescent now; but did she exert her powers, draw the waters above him, he would drown. In Stanza 1, he ennobled her as his monarch, minted her coins, stamped with her worth. Now he is in the dominion of the moon, his masculinity helplessly bobbing, engulfed by briny water. Literally, he will soon cross the channel where the moon tides will determine if his ship will arrive safely or not. Cut adrift by marriage from the masculine structure and landed proprieties of England, he is wallowing in the power of the feminine universe.

But "more then Moone" suggests a translunar force of unchanging potency, without flaw or sully. Seeing himself in the drowning waters of life, gazing up in prayer to his celestial angel is analogous to the damned in hell, who gaze up in the heavens and see the blessed enthroned in glory. So his bluster in Stanza 1 of power and helplessness, wealth and impoverishment, fecundity and sterile distance shrinks to an insecure isolation. Momentarily, he becomes a depraved castaway, wedded to a saint, an unstable plunger into utter fidelity, a sullied confusion beneath the constancy of heaven. The winds of providence are astir. Forgetting all posturing, all resentments and structures, in a gray humility, he prays to his redeeming angel:

> Let not the winde
> Example finde,
> To doe me more harme, then it purposeth . . .
> (ll. 23–25)

Her vision hangs exalted over the oceans, with a faint echo of the courtly love god, then fades, but not into enslavement and distance. She is back on earth, weeping in his arms. And with her return, he has exhausted his freight of guilt, fear, and resentment. They are now joined, two vulnerable human beings, breathing as one, caring for one another in a wash of chaos:

> Since thou and I sigh one anothers breath,
> Who e'r sighes most, is cruellest, and hasts the others death.

The extraordinary force of this poem can only be comprehended in the body of Donne's poetry, and some intuition of his life. A huge circle has been completed here, but with a decisive change. One of the main shifts from Donne's early lyrics to his marital poems is from the elevation of the female figure to a position of authority, and her association with a god of courtly love, an effect most terrifying in "Loves Exchange," though its examples are scattered through the early poems. The marital poems and the poems on the structure of love strip clear this old cosmological machinery of demons and supernatural powers, and secularize the process of love along loosely neo-Platonic grounds, fix an independent authority in the married couple, standing as equals, if not with him in the ascendant. If this shift was not altogether persuasive, it is because of the careful definition of grounds—on native ground, one would presume all this, as well as the pallid echoing of the female to the male.

It is here that "A Valediction: of Weeping" marks a great return. The woman is again in the ascendant, "more than Moone," and able to drown him, to be prayed to, as well as loved. Yet in the early lyrics, the woman was outside the hero's accepted ways, unpredictable by his schoolboy logic. Her demonic counterpart was an upstart "moderne god," demanding the prerogative of Jove, conducting the equivalent of a black mass, and extending his tyrannical power. Here, she is integral to the workings of the universe, not alien to it. Their emotions they share, their fears and insecurities, their love. She weeps as he weeps, not willing him any harm, but innocently providing the sea an example of watery chaos. And the poem finishes with a reconciliation, they weeping in each other's arms as equals, not with a stark enslavement in crippled isolation. Evidently, the compulsion in Donne's psyche to see the woman as above him, fundamentally alien and threatening, a compulsion we can associate with his mother, here shifted to his wife with a huge release of moral acceptance and intimate care. His period of penance was accomplishing its work. He was reconciled with the dark rejections of his own spirit.

Our last poem of parting, "The Expiration," seems unmistakably earlier. It begins in a conventional meter with an artificial kiss, and ends with the hero struggling to formulate a farewell speech, so he can leave. The murky atmosphere suggests a night of sexual love, with no structure, trust, or bond apparent. The young speaker, pompous and inexperienced, thrashes about for an appropriate word, where any language is obnoxious. "Breake of Day" also had a banal, unintelligent speaker; but there the crisp absurdity indicates gentle satire. Here, the language is pompously false, with no clear definition, suggesting an early exercise, the poet of promiscuity, mouthing of death and mystery as he backs out the door.

The opening couplet is unclear and unpleasant. We have no idea what constitutes a "lamenting kisse," unless the young lady was sobbing in her throat, or kissing him too demonstrably, suggested by "Which sucks two soules, and vapors Both away" (l. 2). Addressing her as a "ghost" seems falsely pretentious in a line with so neatly balanced a farewell. And the entire stanza builds up to the unnecessary flourish of "Goe," indeed, is pretentiously enclosed in a reiterated rhyme of "So, so," and "Goe; Goe." So the second stanza piles up mutual symbolic deaths, double deaths on deaths, all involved in "bidding, goe." We wish the boy would just leave.

It becomes clear that Donne's talent came alive to actual events and complex structures of imagery from mere threads of word play. His self grew larger and more open. In "A Valediction: of Weeping," his concealed self is fully manifest; but the "thou" in his poems would still steadily grow to God with his last religious poems. Donne's pilgrimage was not yet over.

# 10

# The Mellow Poignance of Love

Long-married, his traumatic loss of career finally absorbed, Donne wrote several Indian summer love poems, to the Countess of Bedford, Mrs. Herbert, perhaps his wife, lyrics that recall earlier courtly love poems, but softened and changed in key. The demon has lost interest; the woman engages only in simple rejection; the blunt English warrior has softened to more pensive emotions. Donne's lyrics, both early and late, characteristically shape an ego to its occasion. Here, he wallows in subjectivity, sopping up the drift of experience. His early lyrics had a thrust of dialogue:

> I wonder by my troth, what thou, and I
> Did, till we lov'd?
>
> Goe, and catche a falling starre.
>
> Busie old foole, unruly Sunne,
> Why dost thou thus
> Through windowes, and through curtaines call on us?

These project only a hurt human spirit in the mellow wake of experience:

> Blasted with sighs, and surrounded with teares,
> Hither I come to seeke the spring . . .
>
> Who ever comes to shroud me, do not harme
> Nor question much

That subtile wreath of haire, which crowns my arme.

Little think'st thou, poore flower,
Whom I have watch'd sixe or seaven dayes . . .

"Twicknam Garden" softly extends some implications in "A Valediction: of Weeping." Again the woman is a kind of natural force. Indeed, she is pushed even deeper, from an ambiguous "more than Moone," a minor female planet, to grace itself, her garden a miniature Eden. But the cumbersome theological paraphernalia blocks the emotional force of "A Valediction: of Weeping," or "A Nocturnall upon S. Lucies Day." So its stanza shifts from 4 to 5 feet per line, its transitional repeated rhyme dissolving its opening quatrain into couplets.

Stanza 1 begins on a visit to Twicknam Garden, where the speaker has come for a healing; but he is so absorbed in betrayal and rejection, he can hardly discuss it. Its poetic material comes without the clutter of "Loves Alchymie," the taut suspense of "Loves Exchange," the peculiarities of temperament of "Breake of Day," but stays simplified as late Matisse, with the mythic sweep of Shakespeare's last romances. So Twicknam Garden becomes a Garden of Eden, he a curious "anti-garden." "Blasted with sighs and surrounded with teares," all in a passive voice, is touched with exaggeration and lack of reticence, a stylized treatment of misery, not misery itself, a walking garden of male collapse, sighs and tears his wind and rain, a cloud of human winter afloat across springtime vegetation.

Such lyric material we call mannerist. The earlier lyrics had tight verbal involvement, hell-bent flirtations, struggles to maintain dignity. These strangely slack relationships express no crisis in the speaker's life, but come after his pitchpoint of experience. The woman has rejected him without condemnation; he reorganizes his attitude to experience. In "Loves Exchange," he still addressed love, defiantly, submissively, though it had broken him; here, he wistfully addresses future generations of lovers, having no one else to talk to. Yet these slack situations do not express a simple ennui, but the stylized posturing of a great "as if," in symbol and episode. A garden becomes an Eden, a flower the sign of love, an odd skeleton a sign of holiness, symbols of Eden, the serpent, grace, and damnation elegantly piling up in illusory symbols with a mannerist carelessness, like an unnecessary pair of antlers in a mannerist painting. So the speaker becomes a stone fountain to no purpose, plays with a primrose, binds a strand of hair from his beloved around his arm.

In considering the poet, one senses here his age, and a certain marital sheepishness. Critics have tended to dismiss these poems as literary exercises, given his religious concerns, his marriage, the high character of the women addressed. We take them at face value. Many a religious man has flirted before his ordination, if not after. Mrs. Herbert was Donne's senior; but she finally married a younger man than Donne himself. As for Donne's marriage, what with his wife's repeated pregnancies and illnesses at home, she could hardly fulfil Donne's residual inclinations to romance. A literary courtship of a meditative lady seems eminently appropriate. What else, one might well ask, is sublimation all about? Indeed, the stagnant impasse in Donne's life at this time made him peculiarly vulnerable to such pointless flirtations, steadily hedging as he drifted to a religious vocation, facing about, attempting fresh expedients, probing himself and doing nothing. In such a *fin-de-siècle* mood, he might well turn his idle hours to elevated flirtations, his poetry to mannerism.

So "Twicknam Garden" sets out its symbols. The garden spring is somehow the fountain of life, with healing, cleansing, and purifying waters. The visitor, wounded, enveloped by sighs and tears, would slough off all slippery tumult, but is unhealable; indeed, a first principle of treachery, his "spider love which transubstantiates all," proves the reverse of grace. The elixir of depravity, he is malicious and playful enough to bring the serpent, at once making the garden a paradise and spoiling it. The serpent, emblematic of the male sexual organ, would be an appropriate spoiler, flirting with too virtuous a woman.

In the easy wash and flow of myths characteristic of this style, the garden changes between stanzas. In Stanza 1, it is Eden, a primal font of beatific healing; yet even there, it has anomalies. The word, manna, sits oddly in Eden, recalling the

Israelites, wandering in Sinai after the second fall. Indeed, the speaker comes as a returning exile; yet Eden has no exiles. By Stanza 2, the fountain has disappeared. The speaker is more narrowly the devil, mocked by innocent garden growth, not simply an unfortunate man bringing a serpent. Moreover, given the rejection in love that precipitated the poem, the ruler "Love" (1. 15) suggests not God in heaven, but the early courtly love deity, in a locale of mannerist emptiness and permissiveness. Earlier, the speaker confronted the love god, condemned to slavery and mutilation, as in "Loves Exchange," or slyly made his adjustments under him, as in "Loves Deitie." This speaker comes of himself for an impossible healing, under an intangible god. And by now, the empty garden has shifted from Eden to a Stuart aristocratic garden, with statuary, mandrakes, and a stone fountain that works.

By Stanza 3, the speaker seeking a healing fountain is himself the fountain of the garden; the serpent and devil of Stanza 1 is the Christ of love, offering infallible truth to insecure lovers. As Christ was crucified, his blood carried away in vials as spiritual food, so the speaker, crucified in love, is a stone statue, his tears weeping with authenticity. Thus stone tests feeling; statuary reenacts the sufferings of Christ. And having shifted in sentimental pathos from devil to Christ, from wounded, insecure alien to the touchstone of truth, in the closing couplet, he allows a pout of pathetic resentment against the woman who rejected him, indeed, breathes mistrust of the entire female sex:

> O perverse sexe, where none is true but shee,
> Who's therefore true, because her truth kills mee.
> (ll. 26–27)

His earlier poems came upon the pitchpoint of severance; here the deed is long over. The stately, blossoming Stuart garden mocks him to his face.

We have here, then, a crosshatch of blending myths, an elegant Eden, a serpent the Christ of love, God the courtly love deity, an exile amid the statuary of Eden, a depraved, pathetic failure the touchstone of truth. This green bottle full of emblems brings a relaxed catholicity among jaded contradictions. Life here is simultaneous, in a gel, with a mannerist music of frustration. The encounter with the garden only demonstrates that encounter is no longer possible.

"Twicknam Garden" offers then a wistful, mannerist extension of a late recurring theme, that of the lovers as a holy island, apart from secular society. "The Extasie" first hinted this in a wholly secular context, when the souls temporarily rose for an ecstasy of illumination, before returning to bodily love. In "The Good-Morrow," they form a celestial sphere, but exuberantly scornful of the ordinary world, not exiled from it. By "The Canonization," the split is complete. They exist apart, touchstones of holiness and truth, driven out of the world by social harassment. Here, in "Twicknam Garden," the exile comes home for a healing, fallen man to his innocent Eden, and discovers himself to be a lifeless fountain of grace, offering vials of tears—presumably stones cannot give blood. This mannerist pathos and lugubrious self-pity serves to mask a lost and bewildered man. Befuddled, he gropes about for a vital encounter, and finds nothing.

Helen Gardner dates "The Will" among the earlier poems. Lighter in tone, and with a denser music, for all its befuddled pseudo-decision, its items come piled on one another with a careless ease, but in a simplified linear succession, and with too urgent a profusion for any slack mood. Furthermore, the interruption of the bequest and the abrupt decision to die in Stanza 6 have more vigor than the later slack ennui, however playfully the speaker means it here. This poem reads then, not as a late, poignant, mannerist lyric, but an early exercise in this mode.

Its six long stanzas of three couplets and a triplet are all in pentameter, except for a last tetrameter couplet line, introducing a triplet that widens to a sonorous 4, 5, 7 feet per line. This is rather nondescript music, except for the four-line effusive finale. Thus, the many stanzas of series of couplets make the poem one of loose, easy repetitions, with variations, overlong, as befits its good-natured, skeptical speaker, a hearty soul, who finds social irony everywhere, yet loves on in hopeless futility. He finally interrupts his legacy, but only after giving away almost everything; and his decision to die is without bitterness. He at least establishes that he can do something.

So loose categories organize his legacy: Stanza 1, the parts of his head: his eyes, ears, tongue, and tears; Stanza 2, his moral characteristics: his constancy, ingenuity, pensiveness, silence, and oddly, his money; Stanza 3, his civic virtues: his faith, good works, civility, modesty, and patience; Stanza 4, his personal achievements; his reputation, industry, "doubtfulnesse," poetic works, and again, most amusingly, his sicknesses; Stanza 5, his acquisitions; his "physick bookes," his "writen rowles of Morall counsels," brass metals, and English tongue, each item bequeathed where it will be least needed or used, or as a mocking insult—such lyrics have a hoary tradition in English poetry.

The items are too numerous, loosely organized, and good-naturedly funny to stand up to Sir Walter Ralegh's "The Lie." Furthermore, at the beginning, the speaker slips into an easy, pathetic role:

> Before I sigh my last gaspe, let me breath,
> Great love, some Legacies.

Managing in one opening line to sigh, gasp, and breathe, he launches into an exceedingly long-winded legacy. But the "great love" repeatedly invoked places the poem slackly in the courtly love tradition, though its broad interests ease all concern for the speaker's fate. Deathbed confessionals might have a more taut music, and less garrulity.

Finally, after six stanzas of excellence piled on excellence, frustration on frustration, the speaker interrupts himself. He has had it—it is too much! He will bequeath nothing, simply die, and free himself from love. Indeed, the tit-for-tat revenge of the closing triplet recalls the close of "The Message." But there, a clean-limbed speaker is returning to his warrior caste; here, a garrulous gentleman heads for the grave in a slaphappy engulfment he could throw off in a moment, but wouldn't bother to, having nothing better to do. Hence the bittersweet flavor here, as in all the late love poems, of slack chains that only bind one too sluggish to throw them off, a befuddled suspense at an old bond, binding only by default.

But another item in poetic structure makes this an early exercise, anticipating his later mannerism. Each stanza begins with six lines, cataloguing all of him, then a triplet, expressing a surrender to unrequited love. But this division of love from normal life as an alien area, where usual strategies do not hold, is typical of the early Donne, where love is a god apart, tearing his life to pieces. This peculiar dichotomy returns in "Twicknam Garden," but elevated to a sacred role as in so many late lyrics. "The Will" is an early, shallow, and good-natured secular statement of the problem of the isolations of love.

The soft acceptance of death also pervades "The Funerall." The poem has a thin, but deadly etiquette of shrouds, prisoners, manacles, relics, and burials; yet its atmosphere is so dry, astringent, and restrained, it is somehow sane, not at all a Gothic atmosphere. The last line reveals the full situation. The rejecting woman has given a strand of hair for the speaker's arm, a sort of badge, indenturing him to her service, even as an elixir or reliquary.

But an undercurrent of pervasive, skeptical irony reverberates in the conceit. The gesture of giving him a strand of hair as she rejects him as a lover is somehow slack or twisted, binding him in rejection; he then makes a conceit from it, the paradox that hair grows upward, out of the brain, whereas the nervous system grows downward, through the body, making the hair some reverse nervous system of the uncanny dead, a system that grows up toward heaven. So her strand of hair on his arm binds them in eerie intimacy, his second nervous system, that crept up from a better brain, dedicated to art and strength, his wreath, his crown, his viceroy, his outward soul.

Yet a mannerist ambiguity renders suspect his conceit even as he utters it. Even could we accept human hair as some reverse nervous system, the close of Stanza 1, "And keepe these limbes, her Provinces, from dissolution," making them a religious relic, piles conceit on impossible conceit. Moreover, to Seventeenth Century England, such relics were a technique for control used by the Roman Church. So his calling his limbs "her provinces" masks a mistrust of her gift of hair. As the Roman Church bound its provinces with a display of relics; so she binds him to her with a strand of hair. Indeed, her motive is more than mere bondage, but also vain display, to bind him with her manacles, make manifest her power of condemnation:

> Except she meant that I
> By this should know my pain,
> As prisoners then are manacled, when they'are condemn'd to die.
> (ll. 14–16)

This hanky-panky of deification and mistrust, of upward striving and premeditated sadism, is reversed in Stanza 3 onto him, who would be buried with her strand of hair both to save a holy object from idolatry, and bury her dead remains with him out of revenge.

Indeed, this tough knitting of ambivalence and repressed hate is too pervasive to read as a poetic exercise. Our reading of "Twicknam Garden" as a mannerist mask over bewildered pain might be disputed; but the emotions here are simply too blatant. Even the music has a taut flicker, like sudden twists of hair around a man's arm, each stanza alternating 2, 3, and 5 feet per line, with a 7-foot close to crackle with the meaning. Yet his deflected attention onto her hair bespeaks a deflection from the "thou" of love to the material about it. This speaker is already reorganizing within to focus on God, and can hardly focus on a woman in his poem.

"The Blossome" marks the slightest shift of subject matter, from a strand of hair to a blossom; yet both are in some sense the materiel of love. It begins tinsel demure, addressing a blossom he then compares, in an over-worked conceit, to his heart. The blunt, prosaic opening line of the last stanza, "Meet mee at London, then," in contrast to the stylized opening, "Little think'st thou, poore flower," makes clear the work of the poem, to shift from the mannerist flirtation that has distracted him to no purpose to the real life of London.

The poem is a low-key transition poem with a trim, unfolding music. Each stanza has a quatrain and two couplets, rising easily to its pentameters, with 3, 4, 5, 5, 5, 2, 5, 5 feet per line. The two-foot line is a catch of care, a qualification of a mood, a collage of thought on thought. The poem has the static suspense of a tableau, a meditative interlude between two worlds of action. With detached urbanity, the speaker compares his heart to a blossom, delicate, simple, exquisitely innocent, and ignorant of its speedy misery, all in a twilight of easy pathos. At the end of Stanza 2, we learn he plans to leave at dawn for London. Indeed, he anticipates his heart, "subtile to plague thy selfe" (1. 18), will insist on staying. He then insists a heart alone is a ghostly, useless monstrosity no woman can possibly know, love, or be close to. So his is an embarrassment, though he indulges it a bit. Indeed, his farewell to his heart is a farewell to all passionate romance and masochistic frustration, thinned through the years to a wearisome mannerist gesture.

The poem thinks with emblems. Not only is his heart a blossom; but in a tableau, it grows six or seven days (perhaps the length of a visit to western England) until it laughs and triumphs on the bough in diminutive hubris. So the image in line 12 of the blossom struggling to "get a part in a forbidden or forbidding tree" is not merely an emblem wed in a mannerist conceit, but a thinking in emblems. The tree is at once the tree of knowledge in the Garden of Eden, but also her body, in which his heart would like to "get a part," a pathetic sublimation of the sexual impulse.

And yet the critical attempt to reduce metaphysical poetry to the use of emblems is as futile here as the use of strong lines or far conceits. Donne begins his poem thinking with emblems as a convenient technique to express a mentality he had little patience with. At the end, he thinks with prosaic truthfulness, as he instructs his emblematic heart:

> Well then, stay here; but know,
> When thou hast stayd and done thy most;
> A naked thinking heart, that makes no show,
> Is to a woman, but a kinde of Ghost . . .
>
> (ll. 25–28)

The sentimental opening pathos and the blunt closing instructions have in common the equilibrium of the speaker's ego, balanced, on the move, tasting here, blundering through bewilderment there, and all to attain its ends.

The end of Stanza 4 offers an alternative to the overblown life of romance with its futile sublimations:

> Practice may make her know some other part,
> But take my word, shee doth not know a Heart.
> (ll. 31–32)

This low-key allusion to the sexual organ suggests it is superior to the heart, being open to sight and knowledge. The speaker then bargains to meet his heart in London in twenty days time, to test their separate functions. Then he, without his heart, will be "fresher, and more fat, by being with men" (l. 35). They are at loggerheads; but given this prosaic adulthood, with a shift of scene, they will soon function together again. The bond of courtly love will thus be followed by a loving affair, we trust with his wife:

> There, to another friend, whom wee shall finde
> As glad to have my body, as my minde.
> (ll. 39–40)

Clearly, the speaker is closing a visit to an elegant, but removed lady; but against all purpose, his heart wants to stay. He cajoles it, offers to leave and rejoin it. With heart, or without, he has cleared an adult path of solitary sanity that somehow works; though his heart is sequestered elsewhere.

This disengagement from the heart bears comparison with the slack disengagement in "The Legacie." There, unpleasant details clutter the heart, its corners, its color, its patched, second-hand quality, like the clutter of "Loves Alchymie." Its speaker is something of a lummox, a self-righteous reject, nursing his dignity as he retreats behind a far-fetched insult. That is the early Donne, here a clutter, there a taut, eerie, Gothic play with demons and warlocks, a sour, willful, exuberant Elizabethan spirit, encumbered with details, cluttered psychic demonism, emotional cranks, impish, flirtatious schoolboys, warriors of embattled dignity, yet struggling towards reality. Here, his heart keeps its distant simplicity, the speaker his sane, level disengagement. The neo-Platonic interlude of marital poems has relaxed into a Carolingian ease and suavity.

"The Primrose" dallies with numbers on the theme of an ideal woman. A small flower, it opens on a spare, trimeter couplet, where "The Blossome" spreads from 3 to 4 feet. Its step-by-step precision in music is suited to a play on mathematics. Each stanza holds two couplets, then two triplets, four units in a balance of odds and evens, to make up 10 lines, an emblem of a perfect match.

The noun "true-Love" is no longer the deity of courtly love, nor yet a neo-Platonic idea, mingling with the world, as in "Aire and Angels." It is rather a boyish dream of a perfect match in a woman, like a drop of rain fitted into a primrose, making a miniature universe, a "terrestrial Galaxie" a small star in the sky. The overtone of easy, lazy, flawless sex in the image of the drop in the primrose reinforces the sense of a boy's daydream of the perfect woman. Such emblems, hanging in a mannerist ambiguity, serious, yet slackly whimsical, recall Marvell's "On a Drop of Dew"; but Donne had no patience with ambiguity, and struggles for clarity. So, by the end of Stanza 1, he sees his desire is "not a mere woman," but for some unnatural perfection, that "must, or more, or lesse than woman bee."

He then speculates on an ideal match, relying on the folklore that flower petals will betray one's true love. But here, as in "The Blossome," he is most adult and realistic, for all his mannerist verbal play, seeing through the romantic clichés he toys with. Hence his ideal woman will be ideal not by any abstract perfection, but by her good fit to the man. We begin, then, with the fit of a perfect coupling, which seems in some way to hinge on the number ten. Here we find arbitrary Helen Gardner's association of the number ten with a man: "Ten" which is "the farthest number," must surely then be the masculine number, the number of "each man." She offers no basis for this reading. Furthermore, the poem does not discuss ideal man, who might suggest "the farthest number," but small, average, humdrum man, a man comparable to a drop of rain in a primrose, the sort of a man who has no assurance, but wants a superwoman, a subwoman, more or less than a woman, and hangs between a six and a four. Furthermore, Stanza 2 clarifies that he wants a woman true to nature, not an ideal above all thought of sex, or a paltry nothing. In a word, he wants a suitable fit, in bed, at table, and sharing all human experience.

There is an overtone of magic numbers, but no firm evidence. On the contrary, the mathematics here is only for hints and allusions. So his qualification, "Ten is the farthest number," simply gives ten as a wide numerical straddle, the fullness or abundance after which another set of tens begins. It refers not to the man, but to the match, the ideal fit, that woman, to whom "halfe ten" belongs, seeks in marriage.

The poem thus points out a difference between men and women, that men, being changeable, know not what they seek, a six or a four, since they need an odd fit to make up an ideal ten. But women are constant, having the primrose as their emblem, with their true number, five. And being constant, knowing their needs, they finally make the decision. Men come irregular, large and small, odd and even. Half of them the women claim as a good match; the other half they take anyway. Being a combination of an odd and an even, two and three, they can take all men by pieces, whatever combination of two and three they come to.

The atmosphere here is one of gentle triviality, a befuddlement of helplessness, the abstract "true-Love" a forlorn echo of courtly love, as a piecemeal attack reduces the man to acquiescence for lack of an alternative. The speaker is whimsical, casual, detached. Could he muster the sentiment, he would wax pathetic.

"The Relique" extends and plays variations on "The Funerall." There, the speaker would bury her hair with him against idolatry. Here, he speculates his grave may be broken up and her hair found on his arm. The music is mellower than in "The Funerall," yet with a firm structure, each stanza opening with two tight tetrameter couplets, then evolving a speculation to a closing pentameter triple.

Its idea seems a pathetic variation on a theme in "The Canonization," where a harassed frustration led to a fantasy of wish fulfilment that made angels and saints of two failures in life. Here, the conceit has mellowed a good deal. There is no insistence that the canonization be literal. On the contrary, whoever breaks open their grave will think his armlet of hair a lover's mark, to know whom to rejoin on Judgment Day, since the facial features will be gone. The bishop and king will then make them relics, to be turned to for miracles. But this will be a pretty case of mistaken identity. The woman is only a patron, not a sweetheart to be sought out after death. Indeed, she has rejected the speaker as her lover; and he has accepted this arrangement. The confusion if he will be mistaken for Christ (l. 18), or some shameful unnamed lover is therefore deliberate. He would play Christ; but other unnamed desires abash him. So he hides behind the phrase, "a something else." He then celebrates their wise and faithful love, their occasional chaste kisses. The angelology of "The Canonization" has thinned and mellowed to a pretty compliment.

"The Dampe" has too much intensity for this group, and more directly addresses a woman; but its edge of playful banter, taking its demons as rhetorical symbols, not as independent forces, the episode as less than ultimately vital, suggest the poem is a late one. The theme of finding her picture in his heart after death recalls finding her hair on his arm in "The Relique." Also the shift from unnatural romance to the challenge of sex at the close of "The Dampe" recalls the close of "The Blossome." His earlier fantasies of death had more gloom, anguish, demonic pressures; here death is grim enough, but a familiar location. The music is muffled, tentative, its irregular couplets halting forward in a courtly gesture, though a heroic couplet rounds out each stanza with finality.

Even the references to giants and witches, Goths and Vandals, express disbelief and simulated terror—he has his own roster of giants and witches to evoke at will. Earlier, he vigorously hosed the demons from his consciousness in "Loves Alchymie." By this late Carolingian period, he can refer to them with relaxation, being so far away. So the opening stanza has a straightfaced aplomb. Being dead already, the speaker has nothing to lose. The "dampe" is the fatal infliction of the Medusa face of love, killing its viewers; but the casual tone softens the impact.

So, in Stanza 2, he bullies love to challenge its giant and enchantress, annul its own terrifying record, "And without such advantage kill me then" (l. 16). The challenge seems simplistic as a solitary westerner, marching down Main Street in a bandit town. But the gesture is tongue-in-cheek; the speaker knows very well this is a woman, not a man. To set his giants and witches against hers in a fight is lugubriously, suavely funny. And gradually the poem grows more and more bawdy. "Kill mee as Woman, let mee die/ As a meere man" (ll. 21–22) has taunting overtones of sexual intercourse. Her "passive valor" is most appropriate in bed, as "naked" is for the battle of sex, when the odds will make them even. "The Dampe" belongs then to his last love poems, but has a more strident masculinity, a seduction poem, not a poem of wistful disengagement.

These poems register, then, a deep sea change in Donne's disposition. They express a mannerist sensibility, not outright libido. Befuddled, out of sorts, the speaker repeats gestures of courtly love that are too habituated to be sloughed off, too immature to be believed in. His old symbols have lost their binding force. The reading of complex or esoteric numerology into "The Primrose," like the reading of a controlled, purposive meaning into any of these mannerist emblems, is an error. The speaker establishes no truths by the medium of numbers, but articulates a mood by their ornamental reverberations. He no more believes in his numbers than in the heart in "The Dampe," or the strand of hair in "The Relique." He is rather like Thomas Hardy, who, nearly three centuries later used symbols he had ceased to believe in because a fresh vocabulary of experience was not yet available. No object has any necessary significance for him now. No picture is stamped inside him. His heart is adrift. Its surface is a blur.

# II

# Love's Death

Death was a sporadic subject to Donne. After some early exercises, he made only an occasional reference until his final period. Three poems, "The Computation," "The Paradox," and "The Broken Heart," seem schoolboy exercises, as early as any that have survived. Particular occasions evoked two others, "The Dissolution" and "A Feaver." Helen Gardner dates them as late; we are at a loss for clear grounds. The most significant among them, "A Nocturnall upon S. Lucies Day," Grierson associated with Lucy, the Countess of Bedford; but Donne's late love lyrics indicate at most a stylized flirtation, but no emotional charge sufficient to evoke this poem. J. B. Leishman would relate "A Nocturnall" with his wife's death; but the late date, two years after his ordination, troubles him. However, her sicknesses and miscarriages would suffice to precipitate such a poem. In any case, its female figure admirably completes our discussion of Donne's love lyrics. His great other here slips into heaven. It was now toward heaven that he turned his soul.

"The Computation" calculates in years the absence of a beloved. The phrase, "Gone away" (l. 2), ambiguously refers to death, departure, or rejection. The closing line suggests death, but in a mishmash of death and immortality, ghosts and living men, thought, question, challenge, and statement. The five flaccid heroic couplets are too regular to intrigue us, too loose to brace us, and altogether without pace or gathering momentum. Lines 5 to 8 all suddenly rhyme in a flexing of craftsmanly muscles. Its activities are vague and stereotypic, "scarce beleev'd," "fed on favours past," "on hopes," "tears drown'd one hundred," "sighes blew out two," building from twenty years to forty, a hundred, two hundred, a thousand, then a thousand more of blank forgetfulness, all multiples of ten, the number of conventional regularity. The closing question, "Can ghosts die?", brief, muffled, forlorn, registers only as rhetoric.

The conundrum of "The Paradox" is more usual in mystical experience, on which no testimony is possible; one either experiences an ineffable union with the godhead, or its description cannot register. This speaker applies it to love, and to himself as lover:

> I cannot say I lov'd, for who can say
> Hee was kill'd yesterday?
>
> (ll. 5–6)

So love is once-for-all, not a periodicity of ecstasy and death:

> Wee dye but once, and who lov'd last did die,
> Hee that saith twice, doth lye.
>
> (ll. 9–10)

The speaker is dead, then, killed by love, but in a last afterglow, a two-hour corpse, the poem his uttered epitaph.

'The Paradox" is an adolescent exercise, like "The Computation," but with somewhat more jouncy music, heaving forward in ten couplets of alternative 5 and 3 feet, 16 opening lines of generalized propositions about love and life becoming personal in the last two couplets. The poem does anticipate Donne's early love poetry, however. The hidden religious paradox anticipates "Negative Love," the sense of love as a wholly unpredictable experience of overwhelming force, "Loves Exchange."

"The Broken Heart" is stronger, yet still suggests apprentice work. The extreme analogy to a burning flask of powder (l. 8) also recalls mystical illumination; yet menace and insecurity, while thin enough, are first felt here. The poem also opens with generalized propositions:

He is starke mad, who ever sayes,
That he hath beene in love an houre.

(ll. 1–2)

Ah, what a trifle is a heart,
If once into loves hands it come!

(ll. 9–10)

But a personal experience quickly appears, of going into a room in innocent detachment, and being in a moment consumed by love.

The poem is an early, but decisive thrust toward courtly love. When the speaker cites "loves hands" (l. 10), love is not his proposed sweetheart, but an independent demon and alien upstart god, here emphatically masculine, "Hee . . . him . . . he," an armed, brutal warrior, part animal, though his power is expressed through the woman. The later poems kept its sexual identification somewhat more tentative. The speaker, by contrast, is tender, innocent, vulnerable, a male virgin wrecked by love. The image of pike and fry (l. 16) anticipates "The Baite"; but here two fish simply fight for food and life. In "The Baite," masochistic pain and pleasure mingle in an exquisite modulation, the woman a beautiful fisherman or in the water swimming. So the warfare dramatically unfolded in "Loves Exchange" is here concentrated with the fish in one primitive, raw, consuming image:

. . . us Love draws,
Hee swallows us, and never chawes:
By him, as by chain'd shot, whole rankes doe dye,
He is the tyran Pike, our hearts the Frye.

(ll. 13–16)

The love experience is instantaneous, absolute, uncontrollable:

. . . what did become
Of my heart, when I first saw thee?
I brought a heart into the roome,
But from that roome, I carried none with mee.

(ll. 17–20)

Love swallowing, but never chewing us, emphasizes a total helplessness in an oral-aggressive metaphor, and its instant effectiveness, overwhelming whole clusters of men (l. 15), ten in less than an hour (ll. 2–4).

The last stanza is a sober assessment of reality, anticipating the male independence, however ineffective, in the later love poems. It depicts the heart curiously detached, as an item separate from the body as a whole. Thus, in Stanza 2, the speaker cries:

> Ah, what a trifle is a heart,
> If once into loves hands it come!
>
> (ll. 9–10)

He seems describing a drugstore item; as in a more intimate rendering of the detached heart in "The Legacie," he probes for a heart and finds a bizarre, strange object. The heart thus becomes emblematic as an odd, detached, vulnerable item, with no will or intelligence, so is his love extraneous, helpless, uncontrollable before courtly love. Its ending here is most pathetic, all its pieces scattered and flung about. So the speaker can now love in bits and pieces; but ultimate love is lost forever.

In this still apprentice work, the image of "glasse" in line 24 is jarring alongside "ragges" in line 31; though the gap of seven lines prevents a mixed metaphor. Yet musically, the poem marks an advance over "The Paradox." The addition of a foot in line 4 pitches the opening quatrain into a tetrameter couplet and a closing heroic couplet, but without the intimate bite and resilience of Donne's best stanza inventions.

"A Feaver" Helen Gardner dates late by its philosophical allusions, despite its simple tetrameter quatrains; but the courtly love overtones and metaphor of a sudden meteor incline us to an earlier date. The poem was precipitated as some dear one suddenly took sick, its larger meditations perhaps pitched by a coming death. More we simply do not know.

The poem has an honest edge, though its cryptic flamboyance suggests a more sudden than a deep shock, a mistress or a good friend, not his wife. And yet its cosmological allusions muffle or detach the shock of the experience:

Oh doe not die, for I shall hate
  All women so, when thou art gone,
That thee I shall not celebrate,
  When I remember, thou wast one.

(ll. 1–4)

Donne here suggests the mourning as at least in part a discharge of repressed hostility. So at her sudden death, he will feel so cheated and deprived that he will hate her memory.

Stanza 2 thrashes into a denial that she can die, Stanza 3 back into an insistence her death is the death of the world. The conceit that she is the soul of the world, also in "The First Anniversary," is here not merely an exercise of philosophical imagination, but illuminates the temperament of the speaker, illustrating his dependence. He thrashes in far imagery; her imminent death shoots faults through his frame of reference. Indeed, calling her the soul of the world, the world her potential carcass, at once glorifies her and debases the transient, vulnerable world. At her mortal danger, with a metaphysical shudder, he senses the world may be just a soulless corpse.

Stanzas 5 and 6 pursue further implications, that sudden flashes of power are necessarily short-lived. Her sickness and imminent death are not capricious accidents, but inevitable; and yet her transcendent beauty is beyond change (ll. 21–24). Rather than a more tepid, but enduring love, he chooses a brief, supreme love, and thus reconciles himself to losing her. He enjoyed all he could expect, she being well worth his devotions. The poem thus ends with a cerebral, yet effective catharsis.

"The Dissolution" reads as more mature than "A Feaver." Musically, it advances in an irregular, impetuous zigzag without a stanza break, two to five feet to the line, to finish on a seven-foot line, occasionally using couplet rhymes, then a more broken weaving, as befits extreme grief. In "A Feaver," gripped by anxiety, he elevated, abstracted the woman, made their relationship distant and immature. In "The Dissolution," they seem more intimate equals, all their parts in close knowledge. Its psychology is quite dense and advanced, grasping the implications of object loss after libido has been poured into it. That libido now has no object, and hangs on him:

> And those things whereof I consist, hereby
> In me abundant grow, and burdenous,
> And nourish not, but smother.
>
> (ll. 6–8)

He thus has more energy, with no regular outlet, leading to a rather far-fetched final resolution, that, dying, he will overtake her soul like a bullet, since "my fire doth with my fuell grow" (l. 15).

The poem has suggestive subtlety; nevertheless, with reading, it turns unpleasantly self-involved. Eight lines describing their intimate relationship are followed by thirteen of navel-watching, where he analyzes his energy changes, his weight, his system upset. The opening, dismissing his beloved in three words (and two syllables), "She'is dead," has rhetorical shock, but is followed by too diagnostic a self-analysis. "A Feaver," for all its stanzaic regularity and far conceits, thrashes about in an impetuous instability, accepting and rejecting her, recognizing her as a person, projecting her as the soul of the universe. "The Dissolution," impeccably uneven, is finally a sedate series of even, steady sentences, the speaker patiently piecing himself together amid stressful difficulties. And extravagant as is "A Feaver," its abrupt catharsis ends accepting the inevitable. The closing conceit of "The Dissolution" rings hollow. His soul will speed up, not to rejoin, but "outstrip hers." This cautious narcissist will yet win a first in the heavenly Olympics.

These two poems touch on death with sudden shock or astute introspection; but only in "A Nocturnall upon S. Lucies Day," is death an august arrival, not just a sudden loss. It recalls the effective, cumbersome, strongly rhythmic stanza of "A Valediction: of Weeping"; but "A Nocturnall" is slower, more measured and more massive, with nine lines, a middle catch or pause in line 5. "A Valediction: of Weeping" opens with and interposes dimeter lines; as the speaker, wholly involved with his beloved, struggles with his grief at parting. "A Nocturnall" is a threnody, not a dialogue; and requires no such restraint. Yet it lacks the choked, explosive emotion of "A Valediction: of Weeping." A strong dissolution is rather taking place. The person of his beloved has withdrawn and grown impersonal. The world has lost its soul and is a corpse. The speaker, its epitaph, is yet somehow in the placenta of her awesome presence. Life and death are reversing themselves, heaven and earth, as ponderously, he defines himself.

Its feet per line are 5, 5, 4, 4, 3, 5, 5, 5, 5, its rhyme scheme a, b, b, a, c, c, c, d, d. The firm opening quatrain gradually shrinks before death from five to four feet. The couplet rhymes of the closing quatrain allow either two simple couplets, in Stanzas 2 and 4, or an interlocked quatrain building to a heroic couplet in Stanzas 1 and 3. But the key to the stanza is its middle three-foot line. In Stanza 1, it stands in choked stasis, making the stanza heave to a start for line 6. In Stanza 2, it feeds into the last quatrain, making its soft, hissing rhyme a triplet of empty nothingness. In Stanza 3, it hangs amid ongoing lines to emphasize the poignant, uncontrolled openness of weeping. In Stanza 4, commas lightly enclose it, in the swinging, logical catch and drift. In Stanza 5, it closes the first quatrain to allow a four-line finale.

The figure of Lucy allows a strange cathartic release, with flood-tides of expression. Donne's earlier lyrics showed a tension between an alien, rejecting superior, and the speaker's strategy of aloofness, rapid movement, and evasive self-assertion. This tension eased under the rigorous redefinition of the love relationship in "The Extasie"; but "A Valediction: of Weeping" again elevated the loved person to a cosmic force, but now one absorbed into his universe. So "A Nocturnall" offers Lucy as such an animating force. But "A Nocturnall" contains a second woman, not only Lucy, who opens the poem, but his unnamed beloved, who appears in line 23. Indeed, the speaker's evolving relationship to these two women shapes the plot of the poem.

Lucy, whose name means light, establishes the opening antinomy in Stanza 1, she against her wintry day, light on shrunken darkness, a paradoxical opposition increasingly congenial to Donne's pen. In "Goodfriday, 1613. Riding Westward," Christ the life-giver dies on the cross; so Lucy, who is light, radically withdraws from the universe. Indeed, Lucy is in some sense its animating spirit, like Elizabeth Drury in the *Anniversaries*. Thus, "the Sunne is spent," having lost its source of renewal. On a theological level, this is markedly Augustinian, the natural light entirely depending on supernatural, or animating force. As Lucy withdraws, light withdraws. "The world's whole sap," in some sense Lucy's animating spirit, sinks away when Lucy is gone. The earth drinks its "generall balme," as the sun spends his rays, "hydroptique," i.e., without any satiation, drinking for sap or balm with no constant rays.

There is a strong shift of imagery in Stanza 1 from light to water, turning on the pivotal line 5. The first quatrain establishes a motif of light flickering from the earth, "midnight . . . dayes . . . Lucies . . . unmaskes . . . Sunne . . . flasks . . . light squibs . . . constant rayes." The trimeter, line 5, shifts this from transcendant to immanent, from light to water, "sap . . . sunke . . . balme . . . hydroptique . . . drunk . . . shrunke." So, by Donne's dualism, the earth is a blend of inert matter and animating spirit, as in "The First Anniversary." When that animating spirit withdraws, it leaves a universal corpse, "shrunke, dead and enterr'd." By this description, in the natural change of seasons, the animating spirit ebbs as summer turns to winter. So Lucy withdraws, leaving only light squibs, no constant rays.

Stanza 1 establishes a strange blend of utter distance and intuitive rapport with Lucy. The natural phenomena reverberate with human tensions as Lucy withdraws. Thus, the imagery of light and water masks another of sexuality in grave divorce. Male and female in the opening lines move in a large, stylized myth:

> *Lucies*, who scarce seaven houres herself unmaskes,
> The Sunne is spent, and now his flasks
> Send forth light squibs, no constant rayes.
>
> (ll. 2–4)

Elegy XIX projected a woman undressing for bed. Here, Lucy unmasks herself so briefly, the masculine sun remains virtually impotent, his flasks, in some sense his sexual organs, ending forth only light squibs, no constant rays. The shift from light to sap carries overtones of semen as an animating life force; but it builds to the bitter irony and paradox of "beds-feet." "Bed" could refer to the rock of earth inside which water cannot penetrate; but after the interplay of Lucy and the sun, its overtone is of a lover's bed, yet the opposite of sexuality and fertility, a place where life is "shrunke, dead and enterr'd."

Following the later disclosure that the speaker's beloved is dead, this divorce of Lucy and the sun reads as a self-projection. Nevertheless, the speaker's rapport with Lucy has personal poignance. Indeed, Donne's poetry has long antecedents of a dual woman. The images blur fascinatingly on one another. The startling echo and reverberation of "this face . . . this face . . . this face" in "Loves Exchange" demonically echoes the benign opening of "Aire and Angels":

> Twice or thrice had I lov'd thee,
> Before I knew thy face or name . . .

He bargains in "Loves Usury" with the exasperated futility of "The Flea," with a god or woman. "A Lecture upon the Shadow" shifts Love from a listener to a lecture, at the beginning, to "a growing, or full constant light" at the close. Indeed, in "A Nocturnall," Lucy suggests some identification with Donne's mother, the beloved his wife or a surrogate; but our concern here is the structure of Donne's poetic consciousness, not neat biographical parallels; and here again, the two women flicker over one another enticingly.

Yet Stanza 1 begins with Lucy alone, depicting her departure as a solemn, but natural phenomenon in the arrival of winter. The speaker, though in mourning, momentarily absorbs his consciousness in Lucy. Bereaved, estranged, he is in paradoxical rapport with the universe, and suffers no radical isolation. He and nature are one, both bereaved and estranged. Indeed, with the ebb and flow of the seasons, his period of mourning might well come to an end, and he return to normal life. Then, at the close of Stanza 1, the implication of harmony in bereavement turns into a howl of savage mockery. He is the antithesis of Lucy herself. She is the spirit of the world in its life, he its epitaph after its death. She is a living spirit, he a dead word.

Stanza 2 pushes their antithesis. Did Lucy withdraw in the dead of winter, being an animating spirit? He, in the full flowering of spring, will remain gauchely there, a quintessence of nothingness. Indeed, all Donne's metaphysical shudder of savage doubt makes this image dense with denial. After "Loves Alchymie," we have no assurance that Donne gave significance to any essence. A "quintessence even from nothingness" suggests a pomposity of bereavement; and yet the impossible language, delivered in ponderous, even stately lines, communicates a blank denial, the departure of all hope. He is "every dead thing," Lucy's polar opposite; as Lucy recedes, he invades them. Indeed, the old demonic god of love returns in almost clinical terms as a radical life denial. He is in some sense his victim, subject to the raw denial of life:

> For I am every dead thing,
> In whom love wrought new Alchymie.
> For his art did expresse
> A quintessence even from nothingnesse.
>
> (ll. 12–15)

His spirit was created by the destructive force of love, and is therefore radically estranged from Lucy.

Then, in Stanza 3, as he reaches a nadir of denial, "loves limbecke . . . the grave/Of all, that's nothing," suddenly, mysteriously, the second woman appears, no ideal image, god, demon, or animating force, but a particular woman, his unnamed bride, and in an echo of Stanza 1, but with the roles reversed. There, the speaker had paradoxical rapport with the corpse of nature; here, the woman has rapport with the corpse of his spirit; as they keep paradoxical company, weep together, live and love in an endless parting. Indeed, such phrases as "Drownd the whole world, us two" and "often absences/Withdrew our soules and made us carcasses" so closely parallel "A Valediction: of Weeping" as to indicate the same woman. So the steadiness of relationship in the repeated "oft . . . often" incline "A Nocturnall" to Donne's wife.

Stanza 4 then remarks a second and larger bereavement. As in Stanza 1, he felt a paradoxical rapport with the absent Lucy, that sank into savage bereavement; so here, the actual death of his beloved turns their paradoxical rapport in the chaos of their lives into ultimate total solitude. Now he would not even be a man, not a beast, not have any properties, not even be a shadow, and so imply a body and light.

He is at the nadir of his existence, then; but two strands of symmetry anticipate the catharsis in Stanza 5. Firstly, his beloved and Lucy are curious parallels. They do not interact as separate persons—on the contrary, as his beloved appears, Lucy slips away; yet their careers are strikingly parallel. In both cases, a paradoxical rapport in denial arrives at a sudden shock of bereavement and estrangement. Secondly, the flip-flop of reality is repeated and strengthened with too scrupulous an insistence: Lucy is sunk in darkness; life is dead at the "beds-feet"; the speaker is "every dead thing," a "quintessence even from nothingnesse . . . dull privations . . . lean emptinesse . . . re-begot/Of absence, darknesse, death; things which are not . . . the grave/Of all, that's nothing . . . two Chaosses . . . carcasses . . . of the first nothing, the Elixer . . ."

Both strains come to an awesome head in Stanza 5. "None" rhymes with "Sunne" in line 37. But the sun in Stanza 1 was Lucy's mythic comrade, her summer partner and absorber of her spirit, who sent forth his light squibs. But the echoes of motherhood in Lucy identify the sun as the father figure, the sun of the cosmos and source of all earthly life. The huge estrangement and denial this would evoke might well block him off from any possible participation.

But now "None" rhymes with "Sunne," suggesting an identity of polar opposites. Not only is "none" an absence, and "Sunne" all authority and power; but "None" puns with "nun," a celibate female where the sun is the sexual lover of Stanza 1. But the long systematic exorcism of the poem, the ritual penance in the runic repetition of phrases, one behind the other, has built to the pitchpoint of "But I am none," an exorcism of all life, vitality, body, masculinity, and property. Indeed, here the biographical strand cannot be ignored in the poem. Brought up a Roman Catholic, the nephew of priests, Donne fought all his life to establish himself as a vigorous Anglican gentleman; and now penance and exorcism bring him to a shocking self-identity as a female celibate in a forbidden church. His sun, his earthly father, adult, worldly authority, his vitality in life, will not arrive at any fresh springtime, "nor will my Sunne renew."

Then comes the crack. The speaker crosses the ragged edge of existence. Other fallen men may mark time, then rise again:

> You lovers, for whose sake, the lesser Sunne
> At this time to the Goat is runne
> To fetch new lust, and give it you,
> Enjoy your summer all . . .
>
> (ll. 38–41)

But they follow the "lesser Sunne," of physicality, secularism, and social force. In the cycle of seasons, in the continuity of generations, they can anticipate fresh lust. Their lesser sun will fetch from the "Goat" the force and permissiveness passed on in a secular society to permit another summer. But the "lesser Sunne" suggests a greater, indeed, the sun of heaven, the light of grace and eternity.

And which is the sun of Stanza 1? It remains undefined; but its submission to the cycle of the seasons makes it clearly the "lesser Sunne," so awesome at first. And who is the "shee" of line 42? The catharsis is too overflowing with release to identify her with Lucy. On the contrary, her light is inextricably entwined with the "Sunne" on earth. "Shee" is rather his unnamed bride, who "drownd the whole world" with him in tears, when they became two chaoses. She is now with the greater sun, which the blessed share without sin. On earth, the speaker is a "None" nor will his "Sunne renew." His penance is complete, though it has taken his last strand of physicality. But living in spirit, he will prepare for her in heaven, her groom in the world of spirit.

We are present in "A Nocturnall upon S. Lucies Day" at the still point of a vast healing process, a spirit undergoing "a sea change," that still lies on the ocean floor, ignorant, unmoving, apparently dead; but strange new lights of a larger healing are fructifying within. His grace is now elsewhere. The mysterium is in labor. He stands at the end where he stood at the beginning, but on another plane:

> Let mee prepare towards her, and let mee call
> This houre her Vigill, and her Eve, since this
> Both the yeares, and the dayes deep midnight is.

# *Part* IV

## *Special Subjects*

# 12

# The Fragility of Art

An interest in words is necessarily paradoxical. Signs, not substantial things, they signal to the mind, the memory, the will. Who arranges nonsense syllables in iambic pentameters, or serves a menu as the main course for dinner? We do not trust them. Indeed, a man dwelling on words makes us uneasy. He is playing a game; a hurt is oozing out. Yet a child's language is its playground. We like the smack of talk, its knolls and fissures. Not every prattle calls for a diagnosis.

A poet is even more of a puzzle. Do his dense verbal textures, freighted with feeling, indicate more than a maladjustment? When does his fret of dissatisfaction become a hunger for the truth? Blake and Wordsworth regarded themselves as inspired craftsmen; but Tennyson and Browning hung between social engagement and withdrawal into words. Indeed, Browning dramatized a series of verbal eccentrics. And Arnold established so firm an equilibrium, we suspect he was doing penance. But for what? For writing poetry? Wasn't that activity innocent?

To Donne, this antinomy of life and art was no dedication, but a puzzling minor complication, a botched, useless corner of the massive enigma of existence. Sublimation Donne never trusted. In a large, loose way, all things paled before his concerns of spirit; as raw, direct, they engaged his ego. In a sense, as he aged, the activity of art became an emblem for everything earthly, yet also his tool for a direct communication of spirit. His mistrust of the world, his finding it unnatural, insecure, questionably organized, governed his use of conceits and emblems, his selectivity with nouns. Cosmologies were no more compelling than the structure of a stanza. A word and a thing stirred the same metaphysical shudder. His far reaches into language testified to the world he lived in, a construct, mysterious, arbitrary, and finally trivial.

His most serious discussion of the writing of poetry, "The Triple Foole," breaks with the reasons offered by Sydney and others of the Renaissance, to educate and to delight, and advances instead the more modern concept of the psychic wound and its sublimation into poetry. And of its two sinewy, unobtrusive stanzas, the one discusses the poet's purposes, the other his results, each honed to its subject, as it flexes from trimeters and tetrameters, to a pentameter finality. Each stanza has eleven lines, with a sentence break after line 5. The first half presents the problem with laconic brevity, its feet per line 3, 4, 3, 5, 3. Six pentameter lines, with one tetrameter catch in music, then elaborate the conclusion.

In the first stanza, the speaker announces himself a double fool, a lover and a poet. Rueful, familiar, yet never abject, he explores literary sublimation in tight, sinewy language, making no bones that he wants simply to love, with or without wisdom:

> But where's that wiseman, that would not be I,
> If she would not deny?
>
> (ll. 4–5)

Here he scorns poetry, a whining accompaniment to unskilled courtship, folly in two-part harmony. He rather wants love itself, otherwise he will not play the fool. Only his traumatic rejection in line 5 makes him take poetry seriously. The "then" in line 6 marks a fresh turn of attention.

The speaker then probes the psychology of sublimation, offering two metaphors, one suggesting some form of purgation (ll. 6–9), the other a strengthening of self-esteem through discipline and control (ll. 10–11). The first, the more mysterious and interesting, would allay the pain of rejection by drawing it "through Rimes vexation," as sea water purges salt by flowing through "narrow crooked lanes" (l. 6), deep in the earth. The metaphor suggests concepts not fully available in Donne's day. At the least, the metaphor is mechanical, "narrow crooked lanes" suggesting simple emotional exhaustion. The work of poetry would thus exhaust unused excesses of energy, and redress imbalances in his temperament.

But the metaphor says more. "The Dissolution" develops a concept of libidinal energy returning to the speaker with the loss of a beloved:

> My fire of Passion, sighes of ayre,
> Water of teares, and earthly sad despaire,
> Which my materials bee,
> But neere worne out by loves securitie,
> She, to my losse, doth by her death repaire . . .
>
> (ll. 9–13)

"The Triple Foole" also describes energies flowing through the lover that require treatment after pain. The image here is of sea water, salt, dense, and undrinkable. If, after rejection, the lover's inner waters turn poisonous and salty, a stagnant pool, some process or activity must purge them. The metaphor of pouring one's pain over poetry suggests an airing of loss and reinvolvement in activity, a gradual easing and resettlement in a fresh round of needs. So the person moves through slow, tortuous steps, "Rimes vexation," to heal emotional pain. In the vexation of labor over poetry, it deposits its load of poison.

The second metaphor is simpler, more pugnaciously adolescent:

> Griefe brought to numbers cannot be so fierce,
> For, he tames it, that fetters it in verse.
>
> (ll. 10–11)

By reducing his sorrow to verse, the stubborn young Elizabethan warrior establishes his greater strength, and can live on, inviolable. The image, of grief as an animal to be tamed and fettered, recalls the Platonic image of passions as horses under the control of reason. It makes the writing of poetry part of the wholesome development of a Renaissance warrior, not a withdrawal and an escape.

Stanza 2 does not cancel out the sublimation of poetry, but makes it so partial and prone to accidents as to trivialize its effect. For commerce or exhibitionism, someone may set his poem to music and sing it as public entertainment, "his art and voice to show" (l. 13). Thus, his scrupulous healing process would be splashed across the city as moody, sentimental music. Thus, verse is a two-edged sword, discharging and calming passion, and stimulating it afresh. Finally, it reawakens the sentiment of love on a larger, more powerful scale than ever. Indeed, the new vocation will entice the poet. Intrigued by his capacity to give pleasure, he will put private grief to public entertainment and become a triple fool, a foolish lover, a foolish versifier, and a fool as a man-of-letters.

His final judgment, "Who are a little wise, the best fooles bee" (l. 22), allows sublimation some marginal value; but inevitable consequences leave its practitioner the greater fool. This is the instinct of metaphysical poetry, to avoid the plateau of detachment, the vocation of a poet. At a remove from life experience, one will posture and sentimentalize, a triple fool.

"A Valediction: of My Name in the Window" discusses engravings and the power of the art object, not sublimation and the artist's temperament; it is concerned more with magic and sorcery than with aesthetics. Yet its conclusion is also negative; an inscription is powerless, a trigger that evokes empty magical ideas the speaker no longer believes in. The poem occurs in a moment of parting, when the speaker sees his name engraved on his beloved's window. Teased by fantasies of overcoming the separation, he is struck with fears about its dangers. His moment of fantasy turns to panic. The catharsis of the poem then comes with his return to actuality. Thus, under a series of high-keyed whimsical conceits, he meanders from stanza to stanza in an attempt to master a situation, even magically keep it from happening. The conceits here are not free whimsy, but gestures of exorcism; as myriad old superstitions, touched to life at the stress of parting, are examined and found wanting.

Musically, the poem has eleven short tight stanzas. Its rhyme scheme is regular enough, a, b, a, b, c, c; but its feet per line, 3, 5, 4, 4, 5, 4, jostle irregularly forward. These stanzas are not a song, but a string of small, carved jewels, chiseled to their measured meaning. In the poem, a diamond cut the window; so these stanzas are cut to articulate their meaning.

The poem begins with a firm bravado, overflowing with sympathetic magic. The glass fuses their better parts. His name, engraved, lends it his firmness, hard as the cutting diamond. So her glass gives value "to mock/The diamonds of either rock" (ll. 5–6). Indeed, he admires it for being as transparent as he. Lively, euphoric, he shows her reflection in the glass, then, by sleight-of-hand, "loves magique," slips behind the glass and makes them one: "Here you see mee, and I am you" (l. 12). He then pledges his constancy by the glass, and invites her to do the same, "who have the patterne with you still" (l. 18).

Yet these opening three stanzas of giddy whimsy and sympathetic magic also imply falsehood and vulnerability, a hubris laden with tragic irony. He is the opposite of transparent. His firmness is yet unproved; nor has the glass much worth, reflecting only surfaces, and easily broken. Even their joined reflection is so ephemeral as to suggest fragility only.

The euphoric whimsy ebbs in Stanza 4. The easy, sympathetic magic in Stanzas 1 to 3, a casual, impersonal power, shifts to the diabolical power of a name. His name, scratched in the window, becomes a skull, a *memento mori*, a "given deaths head" to preach the mortality of love. The thin inscription, looped and scattered, scratches out his condition, a "ragged bony name," his "ruinous Anatomie." Indeed, his name on glass evokes the thought that his departure will soon tear him to pieces, his soul remaining with her, while his body is torn elsewhere. The courtesy gesture of the valediction in which this is couched makes these lines the more poignant. His words should work to ease her anxieties, give him an invulnerable aura for a secure farewell. Instead, the polarity is pushed to the highest tension, his souls, vegetable, animal, and rational, "Emparadis'd" in her, his little trinity of spirit housed in its Eden, while the rafters of his body plunge into the chaos of travel. Indeed, his "ragged bony name" scratched on her window is in some sense his skeleton. Thus, by force of circumstance, his soul and his bones will remain with her, the parts in between, "the Muscle, Sinew, and Veine,/Which tile this house," will go abroad.

As Stanzas 4 and 5 border on black magic, so Stanzas 6 and 7 glide helplessly into astrology. With each shift of intention, he grows more helpless, she more powerful. This reading would support Helen Gardner's text here, with no punctuation in line 31, a comma only after "so" in line 32, and a comma closing the stanza, making Stanzas 6 and 7 one large clumsy unit. The stanzas in this poem are too short and tight for so many layers of feeling, superstition, and whimsy. In Stanza 8, his repressed fear finally breaks surface, that she may be unfaithful. A large two-stanza unit would appropriately precede it, the last large barrier before the emergence of truth.

The astrology in Stanzas 6 and 7 reinforces at once his helplessness and her power. Thus, the configuration of the stars shapes his destiny, "graved . . . when these starres have supremacie." The word "graved" at once recalls his name inscribed in her window, his fate hanging on it as in the stars, and foreshadows the menace of his coming trip, which may lead to his grave—graved may be his grave. He sees her now as his guardian angel, who can control the influence of the stars. So he begs her to mute her power out of her love. Indeed, he grows so anxious, that he violates the entire purpose of a valediction. Fearful that she may casually destroy him, instead of calming her, he blurts a demand, "Since I die daily, daily mourne."

With this breakdown of dignity, his cheapest fantasies stir up. He sees her throw open the casement window to spy out a fresh lover; as his name on it protests. The rival will corrupt her maid to hide a letter under her pillow; and as she weakens, his name will step in from the window and hide his rival's name on his letter. If she then write a flirtatious reply, his name will flow from the window into her fancy so unawares she will write his name. Thus, he blurts his fears; but they have already thinned and turned ridiculous with the telling, his fantasies a trite parlor comedy, his name an imp, popping about helplessly. But none of his fantasies had substance, not sympathetic magic, the play on names, nor the astrology. All were stagnant pools, cerebral machinery to be aired at parting. Glass and inscriptions are not the bonds to keep them. He has plumbed his dregs of fantasy, and brought up matters he might "murmure in my sleepe" (l. 64). The exorcism is over. He can depart in peace.

It must be remarked, reading metaphysical poetry as a staking-out of a position upon a crumbling metaphysics, that here, sympathetic magic, black magic, alchemy, and astrology are disorganized material tumbled to the surface in a moody pang, to make a serenity possible at parting. The last stanza makes it plain that in sober daylight such ideas hold no substance. Indeed, suspended among careers and religions in an untrustworthy world, the speaker has collected an atmosphere of inscribed names, images without security, inscriptions that work and do not work. Indeed, such tight stanzas controlling a bog of half-expressed ideas indicate a dry, massive control; but they testify to the speaker's extraordinary depth of feeling. He has sunk shafts into his disorganized warehouse of old feelings, to view omnipotence, exotic cosmologies, forlorn helplessness, all caught up in magic and superstition.

Indeed, the moody shift beginning Stanza 4, and the break after a two-stanza unit after Stanza 8, make this poem the gesture of a gallant man, repressing his insecurities with ostentatious confidence, that nevertheless will out. So, as they articulate themselves against him, his invulnerability begins to collapse; and the horrors smack through, dignified, abstracted, yet so primitive and disordered they betray more anguish than any actual expression could convey, locked in its tight, halting music to make it hard to cry. And finally the bathwater overflows. The speaker, a little silly amid his superstitions and bravura dignity, sees her in a seduction skit, and his name on glass popping about to prevent adultery, a combined fantasy of omnipotence and fatuous degradation so pathetic and so grandiose as to border on insanity.

But the poem is an exorcism, designed to enable an intimacy of spirit. It begins with a formal bravura farewell and ends with the farewell of truth, with mute apologies for his deranged thought and ruminations on the omnipresence of death. Between them, a false control clutches up, magic and the written word, a horror underlying it, the fear of helplessness, of love enslavement, betrayal, all exposed, exorcised, to allow a parting of the more truth. The poem is an interlude between gesture and gesture.

"A Valediction: of the Booke" is a rather garrulous valediction, instructing her to write a book of love, a subject Donne never took too seriously. After the tight stanza of "A Valediction: of My Name, in the Window," these nine-line stanzas begin with an iambic pentameter quatrain, a, b, b, a. In the following pinched triplet of 3, 4, 4 feet per line, the middle line drops its opening unaccented syllable, tightening the gradation. The closing couplet then expands to an Alexandrine. "Breake of Day" and "The Message" had such an easy stanza with a pinched middle. A stanza so distracted by its symmetry is not too gripped by its content.

In the other valedictions, a superficial courtesy gesture is balanced against an underlying uneasiness, to be joined in the catharsis of the poem. Only here does no uneasiness underlie the gesture of courtesy. This seems appropriate. He is not commenting on his trip, but suggesting that she spend her time compiling a book of their love. This is not the embattled vindication of a love record as in Shakespeare's sonnets, but a suggestion of how she might while away an hour profitably.

The poem begins on a note of mild and cozy feeling. "Deare Love" is familiar and affectionate; so the "anger" of destiny will show more pique than outrage. He entices his beloved by the vanity of surpassing other poetesses. Indeed, while her competition is superficially grand, its actuality is rather meager. Corinna, temptress of Lucan, is hardly more renowned than Phantasia, the rumored authoress of Homer. As for Lucan's helper, even a modest glory can obscure anonymity. The love-book she will write is steadily expanded through five stanzas into a latter-day Bible of love, source of true law and theology, a little "Universe" (l. 26), from which "Schooles might learne Sciences, Spheares Musick, Angels Verse." Such verbal extravagance attempts marvel, not persuasion. The poem is a late and relaxed one, ruminating material fresher in earlier poems, Stanza 3 their special holiness as in "The Canonization," Stanza 4 the balance of body and spirit as in "The Extasie."

The speaker celebrates his beloved with affectionate distraction, but hides his own complacency. He may coax her to outdo Pindar's temptress, Lucan's wife, and Homer's source; but the comparison puts him alongside Pindar, Lucan, and Homer—rhetoric aside, the books were finally theirs. He wants her to write their annals, but using their letters as sources makes him at least an equal partner in their ultimate truths. His good-natured mockery of statesmen, "Here Statesmen, (or of them, they which can reade)" gains added point by Donne's former aspiration to be among them. Indeed, he gives one stanza to each profession he was eminently trained to and couldn't practice, in a regular way: the theologian, the lawyer, and the statesman. His closing conceit, reading longitude by an eclipse, is a far flight of glory to round out a reassuring gesture of easy distraction. It is pleasant to find Donne so light of heart, writing a valediction, even if his easy levity urges her to write a book, having nothing else to do.

"Witchcraft by a Picture" has neither witchcraft nor a picture. It is spoken by a man terminating an affair, playing with his reflection in her tears to taunt the woman he feels has tormented him. "A Valediction: of My Name, in the Window" began with false assurances to arrive at a limpid truth; "Witchcraft by a Picture" begins with a sharp, peering focus to end in a giddy lie.

At their parting, she is weeping; but her tears arouse in him a vengeful mistrust, not any compassion at her possible suffering. Indeed, he does not see her at all, not even her tears, only his image reflected in them. He taunts her with a mannered play on fire and water, his picture burning on her eye, drowning in her tears. Yet his taunting rage struggles with old insecurities. One of her tears encases his entire image, leaving him small, helpless, completely in her power, as in the old misogyny poems. Though his indignation struggles, her waning omnipotence overshadows him. He seems utterly subservient, locked in her eye like a calf before the slaughter. An aura of witchcraft hangs in the air. He accuses her of murderous inclinations, blocked only by her ignorance of the technique:

> Hadst thou the wicked skill
> By pictures made and mard, to kill,
> How many wayes mightst thou performe thy will?
>
> (ll. 5–7)

The entire stanza is a suspense of antinomies. Behind his gross helplessness, balanced against his surge of indignation, a steady awareness is held in abeyance that he has won already. The first four rhymes register and hammer it home: "there," "in thine eye," "in a transparent tear," "I espie." They have reversed roles, though he scarcely grasps it for his indignation.

As Stanza 1 finishes, it registers. The next lines are of another man, expressing their reversal of roles with a swashbuckling arrival:

> But now I have drunke thy sweet salt tears . . .
>
> (l. 8)

But overtones of black magic, killing by names, even cannibalism invade the poem. Before, her tears contained him, he, helpless as an image in a drop of water. Now he contains her tears, she an easy mouthful to drink down. The aura of magic is abruptly snapped off:

> My picture vanish'd, vanish feares,
> That I can be endamag'd by that art.
>
> (ll. 10–11)

He grasps that she is weeping, helpless, having lost him. This reverses a sado-masochistic relationship between them. Indeed, the phrase, "thy sweet salt tears," has a sadistic overtone—the salt of her body is sweet to him. In Stanza 1, the dependent inferior accepts her killing indifference; at its end, he takes on the independent, aggressive role. Indeed, the last line is exceedingly ambiguous about the memento he leaves behind:

> Though thou retaine of mee
> One picture more, yet that will bee,
> Being in thine owne heart, from all malice free.
> (ll. 12–14)

What will free his picture of all malice? Only her steady knowledge that she has lost him. He is in a beatitude of spite, having humiliated her.

The picture he works with in the poem, like the inscribed name in "A Valediction: of My Name, in the Window," or the book in "A Valediction: of the Booke," have as cheerful or harassed futility, a distraction from the business of life.

The two stanzas have 4, 5, 5, 4, 3, 4, 5 feet per line, that rhyme a, b, a, b, c, c, c, a neat and easy music, with a closed, plunging quatrain and a rising, arch of feet per line in the triplet, a grand finale to a very small stanza, exuberant over its little triumph. Its images are narrowly visual, the most detached and cerebral of the senses. Their speaker, despite his peal of triumph, is a bit too much the social butterfly to trust his judgment about the woman. There finally remain her tears of silent sorrow as he preens and postures in their reflection, flitting from tear to tear in elation. His gestures are a taunt. Spiteful, indignant, he turns into an image, then disappears altogether. Yet his obsessions of cannibalism undercut his claims of impregnability, her tears consuming his image, he consuming her tears, her heart consuming his picture, a self-involved child, playing with manhood. Except as factors in a spiteful gesture of triumph, his emotions, like his images, are nothing.

"A Jeat Ring Sent" uses a pathetic passive voice in the title. His sweetheart has sent the ring back to break off a make-believe marriage. The entire bond was a sham; and now the emblem of that sham is in his hands, the jet ring of a mock-marriage. The speaker looks at it ruefully, whimsically. The poet has long used questionable items to indicate a problematical bond, the flea in "The Flea," the piece of glass in "A Valediction: of My Name, in the Window." So the ring fuses their two hearts, her blackness and her brittleness. But the flirtation has turned to nonplussed embarrassment. He has only the black ring in his hands. In a sour truthfulness, reality breaks through a gauze of romance. The speaker shrinks back, identifying with the cheap ring, whose very material, "jeat," means "cast away," as though saying, "I" am cheap, and nought but fashion, "fling me'away" (l. 8).

For two stanzas, he toys with the unfashionable black ring; in Stanza 3, he puts it on and accepts himself, for all his tarnished record. He still feels close to her, despite her snub: "Circle this fingers top, which did'st her thombe" (l. 10). In his scurrilous way, he was deferential; they broke up at her initiative. He now feels akin and protective to the ring:

Be justly proud, and gladly safe, that thou dost dwell with me,
She that, Oh, broke her faith, would soon breake thee.
(ll. 11–12)

He has lost a sweetheart and acquired a pet, and winces at both experiences. The poem ends when he and the ring are one.

The music has the speaker's clumsy honesty, a dry four-line stanza, rhyming as couplets, with feet per line that expand and settle, 4, 5, 7, 5. The seven-foot line is too ungainly. Line 8 has two contractions. The iambics are prosaic and conversational. The music even has trouble getting started. Stanzas 1 and 2 begin reversing accents:

Thou art not so black, as my heart . . .

Marriage rings are not of this stuffe . . .

The truth registers hard; yet Stanza 3 gets the pace right:

Yet stay with mee since thou art come . . .

He has cleared his moody path in life.

The last poem in this group, a sonnet entitled "The Token," Helen Gardner finds doubtfully by Donne. Its 18 lines make an overgrown sonnet of 4 quatrains. It good-naturedly dramatizes the speaker's indulgence in particularities. A garrulous sentimentalist, he is fundamentally wholesome. So he asks in his last couplet:

Send me nor this, nor that, t'increase my store,
But swear thou thinkst I love thee, and no more.
(ll. 17–18)

Its simple reading is, swear you think I love you, and no other woman; but the lines could mean, swear you think I love you, but do not test it. The command is a flirtatious tease. A man who promises nothing, yet would simply be trusted, he is above belief.

Donne's sense of the art object, then, though slight and derivative, is not simple. He had an uncanny sense of the fixing of human spirit on an object. Thus, he and the jet ring are finally one. His name, inscribed in the window, will not let go. His image in a tear stirs with cannibal impulses and fears. Yet the men whom the art object engages are disturbed, moody, muffled inside their defenses. The activity of art is no glorification of the eternal object, but an enfeebled sublimation of failure, stirring Donne's uneasiness at the shifting bases of security and trust. In "The Canonization," the bittersweet reassurances of poetic immortality come only after the fact of failure. His initial choice was legend, chronicle, a half-acre tomb. And as he grew older, the sense grew stronger of a willful imposition of symbol and meaning on matter. "The Crosse" is a complex take-over of nature by the cross. In "Goodfriday, 1613. Riding Westward," he saw no landscape, only a direction away from Christ. And in "Hymne to God My God, in My Sicknesse," his very body becomes a map, until we cannot be sure where literal becomes metaphoric, where emblem ends and life begins:

> Whilst my Physitians by their love are growne
>    Cosmographers, and I their Mapp, who lie
> Flat on this bed, that by them may be showne
>    That this is my South-west discoverie
>    *Per fretum febris*, by these streights to die . . .
>
> (ll. 6–10)

Indeed, as Donne grew older, his metaphysical framework shifted from two to three parts. The earlier period offered a duality, a clumsy flotsam of the natural world and tentative probes of spirit. But as Donne developed, the material world became like an underpinning we sense, but never quite register. Everywhere about us are emblems, symbols, old ritual objects, pieces of extinct cosmology. And above this is the large, clear thrust of spirit unto spirit, at first for Anne More, and finally unto God. This growth has striking Platonic parallels, the natural underpinning resembling daily experience, and the thrust of spirit the world of ideas. Indeed, the sudden stepladder of existence in "The Extasie" and "Aire and Angels" is so carefully articulated an underpinning for his philosophy of love as to suggest some reading and deliberate imitation of Platonic models. But the growth described here is more elemental, gradual, without any spelling out of parts, indicating the native bent of the man's spirit, whatever its sources. And its final bent is unto a union of spirit so impassioned as to indicate Christian rather than Platonic influences. The parallel Spanish sources, which Donne thoroughly knew, inclined to guide it to the special circumstances of mystical union, thus preserving the structure of the Church. Donne's simpler development, outside the circumstances of mystical experience, is parallel, but more heavily Protestant and Lutheran. Donne's choice, then, at the end of his life, was between a world of illusion and artifice, and God, its writer and maker.

# 13

# Anniversaries

The late love lyrics Donne addressed to a gracious, but lofty lady evince a complex restructuring in the speaker, a mannerist play with symbols, a solitary fumbling around romance, with no risks, no hope, no plan, and no disaster. The "thou" is dissolved to a "she," the confrontation to a constellation of attitudes. So "A Nocturnall upon S. Lucies Day" blurs companion and patroness, sweetheart and motherly spirit, to a light filling an inner heaven. The name "Lucie" suggests a radiant presence more than a person. These poems evince a trend of spirit, a psyche reorganizing itself. His early life, a slow, enormous, painstaking preparation for an intimate encounter, snagged in marriage, misfired. Now a fresh, equally deep reorganization seems under way, disengaging from the woman as his alter ego.

We grope for a bedrock of spirit, its peculiar faults, byways, and sudden canyons, willful tenacities and eerily arbitrary elements. In Donne's case, objects are trivial, landscapes a diversion, natural law a handy metaphor. Never "thingy," his lyrics coiled about, a thin, arbitrary, slashing world, with abrupt presences and hard, dynamic lines. At first, he wrestled, stewed, intuited, and gravitated toward a great encounter of spirit, his marriage. He loved his wife, fathered her children, gave her his support and career; but soon his lyrics began again to intuit out, blindly, tentatively, unsurely. Now the particular woman in his poems became detached, enlarged, undefined, a cosmic presence more than a person.

In this constant, easy openness, Donne was unique among English lyricists; his poems followed the bent of his raw psyche, unloading strata of his being in dramatic lyrics, shifting as it shifted. His great poems, "Loves Alchymie," "The Extasie," "The Canonization," "A Nocturnall upon S. Lucies Day," are at once shaped musical structures and breakthroughs to fresh constellations of experience. His dramatic counterpart, Shakespeare, likewise slightly, but irreversibly restructured his core plot in each of his plays. That these men were close contemporaries, both thorough professional men, both, we have some reason to believe, from crypto-Catholic families, suggests a rare fusion of ego and occasion.

Even "A Valediction: of Weeping" has a periodicity of decor about the womanly presence, an oceanic wash and enlargement of that "subtile knot" of his particular beloved. The extraordinary tear in that poem, as painful as any in our literature, a wound so deeply felt we can feel it in the tissue of the speaker's psyche, is between Stanzas 2 and 3, when he exclaims:

> O more than Moone,
> Draw not up seas to drowne me in thy spheare . . .
> (ll. 19–20)

At that moment, in his psyche, his emotional bride has been torn from his arms to become a cosmic force, albeit its lowest, the moon. His middle period, the manic elation of marriage, the sober pressures of family bond, had been a struggle to exorcise the drama of courtly love, establish a tangible immediacy with his bride. It has been torn now. Against his will and strength, as he leaves her, she rises to a psychic plateau. He is not simply traveling away from his bride; she is sliding back, away, to the cosmos of his innermost forces.

His cluster of late, rueful love lyrics, to the Countess of Bedford, Mrs. Herbert, or whoever, have a strange tonality of emptiness, a mannerist vacuum, a hint here and there of sentimentality, however aesthetically tight. In "Twicknam Garden," the speaker, having been honestly jilted, at once plays Christ and serpent, a scarred refugee in the Garden of Eden, and a depraved fountain of grace. Whatever its sincerity, the poem overflows with a permissiveness of hurt symbols. So, in "The Will," he abruptly terminates a complacent dying, a sweet sorrow sure to last beyond tomorrow. "The Funerall" ends in a pique of pointless revenge, "The Will" on another pique of frustration. He is at loose ends. The alter ego of these poems is a lady he does not know what to do with.

"A Nocturnall upon S. Lucies Day" advances a notch beyond "A Valediction: of Weeping." Its beloved splits into Lucie and his shadowy companion; its globe, a bubble, a tear, an undefined nothing, hardens into a dead, heavy hulk; its perilous equilibrium collapses into "absence, darknesse, death; things which are not" (l. 17), its "more than Moone" expands into the capacious, undefined light of heaven, faintly suggesting a womb. "Her Vigill, and her Eve" (l. 44) echoes, an awed boy, reverent perhaps for the Virgin Mary of his abandoned Catholic faith. So "her Eve" recalls Biblical Eve, created afresh from her husband's body without competitor or Oedipal bar. The woman is becoming mythic, primordial, the female component in his universe.

Indeed, for all the formal structural explication of *Anniversaries* in Louis Martz' *The Poetry of Meditation* (New Haven: Yale University Press, 1954), the personal factor of Elizabeth Drury remains with us, however far this overburdened father is from an adolescent stranger, already passed away; for the female figure has been steadily elevated and distanced, from "more than Moone" to a cosmic light, his alter ego thinned, blurred, and expanded. Elizabeth Drury is, loosely, a parallel to Lucy, a springboard for a fresh undertaking of spirit. Far from the stranger, Elizabeth Drury, surprising us as triggering a major statement, we suspect a more personal alter ego would have been intolerable. The poet was marshalling his ego for other things.

The introductory gesture of "The First Anniversary" demands participation of soul, not contemplation, withdrawal, or humble passivity:

> For who is sure he hath a Soule, unlesse
> It see, and judge, and follow worthinesse,
> And by Deedes praise it?
>
> (ll. 3–5)

This strenuous Protestant attitude, that a soul must "see . . . judge . . . follow worthinesse . . . by Deedes praise it," recalls the later Milton. So "Negative Love" satirizes ineffable attributes as complacent and self-deceiving. So, in "The Extasie," Donne celebrated "that subtile knot, which makes us man," the knotting of one bond of experience. Donne alludes to both poems when he continues:

> hee who doth not this,
> May lodge an In-mate soule, but 'tis not his.
>
> (ll. 5–6)

The soul is an alien lodger until knotted in sight, judgment, noble ideals, and worthy deeds.

This strenuous human model, the integration of Donne's middle period, is here relegated to Queen Elizabeth, whose opening death foreshadows that of Elizabeth Drury, like Lucie and the unnamed companion in "A Nocturnall"; but here, the earthly woman prepares for the female principle of creation. The strenuous human model is clearly to be admired, but also transcended:

> Her death did wound and tame thee than, and than
> Thou might'st have better spar'd the Sunne, or Man.
>
> (ll. 25–26)

But for what? A Platonic world of ideas? A Beatrice over a Martha, visionary contemplative over patient selflessness in good works? With enormous negative capability, the poem confines itself to the exercises of meditation, to survey the world, and redirect the human spirit. Its goals will emerge elsewhere.

The shift from Elizabeth Tudor to Elizabeth Drury is from the ways of the earth, its worldly processes to be shed. A monochrome of dying replaces high, restless aspiration. Worldly vision grays to the lees of life. The earthly queen rises to a heaven of order, creativity, courtesy, and music, with "Quire and Song," from a purposeless constancy of dying:

> This World, in that great earthquake languished;
> For in a common bath of teares it bled,
> Which drew the strongest vitall spirits out:
>
> (ll. 11–13)

This theme of the waning of life on earth, universal decay, the decline from the Golden Age, was common to the Seventeeth Century. Donne's treatment here is instructive, because of his rare attempt at the impersonal depiction of a historic process, as is called for here. His method is fascinating for its failures as for its successes. The Seventeeth Century master in unfolding a historic process is Milton, whose panorama of creation in *Paradise Lost* is large, sensuous, and overwhelming as a Rubens canvas. This was Milton's life-long struggle, to master the scene, objectify his mind, work his language into the interior of process until he could engulf and articulate all creation. He then unrolled a vast epic tapestry, even bewilderment, even tearing ignorance blended and rewoven into the web of experience.

Donne attempts here such a panorama. It does not work for reasons that lie in the peculiar bent of metaphysical poetry. Yet Donne's depiction is large enough:

> There is not now that mankinde, which was then,
> When, as, the Sunne and man did seeme to strive,
> (Joynt tenants of the world) who should survive;
> When, Stagge, and Raven, and the long-liv'd tree,
> Compar'd with man, dy'd in minoritie;
> When, if a slow pac'd starre had stolne away
> From the observers marking, he might stay
> Two or three hundred yeares to see't again,
> And then make up his observation plaine;
> When, as the age was long, the sise was great;
> Mans growth confess'd, and recompenc'd the meat;
> So spacious and large, that every Soule
> Did a faire Kingdome, and large Realme controule:
> And when the very stature, thus erect,

> Did that soule a good way towards heaven direct.
> Where is this mankinde now?
>
> (ll. 112–127)

It is clear that the creative mind here is fundamentally different. From the start, however instant the grasp of scene, it takes place inside the mind, in the process of noting it. Its conflicts are not woven in a large, vivid tapestry, but delivered in a series of prickly alternatives, sudden stabs of surprise, mild metaphysical shudders. Thus, the struggle for survival takes place, not in actuality, but inside the minds of the sun and man. The stag, raven, and long-lived tree are not seen as a simple experience but couched in a comparison of their longevity. We do not stand witness, waiting for the star to reappear, but focus on the mind of a long-lived man who observes it. Lines 121–122 depict nothing, but neatly summarize, introducing the greater amplitude of lines 123–126, where again we are inside a man's spirit, growing toward heaven. Evidently, some catch of inhibition confined Donne to the drama of spirit, even when a simple panoramic depiction seemed called for.

The lapse here cannot simply be laid to the poet's peculiarity of talent. "The Storme," "The Calme" unfold a magnificent panorama, though as a simple journal. The lapse from these to "The First Anniversary" is a shrinkage of attention from the outer world to the level of spirit. Donne is now like a recluse who does not readily traverse the jostling marketplace. He will take to hand only the material of the spirit.

This same withdrawal from immediacy clarifies Donne's treatment of the large wound of creation, so knowledgeable in grasp and detail. Thus Elizabeth Drury represents the animating spirit or soul of the world. Her death reduces the world to an idiot, a shell, a clod:

> Her death did wound and tame thee than, and than
> Thou might'st have better spar'd the Sunne, or Man.
> That wound was deep, but 'tis more misery,
> That thou hast lost thy sense and memory.
> 'Twas heavy then to heare thy voyce of mone,
> But this is worse, that thou art speechlesse growne,
> Thou hast forgot thy name, thou hadst; thou wast

> Nothing but shee, and her thou hast o'rpast. . . .
> Her name defin'd thee, gave thee forme, and frame,
> And thou forgett'st to celebrate thy name.
>
> (ll. 25–38)

The passage so strikingly parallels the fall in *Paradise Lost*, that the two passages might be considered together for threads of contrast:

> So saying, her rash hand in evil hour
> Forth reaching to the Fruite, she pluck'd, she eat:
> Earth felt the wound, and Nature from her seat
> Sighing through all her Works gave signs of woe,
> That all was lost. . . .
> Earth trembl'd from her entrails, as again
> In pangs, and Nature gave a second groan,
> Skie lowr'd, and muttering Thunder, some sad drops
> Wept at completing of the mortal Sin
> Original.
>
> (IX. 780–784, 1000–1004)

Again, Donne's heroic couplets do not measure up to Milton, reading as neat contrasts and balances alongside Milton's simple, masterly blank verse. Donne's lines are not a depiction, but an address to the earth in its loss, a diagnosis and catalogue of its failings; but we remain outside, eavesdroppers to this dialogue. Milton's process of loss seems simpler and less detailed. A vast, flawless organism suffers enormous pain receiving a wound, sighs, trembles, and groans; but the phrase, "all was lost," looms ambiguously. What exactly was lost?—perfection? And why is perfection "all"?—spiritual grace? Is nature then in some sense depraved? The concept is too terrifyingly threatening to be grasped all at once. The phrase is less an explanation than a shift in process, a seed of uneasiness planted in the world. So the incidents of carnivorous animals follow, of irregular seasons, decay, all spelling out the fall as an imbecilization of nature, a shuddering step toward a mechanical existence on losing the shaping will of God. Its lost "all" is its soul.

The same imbecilization of nature, Shakespeare expressed in Ulysses' speech on order in *Troilus and Cressida:*

> The heavens themselves, the planets, and this centre,
> Observe degree, priority, and place,
> Insisture, course, proportion, season, form,
> Office, and custom, in all line of order;
> And therefore is the glorious planet Sol
> In noble eminence enthroned and sphered
> Amidst the others; whose medicinable eye
> Corrects the influence of evil planets,
> And posts, like the commandments of a king,
> Sans check to good or bad. But when the planets
> In evil mixture to disorder wander,
> What plagues and what portents, what mutiny,
> What raging of the sea, shaking of earth,
> Commotion in the winds, frights, changes, horrors,
> Divert and crack, rend and deracinate
> The unity and married calm of states
> Quite from their fixure!
>
> (I. iii. 85–101)

Here, too, is depicted the myth of the fall from an inherent ideal order, obedience, propriety, though here an ideal final cause was never palpable. The discipline is tight. The "medicinable eye" of the sun corrects "evil planets" in their wayward impulses. The fall has no moral overtones. The "medicinable eye" qualifies the mode of evil of the evil planets as a lack of control. Shakespeare's universe here is from the first morally imbecilic. The fall is not from any inherent malevolence, but a bad coincidence of evil planets, giving them the force to upset order, "when the planets/In evil mixture to disorder wander." The evil lies in the mixture, a bad throw of the planets, causing disorder. The earliest of our three poets, Shakespeare was yet the most radical. The lost "all" of nature, its lost soul, was already a given whose consequences he pursued.

We should not deceive ourselves on this subject. The master writers of this period knew very well these formidable changes in the grasp of reality. They sensed the implications in their stomachs, and pursued them each by his bent. Donne in the *Anniversaries*, Milton in *Paradise Lost*, and Shakespeare in *Troilus and Cressida*, all articulated the sudden imbecilization of nature. All three express a controlled, portentious terror, a maculation, a sense of good and feeling nature lobotomized. Its fullest documentation fills the remainder of "The First Anniversary":

> And new Philosophy calls all in doubt
> The Element of fire is quite put out;
> The Sun is lost, and th'earth, and no man's wit
> Can well direct him where to looke for it.
> And freely men confesse that this world's spent,
> When in the Planets, and the Firmament
> They seeke so many new; they see that this
> Is crumbled out againe to his Atomies.
> 'Tis all in peeces, all cohaerence gone;
> All just supply, and all Relation:
>
> (ll. 205–214)

Shakespeare, the earliest and least learned, grasped it in one large vision; Milton moralized and absorbed it into his myth of historic process; Donne documented it with obsessive acumen. To all three, the world has lost its soul.

But parallel as are their statements of loss, they differ vastly in their grasp of consequences. Here, unfortunately, Donne is the least interesting. The interaction of man and nature as one is so complete in *Troilus and Cressida*, the play becomes a black comedy. As nature has grown imbecilic, so man and the processes of history. The speech on order interweaves details on government and family life with natural disorder. So time is loosely a synonym for the processes of society and history:

> Time hath, my lord, a wallet at his back
> Wherein he puts alms for oblivion,
> A great-siz'd monster of ingratitude.
> Those scraps are good deeds past, which are devoured
> As fast as they are made, forgot as soon
> As done . . . to have done, is to hang
> Quite out of fashion, like a rusty mail
> In monumental mockery. . . .
> For Time is like a fashionable host
> That slightly shakes his parting guest by th'hand
> And, with his arms outstretched as he would fly,
> Grasps in the comer: welcome ever smiles,
> And farewell goes out sighing.
>
> (III. iii. 145–169)

Shakespeare, the least formally trained of the three, most searchingly explored implications in man and nature, taking the given as a point of departure. Milton retrenched in a simple, but enormously cathartic gesture. Nature became a botched wilderness, with brutalized habits, except as man tamed and harnessed it. Only the solitary moralist, here, there, refashioned a "paradise within" in reverence and obedience to God's will. This somehow recapitulates the progress of individual life, secular or religious, the loss of innocence and establishment of solitary adult responsibility and fulfilment. Whatever their differences, Milton and Shakespeare both fixed attention on this world, imaginatively inhabited, and came to terms with reality, however imbecilic.

Donne did not. His elaborate diagnosis of the breakdown leads us astray, if it suggests a sense of some new order, coming into being to replace it. Donne suggested none whatever. The old order, now so unsatisfactory, retains what shabby precision it has left by the faint imprint of the old soul, the last glimmerings of the memory of Elizabeth Drury:

> For there's a kind of World remaining still,
> Though shee which did inanimate and fill
> The world, be gone, yet in this last long night,
> Her Ghost doth walke; that is, a glimmering light,
> A faint weake love of vertue, and of good,
> Reflects from her, on them which understood
> Her worth; and though she have shut in all day,
> The twilight of her memory doth stay;
> Which, from the carcasse of the old world, free,
> Creates a new world, and new creatures bee
> Produc'd: the matter and the stuffe of this,
> Her vertue, and the forme our practice is:
>
> (ll. 67–78)

There is no hint of any emerging new world. An uncompromising dualist, even after the loss of Elizabeth Drury, Donne saw the world held together only by the walking of her ghost. Both Shakespeare and Milton always maintained a bridge to reality; but things bored Donne, offended him, made him anxious. His solitary path was not to find order, which he regarded as an arbitrary given, a construct, but to attain a great encounter of spirit. His ardor was visible and constant. The documentation of decay in "The First Anniversary" is no truth hammered out for its own sake, but a refrain in counterpoint to the repeated cry of sorrow:

> Shee, shee is dead; shee's dead: when thou knowest this,
> Thou knowest how poore a trifling thing man is.
>
> (ll. 183–184)
>
> Shee, shee is dead, shee's dead: when thou knowst this,
> Thou knowst how lame a cripple this world is.
>
> (ll. 237–238)
>
> Shee, shee is dead, shee's dead: when thou knowst this,
> Thou knowst how ugly a monster this world is.
>
> (ll. 325–326)
>
> Shee, shee, is dead; shee's dead: when thou know'st this,
> Thou knowst how wan a Ghost this our world is.
>
> (ll. 369–370)
>
> Shee, shee is dead; shee's dead; when thou knowst this,
> Thou knowst how drie a Cinder this world is.
>
> (ll. 427–428)

The imbecilic world gives point to the threnody of pain at its loss of soul. It serves to establish that his encounter of spirit lay not in this world. Then so much for this world! He would find his place with God.

"The Second Anniversary" traces out the consequences in the pilgrimage of the soul to heaven. Its dualism is radical, as spirit sloughs off body. Donne documents the ignorance of his time (ll. 255–280), not to clear ground for a grasp of truth in this world, but to shrug off this world and arrive at truth in heaven:

> When wilt thou shake off this Pedantery,
> Of being taught by sense, and Fantasie?
> Thou look'st through spectacles; small things seeme great
> Below; But up unto the watch-towre get,
> And see all things despoyl'd of fallacies:
> Thou shalt not peepe through lattices of eyes,
> Nor heare through Labyrinths of eares, nor learne
> By circuit, or collections to discerne.
> In heaven, thou straight know'st all, concerning it,
> And what concerns it not, shalt straight forget.
>
> (ll. 291–300)

The elevation from the senses to a grasp of spirit recalls "The Extasie," where no unifying insight was possible until an ecstasy of insight of the detached soul. So her "lattices of eyes" and "Labyrinths of eares," warp all discernment; but heaven offers luminous knowledge. But this is now only a way-station to another, higher knowledge:

> She who in th'art of knowing Heaven, was growne
> Here upon earth, to such perfection,
> That she hath, ever since to Heaven she came,
> (In a far fairer print,) but read the same:
> Shee, shee not satisfied with all this waight,
> (For so much knowledge, as would over-fraight
> Another, did but ballast her) is gone
> As well t'enjoy, as get perfection.
> And cals us after her, in that shee tooke,
> (Taking her selfe) our best, and worthiest booke.
> (ll. 311–320)

We sense here a stirring of spirit (alongside it, the previous passage is almost pedestrian), an impatience with earthly knowledge, "all this waight," a concentration of truth in the texture of a radiant soul, "(Taking her selfe) our best, and worthiest booke," an urgency to get to heaven, bring others to heaven, be heaven herself, its map and blueprint.

So his establishment of the unity of flesh and sensibility, a passage widely quoted as emblematic of the metaphysical sensibility, establishes no fusion of body and spirit at all, but an airy and exotic conceit:

> . . . her pure, and eloquent blood
> Spoke in her cheekes, and so distinctly wrought,
> That one might almost say, her body thought . . .
> (ll. 244–246)

This is not the human condition at its finest—that equilibrium of wholeness was long over. It is rather an extravagant compliment to Elizabeth Drury, for suffusing her body though alien to her spirit:

> Look upward; that's towards her, whose happy state
> We now lament not, but congratulate.
> Shee, to whom all this world was but a stage . . .
> (ll. 65–68)

The "subtile knot" has proven counterfeit. The human condition is in its denial, the temporary imprisonment of soul in alien body:

> . . . slow-pac'd snailes who crawle upon
> Our prisons prison, earth, nor thinke us well,
> Longer, then whil'st wee beare our brittle shell.
> (ll. 248–250)

The progress of the soul is no philosophical quest. Donne's neo-Platonic period, to whatever extent he engaged in it, is over. The poem is pietistic and exhortatory. There are no way-stations, no plateaus, no successive arrivals, stages of preparations for a mystical truth. The poem is a sermon. It maps out nothing. It only vicariously follows the soul to heaven, breathless with relief, its joys increasing, until its intimate arrival at its home with God.

# *Part V*

# *The Religious Poems*

# 14

# The Early Devotions

As the female figure thinned to insubstantiality in his late love lyrics, Donne began sketching a context in "La Corona," and "The Crosse," for a fresh alter ego in God. The two movements overlap. In both, there is the same hesitation on an object, the same way-station, or limited circle of devotion; but the early devotions are without the mannerist ambiguity of the late love lyrics. Following the tradition of *imitatio dei*, the speaker muffles his presence. In "La Corona," each sonnet begins as the last ended. "The Crosse" finds crosses everywhere. Like nets without a fish, these poems shuttle about, weaving a crown, enmeshing a landscape with crosses, devotions too closely threaded for any escape, though the catch is yet to come.

"La Corona" is a hymn of the twice-born, with an induction of prayer, five sonnets on the life of Christ, three, "Annunciation," "Nativitie," and "Temple," of his conception, his birth in a manger, and his first task in the Temple, then two, "Crucifying" and "Resurrection," depicting his close of life, then a closing prayer, "Ascention." The middle five sonnets hang in a delicate equilibrium of three against two; yet the closing sonnet, uniting the speaker with Christ, reestablishes three against three, as he and Christ rise together, fused in glory.

The narrative sonnets celebrate Christ's birth and his ascent into heaven. The experience of dying is exceedingly muted. "Crucifying" avoids the agony depicted in "Goodfriday, 1613. Riding Westward." Its dying is rather a tight constriction, to a fate, a span, an inch, a settling into position before a rebirth into magnificence:

> . . . the immaculate,
> Whose creature Fate is, now prescribe a Fate,
> Measuring selfe-lifes infinity to'a span,
> Nay to an inch. Loe, where condemned hee
> Beares his own crosse, with paine, yet by and by
> When it beares him, he must beare more and die.
>
> (ll. 6–11)

Hence the hushed exaltation throughout, soft pastel colors, on pale gray, washes of rose, flecks of bay green, one spot of blood red, the pale blues of glory. As we circle the seven jewels of the crown of God, the air has the suspense of innocence, of hushed, lyric exaltation, such exaltation as Dante might breathe beginning the *Paradiso*, with depravity washed away, salvation not yet sweeping about him. As Christ was twice born; so the speaker will rise, exalted, singing in heaven his "crowne of prayer and praise."

The opening sonnet is a still-life of crowns, its action a tapestry of coronations. From Donne's pen, the theme is portentious. In "The Sunne Rising," his supreme self-affirmation, the speaker crowned himself:

> She'is all States, and all Princes, I,
> Nothing else is.
> Princes doe but play us; compar'd to this,
> All honour's mimique; All wealth alchimie.
>
> (ll. 21–24)

In "La Corona," he ceremoniously crowns the brow of Christ. But this is Donne's own third coronation. First he made the state his unquestioned monarch, he its instrument and servant, leaving family and church. His marriage, a second self-coronation, terminated his regular service to the state. Now, making Christ his king, he offered a coronation of prayer and praise against a crown of thorns and of glory; as he, his early crown only thorns, hopes for a new "crowne of Glory, which doth flower alwayes" (1. 8). So everywhere crowns pale behind crowns. The end of everything is its crown. All life, motion, and endeavor seeks to attain its crown; and God is the ultimate crown of the lesser coronations:

> The ends crowne our workes, but thou crown'st our ends. (l. 9)

Against this tapestry stand two characters, the speaker, "in my low devout melancholie," and Christ, the treasury of good, "All changing unchang'd Antient of dayes." Their relationship is a balance of opposites. On the one hand, they stand in stark contrast, he low, small, destitute of good, melancholy of joy, a fleck of existence, Christ the possessor and embodiment of good, the prime mover, "changing unchang'd," "Antient of dayes," commander of time and the order of existence. So his offered crown "of prayer and praise" is an embarrassment of superfluity, words from a fleck of creation to the source of all salvation. And yet the speaker would be one with Christ in his crown of glory.

This union and opposition hangs in the pleasure of God, whose grace passes all understanding. The opening verb, "Deigne," suggests the prayer of a liege servant; yet he would legitimate and crown his lord. So, in the second quatrain, a liege fitly rewarded by a "vile crowne of fraile bayes" would share the eternal crown of glory. Indeed, the man's purpose grows increasingly brash. The first quatrain, diffident, reverential, asks only to offer a crown of prayer; the second demands the crown of glory as a reward. So all human purposes, however artless, smack with presumption; all seeming generosities mask naked self-interest.

The sestet would resolve this dilemma by "The ends crowne our workes, but thou crown'st our ends." Whatever our crippling depravity, our final goal is God's purpose. Let us but have the grace to move, let the veil, the catch, the clog be lifted; and all ends are finally the ends of God, all gestures the gestures of salvation:

> 'Tis time that heart and voice be lifted high,
> *Salvation to all that will is nigh.* (ll. 13–14)

Beginning a sonnet with the last line of the previous sonnet comes here with a tightening of emphasis, a sense of dramatic arrival. "La Corona" has a strange double motion: weaving a crown of prayer, it shuttles back and forth in selfless adoration; and yet its every gesture filters through hesitations, harmonizes and meshes its allusions to a purpose. So, by the strange mode of dialogue in this sonnet sequence, the speaker and Christ have the closest harmony, but no confrontation whatever. Christ is rather evoked with an easy buoyance, and the speaker brought into focus with him, like an initiate in ballet. There is thus a sinking of arrival, a falling into dramatic place from sonnet to sonnet. So here, at the end of Sonnet 1, the line, "Salvation to all that will is nigh" is a generalized call to exultation. In Sonnet 2, it narrows to the arrival of Christ in her womb by Mary, at the moment of annunciation.

The evocation of Mary here differs from the late love poems. In "A Valediction: of weeping" and "A nocturnall upon S. Lucies day," the speaker struggles with mixed success to confront a quasi-angelic woman. Here, Mary is an object of identification, not an alter ego. He stirs to follow, imitate, become a part of God, and identifies with Mary as containing in her womb the divine word made flesh. So he would embody Christ, be the divine made flesh. Indeed, the female identification comes here with no catch of uneasiness whatever. The speaker would use any metaphor, any figure that might bring a more meaningful relationship with God.

Hence the poetic tone of "Annunciation." The episode is deliberately blurred, with no sense of time, place, or appearance, only its inwardness. So Mary's possible emotions are avoided; he wishes to reverberate with the import of the event, not its drama. The repeated "thou . . . thou . . . thou . . . thou" ambiguously addresses Mary or his own spirit; as the speaker seeks to imitate her sluggish fertility, roll with her gesture, conceive with her conception:

> Ere by the spheares time was created, thou
> Wast in his minde, who is thy Sonne, and Brother,
> Whom thou conceiv'st, conceiv'd; yea thou art now
> Thy Makers maker, and thy Fathers mother;
> Thou'hast light in darke; and shutst in little room,
> *Immensity cloysterd in thy deare wombe.*
>
> (ll. 9–14)

Sonnet 3, "Nativitie," continues the mood of subdued receptivity of "Annunciation." Its nativity scene is suggested without vivid detail, only a quiet naming of the elements, "th'Inne . . . this stall . . . Starres . . . wisemen." The mood is of muffled disquiet, not of glory. Question follows question, not to give information, but to harmonize the anxieties of the reader with scene, engage him until he joins in the softest of prayers:

> Kisse him, and with him into Egypt goe,
> *With his kinde mother, who partakes thy woe.*
> (ll. 13–14)

The transition to Sonnet 3 again brings the sense of slipping closer to the core of existence. The closing line of Stanza 2, "*Immensity cloysterd in thy deare wombe*," is addressed to Mary, the immensity a ponderous, but alien presence in the cloister of her belly. In Stanza 3, "thy" still refers to Mary; but "immensity" has shifted and enlarged to the subject of the sentence. So, as by a gravitation, the reader slips toward religious substance.

The effortless flow of Sonnet 1 is now over. Questions skip about, as the witness identifies everywhere in the scene, with Jesus in the manger, "But Oh, for thee, for him, hath th'Inne no roome?" (l. 5) in the next line with Mary, caring for him, three lines later with the shepherds and magi, gathered in contemplation (ll. 9–10), then with all mankind by original sin (ll. 11–12). As in a hall of mirrors, the reader sees himself everywhere, until he will go into Egypt with Christ under the aura of Mary, who shares his woes.

Such poetry hangs in subdued transparency. Its lines flow in, out, and about the scene, at the manger, over the Middle East, with stars and wise-men, across a wash of days, among piteous mankind, hungering for a mother. So a subdued pity and concern is released for a fragile valuable, easily lost. The pangs of pity in the manger (l. 5) touch off a more general pity for God's restraint (l. 10). God's pity for man, twice repeated (ll. 11–12), evoke ours to go with him into Egypt, like power in a battery, flicking between opposite poles.

And again, the transition line opens a portal for us, draws

us deeper into the scene. In Stanza 3, the line is general to anyone, to share care and responsibility with Mary, "*With his kinde mother, who partakes thy woe.*" In Sonnet 4, the line belongs to Joseph, who stands in the midst of the scene, careful, concerned, helpless. The marvel in Sonnet 4, "Temple," is the marvel of manhood. Joseph, earthly man, stands in marvel at divine man, his son and full of grace. Indeed, the question, "whence comes it?" has a subdued transparency. Who asks it?—Joseph?—the reader of the poem? Indeed, what is Joseph, awkwardly a father and not a father? But the reader filters through Joseph onto the birth of grace, his, yet outside him, divine, yet manly, ripe human experience outside of time. So the reader absorbs the scene. It happens. God's work is under way.

More traditional than Milton, and radically dualistic, grace concerned Donne more than works. Hence his choice of verbs:

> Blowing, yea blowing out those sparks of wit,
> Which himselfe on those Doctors did bestow . . .
>
> (ll. 3–4)

A newborn baby, frothing at the mouth, confounds the Temple, blowing sparks of wit. So radical innocence, the self-sufficient Word, gallops into being:

> The Word but lately could not speake, and loe
> It sodenly speakes wonders . . .
>
> (ll. 5–6)

All of "La Corona" is a pageant of birth. So the divine word is here born. Indeed, as Sonnet 1 weaves coronations; so all of "La Corona" is a tapestry of births, Christ on earth, Christ in glory, the speaker, the inspired Word, the "strong Ramme" and "Mild lambe" in exalted tapestry. Indeed, the subdued gentleness of the sequence, its pastel colors and muffled slippage from sonnet to sonnet, weaving a crown, all have the texture of fantasy, that the birth of spirit is without pain, grace delivered in subdued exaltation.

The sestet answers the question, "Whence comes it" (l. 6) in two negatives. Christ's manhood was manly, not simply divine; yet it escaped the passage of time, power instantly marshaled for extraordinary business. By contrast, Milton depicted in *Paradise Regained* a series of foreordained tests, to establish the straits of manhood. A child, sitting, "Blowing, yea blowing out those sparks of wit" would ill suit Milton. But Donne conceived of radical innocence, arbitrary, decisive grace, from which the work of life then flowed.

The transition to Sonnet 5, "Crucifying," is again a slippage toward the center of godhead. Closing Sonnet 4, "*By miracles exceeding power of man*," touches on Christ's career, alluding to distant miracles. The same line in Sonnet 5 has manifest miracles in the midst of a short, stormy life of faith, envy, affection, and murderous hate. The first, key verb, delayed for emphasis to the end of line 2, is "begat." So Christ works to beget grace; as "Blowing, yea blowing," in Sonnet 4, begat the Word.

In the second quatrain of "Crucifying," the evil impulse, the manifestation of pride, is not to harm or cause pain, but to reverse dominance, maculate the immaculate, prescribe fate to its master, pin down infinity to a span, an inch. The intent is not murder nor crippling, but a strict constraint. The evil want God pinched, limited, to establish rebirth and immortality as the idea of an overreacher. They doubt God's fecundity, and would define His place, absorb the reader by an awesome fascination:

> But Oh! the worst are most, they will and can,
> Alas, and do, unto the immaculate . . .
>
> (ll. 5–6)

So sluggish apathy contrains the reader, unable to move about in grace.

The sestet slips us again from the periphery toward the center of holiness: "Loe, where the condemned hee/ Beares his own crosse." Constant is the sense of constriction, of sluggish flesh. The commas come as irregular, heavy steps and pauses:

> Beares his owne crosse, with pain, yet by and by
> When it beares him, he must beare more and die.
>
> (ll. 10–11)

Christ's exertion was the exertion of the poem. It comes to a standstill after line 11, while the body is hoisted onto the cross. In line 12, with Christ on the cross, we sense ourselves at one with him in his sluggish freight of death. As he was lifted onto the cross, we would be lifted after:

> Now thou art lifted up, draw mee to thee . . .
>
> (l. 12)

The last exertion of the poem is the oozing of a drop of blood from Christ' body onto his dry soul.

The prayer closing Sonnet 5, "*Moyst, with one drop of thy blood, my dry soule*," becomes a reality in Sonnet 6, "Resurrection"; as "moyst" changes from a verb to an adjective. Until Sonnet 7, the speaker hangs in exceeding quiet in a twilight between grace and glory, the blessing and the seal, crucifixion and resurrection, a suspense of patience and prayer before "the last, and everlasting day."

The repetition that begins Sonnet 7, "Ascention," again slips toward holiness. "Salute," at the end of "Resurrection," is subjunctive, praying for an unsure event. In "Ascention," it is an imperative that lovingly bullies the sluggish for not grasping a reality already there. It jostles them to look up, cudgels them into participation by imitation. In Sonnet 5, Christ sluggishly bore his cross, then was lifted as an inert body. In Sonnet 7, he is the model of the vigor to soar:

> Nor doth hee by ascending, show alone,
> But first hee, and hee first enters the way.
>
> (ll. 7–8)

In the octave, he exhorts the human masses to join in the resurrection. In the sestet, he becomes their collective voice, addressing heaven with a marching beat, "strong Ramme . . . Mild lambe . . . Bright torch." He is now again astir. As angry soldiers once hoisted Christ's body to a death; so his muse raises the Holy Spirit to life (l. 13). So the opening prayer ineluctibly returns, but now as the joyous hymn of an equal:

> *Deigne at my hands this crowne of prayer and praise.*

So "La Corona" is a formalized prayer, inching forward with subtle shifts of meaning, a string of poetic beads, a closed double circle of constriction and release, limit and rebirth, Christ and the reader. Missing is only the ego and body of the speaker, his hot mistrust, constricted to an episode. Muted in a suspense of silence, he draws a circle of religious experience in prayerful monotone, a world of values he will soon enter.

So "The Crosse" projects the emblem of Christ, the cross, but not his figure and life. Its opening lines are a formal exhortation, advanced in four couplet questions:

> Since Christ embrac'd the Crosse it selfe, dare I
> His image, th'image of his Crosse deny?
> Would I have profit by the sacrifice,
> And dare the chosen Altar to despise?
> It bore all other sinnes, but is it fit
> That it should beare the sinne of scorning it?
> Who from the picture would avert his eye,
> How would he flye his paines, who there did dye?
>
> (ll. 1–8)

This progression could have any order. It is hortatory, not informative, to jostle the reader's lethargy, with increased emotional impact, tangle him to confront his own inadequacy, the cross he scorns, Christ in pain.

By line 8, the cross has registered. He then internalizes it until he himself takes its form:

> Who can deny mee power, and liberty
> To stretch mine armes, and mine owne Crosse to be?
>
> (ll. 17–18)

He now sees crosses everywhere, in nature, marine travel, astronomy, human behavior, in sickness and health. The process of transmutation is like a "dissolve" in the cinema, where one scene becomes an entirely different scene. So all reality becomes a construct of crosses. Indeed, the fixity sticks the image to its beholder and absorbs him:

> For when that Crosse ungrudg'd, unto you stickes,
> Then are you to your selfe, a Crucifixe.
>
> (ll. 31–32)

This process, if a meditation, is not successful. Its simple-minded dissolve leads to nothing. The opening four exhortatory questions do link the cross to Jesus; but thereafter, Jesus simply disappears from the poem. Far from expressing any grasp of God's presence, the crosses steadily thicken like a fetish. Brute reality seems fading and coagulating into emblems in Donne's poems. Here the entire poem is such a process; but the emblem has no reverberations other than those the reader brings to it. The poem is an extended trigger.

The obsession increases, and soon goes against the grain of nature, attacks its flank, cancels it out. Soon carving a cross only uncovers the cross already there (ll. 33–34). Inside a person, the cross replaces Christ's image (ll. 35–36), making divine experience imbecilic. The cross crosses or cancels out human nature (ll. 41–42), also the senses, for avoiding "Harsh, hard, sowre, stinking" (l. 47). Heart is made inert, as are strong feeling, wit, active intelligence, selfhood, even the human ego. St. John of the Cross prescribed such a systematic dismantling of selfhood; but the process here is more pathetic. St. John of the Cross fully grasped what selfhood was, physically, emotionally, intellectually, and carefully evacuated his selfhood to allow a divine seizure. Here, Donne simply locks himself in a symbol, ticking off the factors that cease to function. Indeed, the final symbol of a cross is a grave-marker. There is even irrelevant black humor in his sardonic closing reference to children, considering the burden of Donne's own children:

> That Crosses children, which our Crosses are.
>
> (l. 64)

This is a strange moment in creativity, a ticking off of effects that are finally a negation. So, hanging between a wrecked career and another as yet indifferent, Donne plays with an image with the congealed automatism of lifeless allegory. A fanatic without a cause, he hangs strangely free; an impassioned lyricist, he has no body to celebrate. A dualist, his earthly self crossed out, trammeled in a shell of crosses and contradictions, he would open to another world, but nothing as yet opens; he readies himself, but nothing happens. Eerily at rest, he flutters across a landscape of crosses, and finds only more on the horizon.

# 15

# Holy Sonnets: 1

The first six *Holy Sonnets* in Helen Gardner's edition, numbers II, IV, VI, VII, IX, and X in Grierson's edition, meditate on death and divine judgment. Immediate, difficult situations fill *Songs and Sonnets* that the speaker comes to terms with; here, wallowing in a purposeless chaos, he struggles to define some future he is helpless to control. "La Corona" moved steadily forward, maintaining a subdued, silver clarity; these sonnets thrash about in arbitrary lunges. Judgment day, animal ethics, menacing death loom up, then slide into gray unawareness. Amorphous presences flare up and sink in acquiescence; God, demons, the flesh, the earth, churn in turbulent, unreal fury.

The speaker here is ego and object, plaintiff and disputed property. Nothing meshes, not his energies nor his trust in God; as he tries legal postures, pleas, confessions, cries of outrage, confrontations. This is not Gerard Manley Hopkins territory. Its landscape is more hollow, ghostly, confused, with forbidden ideas to be floundered in, and no sure footing; yet there is something of the same sense of inscape. Helpless in his sinful condition, the speaker prays without a will for grace, projects visions not knowing who listens to his prayers. These sonnets flare into speech, then fall arbitrarily, with fitful clarity. Their "I" is a balloon cut loose, impulsive, dutiful, persuaded of guilt, vaguely restless but ignorant of itself. Yet with each false start, a twinge of reality jars it toward a slightly more honest direction, attuned to the will of God.

Sonnet 1 begins, offering a legal settlement on grounds spelled out through the octave:

> As due by many titles I resigne
> My selfe to thee, O God . . .

But this "I" and "selfe" are not the same. The "I" keeps itself carefully defined; the "selfe" is a piece of unknown property, at most registered in an attorney's office. Serving as legal guardian, the subject, the I, surrenders itself to God, the passive receiver. Knowledgable, responsible, it then defines impeccable grounds. God made the self for His ends, then redeemed it, His son, His servant, His sheep, His image, once temple of His spirit. Thus a respectful litigant offers a trim, final settlement of a messy legal tangle.

Two stark, formal questions, end-stopped in lines 9 and 10, present the antithesis. The offer is impossible; the devil has already usurped the self; the "I" is a presumptuous poseur.

The closing four-line synthesis then tacitly drops the offer, and prays to God to rise and overcome the devil; yet a resentful grumble emerges that Satan's hate may win over the love of God. So the opening legalistic clarity ends as a whimper at being rejected unfairly. This huff of dissatisfaction still cannot pray; but progress has been made. At least, God is now the subject, the speaker a passive acquiescent.

The poem has a highly formal relationship between the speaker, God, and the devil, under a dominant legal metaphor, with landed property and usurpation. It opens with a formal presentation, the speaker acting as a proper agent. Exposed as usurped property, not an agent, he then prays to God to act as agent and redeem him from usurpation. Through this metaphor of property echoes the doctrine of original sin; sin, like property, can be passed from generation to generation automatically.

But behind this legal metaphor stand other relationships to God of greater intimacy, that make it a formal façade; thus, a family metaphor stands behind it, that appears and disappears in double focus throughout the poem. Thus, in the line—"Why doth he steale, nay ravish that's thy right?"—"steale" refers to man as usurped property. But what of the second verb, "ravish?" Is it still property, stolen and also damaged in theft? Or is this family now, not theft and property injury, but rape and enforced adultery? So, the final prayer, that God "rise and for thine owne worke fight," refers to property; but then the uneasiness that God may not choose him, though He loves him, is a family metaphor, the fear of being rejected for another love.

So the opening resignation of selfhood begins as property, claimed by many titles; but itemized, they begin to slide in meaning. "Made by thee" suggests simple property; "for thee" not quite so sharply. "When I was decay'd/Thy blood bought that, the which before was thine" also means property; but the bond is becoming sticky. But in the second quatrain, the first and fourth, "thy sonne," "thine Image," simply mean family; and even "thy servant," "thy sheepe," read as extensions of family. Standing between two large metaphors, the speaker undertakes to register property, deliver it flat, unmistakable, dominant; but knowing his gesture of surrender cannot work, he betrays the more subdued family metaphor, without even the courage to articulate it clearly.

The poem is thus forced, muffled, formalized. Helpless, the speaker addresses God, yet feels Satan inside him. So he slams out lines in a frozen gel. In his secular love poetry, he rose to any challenge; the woman stayed passive, though she made him prickly, uneasy. Here God is the active one; he can only agitate. His hands tied, he lifts them in prayer.

In Sonnet 1, the "I" and "selfe" thinly wrenched apart, as the speaker addressed the distant, unfelt divine presence. Sonnet 2 splashes more blacks and reds, as his own soul writhes in a gray fog. Both sonnets are strongly formal, with the same balance of eight, two, and four lines for thesis, antithesis, and synthesis. Yet a vehemence begins to stir in Sonnet 2. Its antithesis flows with more continuity and thought, after a semicolon. In Sonnet 1, the antithesis came as two end-stopped questions. The opening outcry, "Oh my blacke Soule" is a formalized judgment, a public outcry, not an intimate address, and built into a closed, tight couplet; yet the words have the smack of dramatic confrontation. The speaker is, as it were, stepping into the lawcourt of Sonnet 1.

In the opening couplet, the black corpse of his soul rises in an atmosphere of menace, an embattled Dürer-like pilgrim, stiff with sin, to the summons to a tourney by the herald and champion of death. Two similes—that he is a traitor fled abroad, and a condemned thief before execution—reinforce the sense of danger, urgency, panic, that he is lost and damned. He is still an abyss away from his large task in the *Holy Sonnets*, to mesh with the machinery of the spiritual world, become an instrument and vessel of salvation; yet here, his first stirring is palpable.

Sonnets 1 and 2 are strikingly parallel in structure, the octave offering a thesis of the speaker rising to action, then a two-line antithesis of a dilemma of befuddlement, then a closing synthesis of humble prayer. Yet in Sonnet 2, the speaker is growing attuned to his condition. He addresses his own soul, instead of simply praying for help. And during the sonnet, as his condition changes, his familiarity grows. "My blacke Soule" in line 1 becomes "holy mourning blacke" in line 11. After the shadow of red of sickness and death in line 2, he blushes for shame at himself in line 12, prays for the redemptive blood of Christ in lines 13–14. The ghostly illusion of violent distant action becomes the subdued, vicarious, but intimate readiness for God's grace.

In Sonnet 2, the soul rose dramatically after death; in Sonnet 3, the entire poem is one long narrative of death and judgment. Its language and its dialectic are lighter and less formal; but the structure is unmistakable. The octave presents the thesis of the arrival at death, body and soul each disjointed to its place in the act of dying. The next quatrain presents the antithesis, in their reception, the soul in heaven, the body in the earth, his sins in their breeding-place in hell. The closing couplet then slams home a defiant demand that the dream be made a reality, his soul be judged by his gesture of abandonment of "the world, the flesh, and devill." Logically, the closing couplet makes no sense. If his resignation in Sonnet I was useless because the devil had usurped his self, then what abandonment can be trusted now? But the progress here is not by a logical development, but by starts of attitude. He is ignorant not of the conclusions that follow, of the universe he inhabits, but what his premises are, of his own condition. So he starts about among terrifyingly naked alternatives, seeking to catch himself by surprise. Yet jumping in this seemingly random fashion, he meshes himself to the will of heaven. Thus, in Sonnet 1, he formally resigns himself; in Sonnet 3, he abandons the world, flesh, and devil. What the second abandonment has over the first is vehement persuasion.

Yet despite its drama of judgment, Sonnet 3 is the lightest of the *Holy Sonnets*. The deaths-head pilgrimage at the summons of sickness in Sonnet 2 thins considerably in Sonnet 3, line 2. His very opening struggle for life alludes only to plays and a foot race. So the repeated word "last" in lines 1, 2, 3, and twice in line 4, is generally terminal, the either-or of a final halt. Here, it establishes a pace, gradually shortening to a "last mile," "last pace," "last inch," and finally a "last point." At this point, presumably, the body goes sprawling. So the second quatrain is perversely funny, anticipating a bit of sleep as "gluttonous death" unjoints him, body and soul. By lines 7 and 8, when he is all unjointed, his "ever-waking part" contemplating God, while his various "joints" shake with fear, he does not betray whether his sleep has been interrupted.

This humor is odd, half-meant, not quite savage enough for straightforward gallows-humor. His poses of Sonnets 1 and 2 are now registering. He treads a stage self-consciously, yet more than half means it. So the sestet yields a serene statement of acceptance, his soul soaring in prayer toward heaven, his body sinking to earth, his sins, washed off by grace, to hell. There is a Dürer-like force in the closing couplet, "the world, the flesh, and devill," clustered together, arms outstretched, jaws agape, receding as his soul rises singing to heaven.

Sonnet 4 might begin just here, after Sonnet 3, with his soul rising to judgment; but this is now generalized to a universal Day of Judgment. Indeed, this generalization marks his attunement and meshing in Sonnets 4 to 6. In the first three sonnets, the speaker was knotted in himself: "I resigne . . . my selfe . . . first I was made . . . Oh my blacke

Soule! . . . my playes last scene . . . my pilgrimage . . . my race." In Sonnets 4 to 6, he prays in attunement to the universal human condition.

Nearing heaven, his ears purged of dross, his soul hears an angelic trumpet-call, blaring out a summons of stunning immediacy. Embarrassment, timidity, are gone, and formal detachment. In Sonnet 3, "the world, the flesh, and devill" clustered below, their mouths agape. Now in impetuous ardor, four angels cast their trumpets; and an infinity of souls rise and reenter their scattered bodies. All historic time is reduced to a catalogue of killings:

> All whom the flood did, and fire shall o'erthrow,
> All whom warre, dearth, age, agues, tyrannies,
> Despaire, law, chance, hath slaine . . .
>
> (ll. 5–7)

So the blessed embrace their future, those who "Shall behold God, and never tast deaths woe" (l. 8). Presumably, the damned have no future.

The thesis of Sonnet 4 is again vehement, illusory action in the octave. The speaker would by a force of spirit evoke Judgment Day. Its antithesis of befuddled helplessness in lines 9 to the first half of 12 falls back on his fallen condition for possible penance. He stands now in prosaic reality, sluggish, evasive, finding reasons in his very helplessness not to move, since in heaven all action on his destiny is ended.

The synthesis of prayer in the last two-and-a-half lines has a muted sincerity; as the opening vision was charged and ecstatic. Standing on "this lowly ground," the speaker asks for a lesson in repentance. The antithesis was an awakening to reality after a giddy, manic vision. Aesthetically, it is a poet's gesture of craftsmanlike equilibrium, balancing extremes of temperament. Standing now on a glum, flat truth, sensing he requires a fresh stirring of soul, he begins at last to pray in earnest.

In Sonnet 4, the speaker expands his grasp in a radiant vision to a universal judgment of all mankind. In Sonnet 5, it embraces plants, animals, the spectrum of life, but in a huff of disquiet at divine judgment. In Sonnet 1, a pathetic, self-involved mutter closed the sonnet. Here, complaints of some apparent validity are finally resolved in the sestet.

The octave, the thesis of the sonnet, presents two sets of two contrasting items. The first half of each pair, "poysonous mineralls" and "lecherous goats," is naturally evil; the second, the tree of knowledge, the envious serpent, is depraved, participating in original sin. Chafing, he demands to know why his guilt should be greater than theirs. Surely all sins stem either from appetite or depravity; and animals share both. Why should intellect justify condemnation only of man, when the body does the sinning, animals' and man's alike? Moreover, condemnation is a perversion of God, to threaten him in stern wrath, when mercy is so easy and so glorious.

A one-line antithesis answers this aggressive disquiet, "But who am I, that dare dispute with thee?" The shift from "hee" in line 8 to "thee" in line 9, linking octave and sestet, recalls the ending of *Job*, where endlessly long, disquieting demands for justice dissolve into shocked self-abasement at the voice from the whirlwind. The confrontation between "I" and "thee" is at last commencing, and with startling immediacy, not in the legalistic depositions of Sonnet 1.

The synthesis, in the last five lines, begins with a twice-repeated, "O God, Oh!" But now divine forgiveness and human repentance join in a single redemptive flood of "thine onely worthy blood,/ And my teares." So, for all their fumbling, their dark withdrawals, their manic visions that collapse into lethargy, these sonnets have coaxed his slumbering spirit into a taut movement of rapport with his environment, engaging God in a direct confrontation. Without vision or self-abasement, he closes, bargaining:

> That thou remember them, some claime as debt.
> I think it mercy, if thou wilt forget.
>
> (ll. 13–14)

On the last fringes of his inner unknown, in a twinge of reaction, in Sonnet 6, the speaker spins about and confronts the figure of death, as it keeps shifting between an independent antagonist and a component in his disposition, expressing a muted demonism, a half-detached autonomy, part internalized devil, part inner shadow, physical death and a clog on his spirit, killing him, reducing him to lethargy and despair.

Structurally, Sonnet 6 is of an odd sort. We have remarked Donne's extraordinary equilibria of self and other, lyric and dramatic, inner and objective experience. Here his equilibria keep shifting ground, between shadow and substance, antagonist and self, confrontation and utter isolation, an inkblot and the ego that confronts it. It thus moves by a series of startled confrontations and slow, uneasy releases. Like a disturbed man whose mirror image keeps threatening him, it gradually blurs, then starts up again; but the image may be a patient, wily enemy, and not simply part of the wallpaper of living.

Indeed, this very ambiguity about the autonomy of evil and death was a subject of medieval bewilderment and debate. Yet despite an official position that evil was a deprivation, an inner denial to be overcome, in common parlance, it was an independent enemy and no nonsense. So here, the aroused speaker keeps confronting death, whereupon it gradually blurs out of sight. He starts up again; it again blurs, yet never disappears.

So the opening octave confronts death in the shock of oncoming conquest. The speaker gives it the lie direct, as in the defiance of a joust. His abrupt opening, "Death be not proud," with its negative imperative of the verb "to be," would settle the matter finally, get rid of its being. It then denies death pride, the cardinal sin, chaining life in this world, also the animal attributes, "Mighty and dreadful," the traditional domain of masculinity. So he denies death the world and the ferocity to possess it. But the second couplet makes death a lie. Subtly, death blurs into its ground. If death cannot kill, then it must have another function entirely. So the third couplet draws an analogy to rest and sleep; if they give pleasure, then so must death. Indeed, "our best men" regard death as choice company; it rests their bones, delivers their souls, and kills nothing. So death has been internalized from a confrontation to a biological process. A shadowy butler, it slips from view, serving pleasure and rest, in his bones and in his soul.

In the sestet, the "Thou" of death looms again, now ineffectual, a mere slave, yet annoyingly still there. The speaker somehow cannot leave him alone. So he holds firm before an encompassing inkblot, that draws his every ounce of manhood. Yet again, absorbed by the process of confrontation, the antagonist becomes ubiquitous. Line by line, its items are gentler, more alluring, building to the word "stroake" (l. 12), perhaps a violent blow, or else a caress in the easy rhythm of living.

This thesis and antithesis are more dramatic than structural, the octave confronting death as a conqueror, the sestet as a slave. Both reduce him to a process or shadow. The ubiquitous presence would seem altogether boxed in, a creature of spirit and a slave of flesh, with poison and poppies, sicknesses and charms. This then should do it. The speaker has blocked death off, annulled it, canceled its existence, absorbed it into the rhythm of life. Yet line 12 stirs with uneasiness. "Why swell'st thou then?" "Swell" may be the swelling of pride, the empty braggadocio of a sullen imbecile, denying his own defeat. Or else the swelling of a blister or a sickness, prefiguring death even as he denies it exists. More simply, the inkblot is swelling again, mysteriously assuming new, threatening shapes, more ubiquitous modes of attack, refusing to be still, accept any settlement.

The last couplet attempts a resolution, marshaling his literal faith in the resurrection:

> One short sleepe past, wee wake eternally,
> And death shall be no more . . .
>
> (ll. 13–14)

Death must be an illusion then. The swelling must fade from the walls of his existence, his metaphysical shudder with the *Blue Fairy Book* and the Brothers Grimm. That ubiquitous threat is but a prelude to immortality, an uncontrollable thread in the process of living. He will yet pass the straits where death does not exist.

The closing phrase, "Death thou shalt die," at once hammers home this defiant triumph, and makes it a grotesque lie, fixing the eternal conflict between man and death. Indeed, its symmetry with the opening phrase, "Death be not proud," encloses the poem in a secluded cell of feeling; yet it also suggests repeated confrontations, spasmodic focusings on death, which then slip out of focus. Nothing is finally settled then. Sleep, quiescence, the clutch for immortality, are all but lapses of attention. Whatever his position and attitude, death starts up as before. The shadow insists on its own body.

Yet slight shifts in tone indicate a movement. So, the bald opening address, "Death," closes on the familiar second person plural, "Death thou;" as he settles into death. "Death be not proud" denies death this world, the proper arena of pride. This is a narrower and more extreme taunt, stripping death of any plume of achievement. The second phrase, "Death thou shalt die," coming after "wee wake eternally," denies death any existence in the world of spirit. The poem has evidently enlarged the speaker, simplified him, made him more elemental to the very fabric of life. Indeed, the closing phrase, "Death thou shalt die" expresses the frozen future, not any particular moment or event. It defines life, not death, as an eternity of confrontation and elimination of death. Life is the gesture of death dying. This is the arrival of the metaphysical poet. As he settles into himself, without a crutch of assurance or support, his life settles into the gesture of stamping out death. The metaphysical shudder has steadily dislodged all halfway houses. He now stands, confronting death, the strenuous existential believer.

Balanced against the opening phrase, then, the closing words suggest a catharsis of self-definition; balanced against the first half of the last line, they explode with contradiction, triumph, beleaguered defiance. The synthesis of the closing couplet calls for a release into eternity. Death shall simply fade away. Indeed, throughout the poem until the last couplet, he addresses death directly, insistantly repeating "thee," "thou," "thou," "thou," "thou," always at bay, confronting the suspect illusion. But now he has exorcised the ultimate demon, and can first refer to death in the third person. There is nothing to confront! Nothing to talk to! Nothing to watch out for! Eternity is upon us! "Death shall be no more." And instantly, the confrontation springs back, "Death thou shalt die."

These two deaths of the last line are the two modes of his life experience, confronting death and standing in faith beyond it. Indeed, the very pace of the poem has speeded to this point. Thus, the first startle and relaxation took eight lines, the second four, the third one-and-a-half. Now it returns on the instant. No final resolution is possible. Neither death nor its absence can be brushed aside. There is only his towering defiance, a strong soul, utterly awake, in the murky chaos of life on earth.

# 16

# Holy Sonnets: 2

The unfolding "I" of the *Holy Sonnets* quivers alive, flagellant and unpredictable, amid starkly immediate visions. Whole domains of turbulent experience are incorporated and rejected with wayward jumps of attention, his hour of death, his pilgrimage to heaven, judgment day, the confrontation with death. The poems seem random in direction; yet the speaker's very mistrust of programs of reality and categories of thought is a program. As Rimbaud systematically sheds all fixed categories for a naked immediacy of grasp; so Donne resists all identifications, thrusts aside all anchors of security, uses words as ramparts, knives, masks, presumptions, to waylay God in a naked confrontation. He refers to Christ in Sonnets 1 to 6, but as Christ related to his own tumult of spirit. In these six sonnets, his aim is to blend his own with the life of Christ.

In Sonnet 7, he swings into precipitous, futile action in a premature attempt to identify with Christ. This follows the pattern of the dialectic in the first sonnets, of a thesis of premature action, an antithesis of befuddled helplessness, and a synthesis of prayerful wonder. Thus, here, he projects himself into the crucifying rabble, spitting orders, "Spit in my face . . . pierce my side . . . Buffet . . . scoffe . . . scourge . . . crucifie . . ." A mistake has been made, an innocent crucified; then let him die, one of the guilty ones, and even up the score.

But even the gesture of apparent selflessness betrays the

presumption of the speaker. He would thrust Christ aside and take his place, when he has neither the vision nor the grace. So the antithesis in the second quatrain repeats "my death," "my sinnes," "I crucifie him." Nor can he give grace, being a creature of self-glorification, whose most presumptuous act may be the attempt to take the place of Christ. His gesture, then, is the well-meaning stubbornness of depraved ignorance. So his ineffectual stumbling exposes three levels of spiritual excellence: Christ, the impious Jews, and the random pagan sinners. This follows the doctrine that the Jews kept the Law, but remained impious, having no grace; but he, glorified in pride, crucifies Christ daily by his daily sins. So he stands among the lawless depraved, befuddled, presumptuous, despairing, beset by sins and incapable of penance.

For all his passionate pretense of indignation in the octave, the sestet offers a staid contrast. Bankrupt, he would glide into harmony with God's ways, but hasn't the knack of participation. The verbs in line 9, "let mee . . . love . . . admire," have a poignant imbalance. He is an awkward misfit, who can at most "admire," fix his admiration on Christ's strange love, its gratuitous *agape* undeserved by earthly sinners. And even such admiration is still only an object of prayer and permission. He, as it were, wishes to wish to love.

All that the first six sonnets settled, then, is that he now has a fresh direction, to arrive at God. Yet staid and listless, he grasps the hypocrisy of the Jews as legalized thievery. Jacob, the weakling, dressed in a sheepskin in harsh pretense of humility, to steal the family birthright—Almighty God dressed in corrupt human flesh to suffer crucifixion. His admiration is thus captured; momentarily, he fades and recedes before the divine figure, "admiring" this "strange love." Yet the gesture is unsettled and paltry. He attempts to locate him self vis-à-vis the Jews in this sonnet as he does vis-à-vis the animal kingdom in Sonnet 8. Full of jealousies, grandiosities, misgivings, he chafes about, having no clear sense of his place.

So, in Sonnet 8, he faces about before the superiority of the animals to the men they serve. But at least the narrow "I" of Sonnet 7 has widened to all mankind. Thus, the "mee" and "I" of line 3 are couched as an exemplar between "wee" in line 1 and "whose whole kinde" in line 8. But such impersonal meditations go against the grain in Donne. The accents in the first quatrain, particularly in line 3, are metrically blurred and clumsy, without a tough, biting intellect to shape them. "Creatures" is a vague noun, too distant to refer to animals, too animated to refer to aught else. So "prodigall elements" is too abstract to grip the imagination. There are too many Latinate polysyllables. Beginning his line with "simple," enclosed and set off by commas, with metrically reversed accents, makes it stand apart, cleverly set, simple, yet unpersuasive. Hopkins, in "Thou art, indeed, just, Lord," wrote with a limpid, persuasive simplicity; But Donne's mind was too toughly knotted for such impersonal moral truths, too Gothic for any classical, stylized statement.

The second quatrain expands on the first somewhat more persuasively. The horse, the bull, and the boar have more visionary force than the abstract creatures and elements of the first quatrain, and distantly echo the warhorse and Behemoth of *Job*, in a situation of Job-like abandon and querulous demand. Yet an abstract polysyllable like "subjection" belies any actual horse's experience. Musically, attributing secret might and pretended weakness (l. 7) to the bull and boar dulls its verbal thud in a meandering three-line question. Further, there is no bite of experience here. The horse, the bull, and the boar are out of old books and sermons, so their ferocity, so their patient self-control. The speaker, as it were, falls back on old sermons to express a dull, schooled conviction of weakness, a perfunctory disturbance that man is inferior to the animals, his natural servants.

The antithesis in the sestet catches fire. It adds not one idea; on the contrary, it repeats and reinforces the octave, but now suddenly grasped, in a twinge of personal awareness. The accent, badly muffed in the octave, grows suddenly intuitive:

> Weaker I am, woe is mee, and worse than you . . . (l. 9)

The word "weaker" weakens, violating the metrical accent. So "I" grows weak, engulfed, almost obliterated by a contraction to "Weaker I'am." In the middle phrase, both "woe" and "mee" are long, open vowels, dragging out their forlorn, self-indulgent emptiness and stagnant emotions without a closing consonant, lightly balanced by the word "is"—"woe is mee." The antithesis, here, then, is the shock of grasp, the startled crystallization of his impossible abasement, as in Sonnet 5, where he starts up, "But who am I, that dare dispute with thee?" (l. 9).

The synthesis, as usual in the Holy Sonnets, contemplates God's ways in prayerful wonder. Hemmed in by a wall of alliterated "K"s—"Created," "Creator," "Creatures"—he finds "Created nature" not paltry, like himself, but subduing "these things" (l. 12), all creatures and prodigal elements, to man. Behind the horse, the bull, and boar, then, stands nature, who subdues them, as they could subdue man; and behind nature stands "the Creator," who made the supreme reversal—he who could subdue all, dying for man, his lowest creature. The turning toward God thus intensifies a notch. His wish for admiration in Sonnet 7, line 9, becomes redoubled into a "wonder at a greater wonder" in Sonnet 8, line 11; as shocked discovery settles to accepted instruction.

The absorption into Christ's fate rises in Sonnet 9 to an onrushing one-line question, "What if this present were the world's last night?" But the shock of such contemplation splinters him into a confusion of presences:

> Marke in my heart, O Soule, where thou dost dwell,
> The picture of Christ crucified . . .

Thus his vision evokes a host of voices in disarray. He is one presence, his soul another, his heart an objectified third, with a fourth presence stamped upon it that he wants to absorb them all, the image of Christ, muddling all purpose and clarity. Is the speaker depraved? Then why is Christ stamped on his heart? Has he grace? Then why the choked hesitation? Are his feelings talking? Then why is his heart apart from his soul? And why is he outside it? But this is the disorganization of a human presence with a goal, and no means to attain it, falling apart under the force of a vision he can scarcely grasp and dares not let go. A wayward human consciousness, unsure of its will, its memory, its sense of structure, trapped among terrifying images, with the unpredictable urgency of a Hamlet he guesses, probes, confronts, evades himself and runs scared.

His vision of Christ is in terms of a conflict between the attributes of justice and mercy. He ponders if Christ's tears, wept in compassion, can quench the "amasing light" that betrays his sins, if Christ's blood, poured for his atonement, can fill his frowns, clenched in judgment, if the tongue that prayed forgiveness for his enemies in crucifixion can adjudge him to hell.

The repeated "No, no," opening the sestet, is too perfunctory to exclaim anything, yet transcends a mere logical reply. Muffled, it shrinks back—from what, the vision of Christ? His own sinfulness? His free panic?—into an inert pile of proverbs, using simplified analogies. But despite his muffled disengagement, the sestet strongly suggests a repentant courtly lover. The qualification, "profane," suggests he once regarded "mistresses" as "holy." Rejecting "my idolatrie" suggests he was once a worshiper. Despite his stiffly archaic and proverbial tone, he still shudders with the more destructive aspects of courtly love, associating "idolatrie" and "profane mistresses" with "wicked spirits" and "horrid shapes." And once again, he is reversing sexual roles in the religious lyrics. As once he spoke to his mistresses, so now he speaks to his soul, a mistress presumably to Christ, anticipating Sonnet 10. So he schools his soul in the arts of discernment in courtship:

> so I say to thee,
> To wicked spirits are horrid shapes assign'd,
> This beauteous forme assures a pitious minde.
> (ll. 12–14)

His soul can trust her coming lover.

Judging these sonnets as separate, complete poems, their periodic, muffled sections, like the start of Sonnet 8, the sag at the close of Sonnet 9, read as blemishes; but read as dramatic shifts and outbursts of spirit, they tumble after one another in moody meditation, a spasmodic confessional of fragmentary voices, some withdrawn, some presumptuous, some sullen and mistrustful, but all attempting to engage the divine spirit, one touching the next one loose. So the school-masterly "I said to all" and "I say to thee," closing Sonnet 9, explodes in the next sonnet in a desperate hammerbeat of Sonnet 10. "Batter my heart, three person'd God," begins the sonnet with two feet, then a comma, two feet, then a comma, the accent beginning and ending each phrase, like a Beethoven orchestral opening, to slam out toward God at the end of the line, "for, you . . ." then hurtle without a line break into the cluster of polite verbs in the next line, "knocke, breathe, shine, and seeke to mend."

But the transition from Sonnet 9 is more than just musical counterpoint. The problem is engaging God. Here pious intent is not enough, nor any patching up of difficulty. The speaker suffers depravity, not ignorance, radical inertia, not bad direction. Only utter violence will penetrate his heart. A rape is called for, not a seduction. So the muffled allusion in Sonnet 9, "Marke in my heart" (l. 2), comes to a desperate focus, "Batter my heart." In Sonnet 9, he compares his heart to profane mistresses, insecure objects of idolatry, not necessarily subject to respectful, legitimate love. So here, he calls upon God to ravish his heart.

Indeed, all the intermittent gathering forces of Sonnets 7, 8, and 9 come to a crisis, not fused or reconciled, yet all there, and finally awake, standing at bay. The address, "three person'd God," is no theological construction, but an exasperated summons that all the parts of God slam into his stony heart —he needs every ounce of weight in that slam, his heart is so stony thick. So the lists of verbs, "knocke, breathe, shine, and seeke," then "rise, . . . stand, o'erthrow . . . , and bend," then "breake, blowe, burn, and make," are not fury in motion, but the harassed frustration of an immobilized spirit, straining, as it were, inside God's muscles for what he finds impossible. Unable to move in grace, he slams verb after verb at God, taunting, confronting, demanding a reply.

The basic structure of the *Holy Sonnets* holds good in Sonnet 10, with an opening thesis of precipitous, urgent, and unsuccessful action; but so closely does he now identify with God that his opening thrust is shifted to Him. The second quatrain comes to the same helpless frustration, but delivered with all its anguished awareness, not sunk in a fog, or clinging to muffled proverbs, but in an image of a captured town. So the intermittent quality in the *Holy Sonnets* is here charged awake. The frame of reference shifts from military violence, to enforced government, then to sexual love in the sestet, not as blurred voices, but in a single huge grasp of his entire situation. Helpless, at bay, in sharp focus, desperately turning between God and the devil, his nature enslaved, his reason untrustworthy, he gasps in despair, "but Oh, to no end"; yet even the luxury of despair he can no longer afford himself.

Then, in the middle of the sonnet, at the octave break, caught up between comma and comma, something crumbles inside him. Where before he would admire, now he suddenly loves God, and dearly. And it is not even a discovery, announced with a paean, but already a presumed truth, prefixed to a desire for God's return of love. So the metaphor of the usurped town, one of property and legalistic relationships, dissolves into the image of betrothal, one of a love relationship. Now the speaker nakedly takes the female role to God, with a complex syndrome of helplessness, enforced betrothal, and a demand for the lover's initiative, even unto rape. Only Donne's urgent language betrays a strident, awkward, masculine spirit, clumsy with anxiety and articulating too brazenly the call for rape to fit congenially the female role.

This reversal of role is so striking as to merit attention. What is literal and what a metaphor in such matters varies from poet to poet, and can never be automatically presumed, even from close contemporaries. Nevertheless, the sexual component obtrudes in the religious poetry of this period. This is because the charge of the personal metaphor beats much stronger in this century of counter-Reformation and Puritan militancy. But projecting strictly the relationship of God to man inevitably charges grace with emotional bonds of a more human kind. Whatever its theological dimensions, to the psyche, grace means quite simply God's commitment to love, indeed a form of marriage, and one in which man naturally has the female role. God gives grace to man, not the reverse. Yet the components in the divine figure are large enough to allow some flexibility in their sex. So, even ignoring the hosts of demi-divinities of the speculative mystics, God the Father has essentially masculine aspects, the Holy Spirit essentially feminine. Thus, *Paradise Lost* begins invoking the female aspects of divinity, the heavenly muse and Holy Spirit. Only then, the masculinity of God manifests itself destroying Satan:

> Him the Almighty Power
> Hurld headlong flaming from th' Ethereal Skie
> With hideous ruine and combustion down
> To bottomless perdition . . .
>
> (ll. 44–47)

Indeed, the multi-faceted close of *Paradise Lost* suggests a kind of birth, the garden womb of Eden gone dead, as Adam and Eve are delivered to step into the real world:

> Some natural tears they drop'd, but wip'd them soon;
> The World was all before them, where to choose
> Thir place of rest, and Providence thir guide:
> They hand in hand with wandring steps and slow,
> Through *Eden* took thir solitary way.
>
> (XII. 645–49)

But *Paradise Lost* began twelve books back with an impregnation:

> Thou from the first
> Wast present, and with mighty wings outspread
> Dove-like satst brooding on the vast Abyss
> And mad'st it pregnant:
>
> (I. 19–22)

Thus, despite the magisterial paternity of God, *Paradise Lost* seems framed between the pregnant universal spirit, and the final delivery of Adam and Eve from Eden, the entire epic, as it were, the birthpangs of Man. But this period constantly played with the male and female aspects of divinity. Their presence in Milton is not what is remarkable, but rather how strictly he confined himself to the parental metaphor. No romantic interlude between man and God intrudes here, nor, to my knowledge, anywhere in Milton.

Indeed, Donne stands in such stark contrast to him, as to merit some exploration. Thus, the divine figure may clearly be male or female, its relationship to man parental or romantic. Perversions suggest themselves, especially in certain Seventeenth Century poets, as the man takes the female role; but they do not necessarily follow. Even in the baldest projection, the male and female aspects still represent the entire man, who is bisexual. Indeed, we may speculate that the ratio of male to female components in the divine figure roughly approximates the ratio of male to female students in a good, mixed, Ivy League university; the instinct for wholeness determines such ratios.

The other alternative, of the relationship being parental or romantic, is equally suggestive. So, the parental metaphor suggests orderly structure, hierarchy, and enduring commitment, the romantic metaphor mystical experience, insecurity, and the suspension of any hierarchy of being. Hence Milton would eschew the romantic metaphor, being the least mystical of religious poets, the most concerned for proper personal order.

The role of Christ is likewise significant here, in understanding the personal metaphor. When Christ is projected as emblem or model, it may be as a supreme career, or for his gift of grace and salvation, as God's only exemplary son on earth, or as the overflow of grace into a depraved universe. Milton here is consistent. To Milton, Christ had an exemplary career, of creation and triumph over Satan; his crucifixion is a minor moment in *Paradise Lost.* So *Paradise Regained* straightforwardly depicts Christ determining his career against the temptations of Satan. In Donne, the reverse is true. Christ's career never gripped Donne's imagination. Again and again, the *Holy Sonnets* dwell on the paradox of the divine becoming flesh, to die for human sin:

> God cloth'd himselfe in vile mans flesh, that so
> Hee might be weake enough to suffer woe.
>
> (VII. 13–14)

So, in "La Corona," only "Temple" deals with Christ's career, and that with an odd verb:

> Blowing, yea blowing out those sparks of wit . . .
>
> (4. 3)

"Blowing" suggests not the strenuous pursuit of a career, but a miraculous overflow of grace, blowing wise bubbles, sparks of wit.

Both personal and doctrinal elements are relevant here. Milton, burdened with his vocation as priest, poet, educator, a statesman under Cromwell, envisioning the reshaping of England, would see Christ as an emblem of excellence, shaping the universe by the celestial compass as he would shape the soul of England. Donne, to whom poetry was never a vocation, whose marriage irrevocably shattered his commitment to statecraft, wrote "La Corona" and these *Holy Sonnets* in the twilight period before his ordination, having no sense of vocation to project onto Christ.

But also in doctrine, Milton, as an Arian and an Arminian, presumed the potentiality of grace, let it only be actualized by self-discipline toward a divine end. To him, Christ is therefore a model of a career of good works. Donne, a fideist and a dualist, who took nothing for granted, not knowledge, nor structure, nor a sure sense of God's grace, but darkly brooded on the essential breakthrough of spirit into flesh, God's grace into his stony heart, made Christ his pivot or fulcrum for the moment of grace in bringing him salvation.

Given his strong self-reliance, his carefully structured monism, Milton would understandably confine himself to the parental metaphor, male or female, about God. But Donne, concerned with the union of polar opposites, the moment of the passage of grace, would incline to the romantic metaphor. Indeed, Donne's entire life bent to such an intimacy of spirit. As "The Extasie" labored to structure a universe that made possible enduring sexual love; so the *Holy Sonnets* shift about to allow for an enduring gift of grace. We sense no mystical illumination in Donne; yet his disposition found the mystical approach entirely congenial. Indeed his life overlapped that of St. John of the Cross. So the systematic deadening of selfhood in "The Crosse" strikingly resembles the processes in St. John of the Cross.

But once we allow the romantic metaphor, the question of sexual role inevitably ensues. The romantic metaphor, in which an adult human male engages the female aspects of divinity, simply does not occur to our knowledge. The Holy Spirit remains safely maternal, engaged in birth and nourishment, but it is never female in the act of love. Centuries of the strongest Oedipal inhibition would forbid this; the Holy Spirit joined in God the Father is simply not to be tampered with. But the reverse is found over and over in this period. Indeed, the doctrine of salvation by grace would impose this, grace, as it were, being a divine semen of rebirth and rejuvenation implanted in man, with the initiative entirely in God's hands. This, the mystics would find particularly congenial; so that St. John of the Cross takes a blatant female role toward God in his imagery.

But male or female, the romantic metaphor suggests danger, even the suspension of all hierarchies of being. The parental metaphor is congenial to a more Catholic harmony, God the Father presiding over a happy household of men; but the romantic metaphor suggests a drastic either-or. Engaged in an act of love with God, a man feels his civic loyalties and worldly experiences fade to superficial pleasures, illicit seductions. Hence, the romantic metaphor in St. John of the Cross comes with a total emptying out of all personal being. This relative danger in the romantic metaphor we find in Sonnet 1, a quietly meditative sonnet, legalistic, conventional, where God is given the parental metaphor:

> I am thy sonne, made with thy self to shine,
> Thy servant, whose paines thou hast still repaid,
> Thy sheepe, thine Image, and till I betray'd
> My selfe, a temple of thy Spirit divine . . .
>
> (ll. 5–8)

The parental metaphor comes encrusted with home and orderly growth. The romantic metaphor belongs to the devil, and comes stark, with no embellishment:

> Why doth he steale, nay ravish that's thy right?
>
> (l. 10)

At first glance, the word "ravish" has an overtone of dishonesty—if the devil ravished him, he must be innocent of sin. He was not ravished, but seduced and voluntarily fell. Yet "ravish" suggests a general sluggishness of heart. In Sonnet 5, the speaker complained:

> Why should intent or reason, borne in mee,
> Make sinnes, else equall, in mee, more hienous?
>
> (ll. 5–6)

His intents are apparently distant from his heart; his flesh, his passions, they do the sinning; his reason only nods permission. So, here, there is a third-person estrangement in the complaint, "he steale, nay ravish that's thy right." But in Sonnet 10, the word "ravish" is transferred to God, in a plea for divine action, a shift so striking, the entire sonnet sequence can be arched from the diabolical "ravishment" of Sonnet 1 to God's true "ravishment" of Sonnet 10. In Sonnet 1, he stood under God's presumed fatherly protection, legalistic, pietistic, conventional, complacently evasive, pleading helpless ravishment. It did not work. By starts and fumbles, he kicked awake his temperament until, anguished, jammed in, desperate, ignoring all decency, all convention, whatever the threat to the tainted hierarchy of order, the disruption of God's household, he cries for God's ravishment, a radical infusion of grace.

Such nakedly sexual language makes us inevitably ask where the metaphorical commitment of faith ends, and a masked perversion begins. Our guideline can only lie in the language, the degree of fascinated dwelling on the components of the goal sought. By these criteria, even allowing for an enormous latitude, the poems of Crashaw read as suspect; his degree of fixation, repeated poem after poem, both secular and sacred, transcends mere convention. Donne suggests the opposite. All his life, Donne's hunger for clarity of spirit struggled with his sense of isolation. Radically, desperately, by passive, intuitive fumbling, he struggled to clarify his ego and arrive at utter intimacy of spirit. His first great gesture was wholly secular, in "The Extasie" and the poems of emotional marriage. Now, in a huge submission to his religious sources, he set about to subdue his pride and attain genuine humility. The romantic metaphor here reads as a gesture of radical self-effacement. Indeed, its desperation is simply appalling. To the Elizabethans, a strong ego was a male characteristic. To subdue his ego and absorb the spirit of God, Donne would eliminate his very sexuality. The taut confrontation with God's spirit is stark as with death in "Death be not proud."

All of Sonnet 11 is a diastole of formal instruction following the systole of agonized feeling in Sonnet 10. In Sonnet 9, the speaker addressed his soul, "Marke in my heart," and again, "I say to thee." In Sonnet 11, he again admonishes his soul:

> Wilt thou love God, as he thee! then digest,
> My Soule, this wholsome meditation . . .
>
> (ll. 1–2)

But this renewed instruction brings to fulfilment a curious process of clarification, settling into place much of the material of the earlier sonnets. The machinery of Donne's temperament has at last meshed into gear, his soul speaking in clean, agonized urgency in its turn, his intellect admonitory and clarifying in its turn. So the phobia of "gluttonous death" in Sonnet 3 here rises to a wholesome, "digest, My Soule." The usurped "temple of thy Spirit divine" in Sonnet 1 is redeemed as "doth make his Temple in thy brest." The plaintive "thy sonne" in Sonnet 1, grounds for self-abandonment, here is renewed as God "Hath deign'd to chuse thee by adoption,/Coheire to'-his glory." The attempt to thrust Christ aside in Sonnet 7, with overtones of sibling rivalry and frantic helpless action, here settles as God first "begot a Sonne," then adopted the speaker "coheire." His obsessive image of himself as a usurped city is healed as Christ died, "Us whom he'had made, and Satan stolne, to unbinde" (l. 12). The sonnet closes on a note of serene self-transcendence; for the first time, God and man exchange images in the intimacy of self-surrender:

> 'Twas much, that man was made like God before,
> But, that God should be made like man, much more.
>
> (ll. 13–14)

Sonnet 12 completes this process of clarification in a stately procession of couplings, emblematic of the coupling of God's will with the speaker. There is a cabalistic grace of couplings here, an elegance of junctions after the disrupted clashings before it. Two by two come assurances of a healing. Father and son share one kingdom, where the son has a double interest, a jointure that the son in turn shares with the speaker. The lamb, who was twice-slain, left two wills, invested with the legacy of a joint kingdom. So grace and the Holy Spirit revive the victims of law and letter. So the speaker is a disrupted two that must come to a coupling. The two of body and spirit, torn apart, must arrive at a jointure of body and earth, spirit and God. A first innocence and grace must be completed by a second of salvation. The isolated ego of the speaker must be joined to that of God. So the last command is "all but love," the coupling of two in stately permanence.

His closing prayer, "Oh let that last Will stand!" expresses simple piety, with no pretense, no tortured frustration; yet the word, "Will," reverberates with overtones. A will is a dying testament. So the death of Christ was his will of grace to be distributed among men, making God's will supremely alive. So the speaker, mistrusting reason, wanted only a will for grace. The entire bent of the sonnet sequence was to blend his will to the will of God. As the first six sonnets arrived at a denial of pride to death, so the second built up to the dissolution of man's will in God's. There is therefore no possessive to the closing will, no qualification, no confrontation between man and God, but a single will, belonging to them both: "Oh let that last Will stand!"

# 17

# Holy Sonnets: 3

The sonnets of 1635 begin with an air of finality, not with the successive layers of consciousness of the earlier twelve; but the finality is deceptive. The sonnets come in loose, but organic clusters, not as solitaries. The first stand as carefully sculptured summaries of the poet's condition, brief and prayerful; but soon they begin to stir.

Sonnet 1 is less vivid than Sonnet 1 of 1633, with built-in contradictions. There an octave of formal resignation to God is canceled out; as two questions betray there is nothing left to resign—the devil has it all already. Yet contradictory or not, one thought naturally follows another, an attempted resignation, a catch of insecurity, a helpless, solemn prayer. Sonnet 1 here has a more rhetorical ring, beginning not with a legalism, but an appeal to property interests:

> Thou hast made me, And shall thy worke decay?
> Repaire me now, for now mine end doth haste . . .

Lines 3 to 8, unto themselves, would be exceedingly moving, a trapped, running victim, depicted with the stark simplicity of a Dürer engraving; and two monsters, death and despair, stand before and behind him, so terrifying he cannot move his eyes about to seek escape. So sin weighs down his enfeebled flesh to hell. Did the poem begin with line 3, the impact of this scene would be overwhelming; but the opening couplet makes the entire passage not a sudden, shocking experience, but a vivid set-piece, clarifying his predicament with rhetorical amplification. We grow uneasy; men with dim, petrified eyes, trapped between death and despair, do not usually argue so well. Indeed, we wonder, given his dim, paralyzed eyes, whom he was addressing in the opening couplet.

Yet for all his rhetorical despair, Donne's wilful ego here at least stands in strong-etched clarity, not pathetic, not sentimental, yet altogether static. He turns about, with elaborate shifts in direction, but has no true movement of spirit. These are the strokes of an orator, not the shifts of a wayward spirit. The speaker knows his role in life. But our uneasiness about his stance is beside the point. Earlier, Donne's confessional sonnets read as poignant dramatic monologues. Here, they are set pieces, carefully shaped offerings of prayer. When a minister sinks in despair during a religious service, no psychiatrist is called on emergency. Let his humility have the ring of finality; we trust he will rise of himself to complete his service.

Sonnet 1 here uses the paradox of double gravity, a cliché of religious writers. Its opening lines project a violation of natural direction. Following the early marital poems, one should take Donne's geometry as literally as possible. These opening lines are thus a dramatization of the opening lines of "Goodfriday, 1613. Riding Westward:"

> And as the other Spheares, by being growne
> Subject to forraigne motions, lose their owne,
> And being by others hurried every day,
> Scarce in a yeare their naturall forme obey:
>
> (ll. 3–6)

So here, the jangling foreign motion makes him run toward death, which meets him in collision. His sight petrifies. He wastes away, and weighs toward death, his spirit subject to the gravity of matter, downward, towards the center of the earth, toward hell.

Thus, sin has misdirected the speaker's normal movement upwards, toward God. Now only His grace can restore its natural direction. The closing couplets follows grace with the image of the wing, suggesting a soaring of blessedness after the moment of grace. By line 14, the soaring wings are transformed to iron drawn by an adamant, irresistible, and universal force, as he settles into a condition of grace.

So the poem suggests the resurrection of the body. Thus, Donne refers to his flesh as subject to the paradox of perverted gravity:

> Despaire behind, and death before doth cast
> Such terrour, and my feebled flesh doth waste
> By sinne in it, which it t'wards hell doth weigh . . .
>
> (ll. 6–8)

Such a dualist as Donne could consign the body to the grave, and remain with his soul. But by the resurrection of the body, the flesh would also have a gravity towards heaven, did not sin weigh it toward hell.

Sonnet 2 of this group projects the same predicament. Its opening couplet suggests a unified being, the ideal self before the fall, a "little world made cunningly," the word "cunningly" recalling the "subtile knot" of "The Extasie." The speaker thus began, a little world of two parts, material elements and an "Angelike spright," his soul, bound together. But by the betrayal of sin, he has been split apart into two parts, each consigned to death, recalling the fragmentation of death in Sonnet 3 above. Indeed, his even poignance, sighing over "both parts" betrayed by sin, suggests the resurrection of the body. Otherwise they would not be equally to be mourned.

With the second quatrain, the speaker is in a fallen condition. His first impulse is to use natural means to redeem himself, to stir his sluggish spirit, now weighed toward death. He turns rather grotesquely toward contemporary astronomy to stir him with new visions of heaven. The quatrain is laden with irony, but too sluggish to register its bite. It is surely pathetic to turn to contemporary astronomers as sources of grace, humility, and prayer; yet the lines haven't even sufficient persuasive resonance to register:

> Powre new seas in mine eyes, that so I might
> Drowne my world with my weeping earnestly,
> Or wash it, if it must be drown'd no more:
>
> (ll. 7–9)

The effect of the second quatrain is finally not grotesquerie, but slack torpor, as Donne occasionally indicated in the *Holy Sonnets*. By human means he cannot move. So the quatrain utters a perfunctory sentiment, then complacently glides into the sestet, coming to a halt on line 9, not line 8.

Only with "But oh it must be burnt" does the speaker feel a catch of horror. This shift from tears to fire is analogous to the earlier distinction between the overtones of seduction and ravishment. At first, the speaker would weep, somehow stir himself into a rapport with God. It drags to a halt. Now he grasps his need for a radical infusion of grace. In an instant, there stands revealed by implication his own depraved condition. He is burned already, made radically foul by lust and envy, the two deadly sins of earthly denial, a hunger for women's bodies and men's property. The speaker now calls on God to burn him out, fire on fire. Indeed, line 13 leaves ambiguous whose is the fiery zeal, God's, who would burn him, or the speaker's, possessed by religious zeal. This ambiguity has a taut compression. The speaker and God will have a single will, as the end of Sonnet 12, "Oh let this last Will stand!"

This image of fire, repeated over and over in the sestet: "it must be burnt . . . the fire of lust and envie . . . burnt it heretofore . . . their flames . . . burne me ô Lord . . . fiery zeale . . . eating," establishes the feeling tone of an extreme fanatic, one who would, like St. John of the Cross, altogether excoriate the old man. Donne's contemporaries found water an adequate image for grace; but Donne, to attain a second birth as a Christian, would altogether burn out the old man in a process of healing that is a self-consumption.

In Sonnet 3 of this group, at first reading their strongest, the most deeply personal voice finally breaks forth in craggy, individual speech. The speaker looks back with bitter truth upon his years as a lover, with neither present joy nor any future investment, only sighs and tears. Nor is his present changed, only his once profane discontent is now become holy, his showers of rain in his period of idolatry are now shed over the rejection of God. The sensualist has memories of old days:

> The'hydroptique drunkard, and night-scouting thiefe,
> The itchy Lecher, and selfe tickling proud . . .
>
> (ll. 9–10)

He remembers only sighs, tears, and vehement grief. Making all due allowances for a selective memory and moralistic exaggeration, the personal flavor of the sonnet makes dubious the picture of an early lecherous Jack Donne, now the repentant roué. Nor does this coincide with his early love poetry. His promiscuity poems are boyish, theoretical exercises, not the texture of fleshly promiscuity. His love poems are artful, manly exercises, but overcast with insecurity. They are winning, not for any galloping triumph of ardor, but for the smell of immediacy about their sober, manly ego. Their divinities are characteristically harmful, and in league with the female figure. And even his radiant marriage poems, so light of touch, with such fine clarity of structure, discover fresh vistas of experience, not the habits of an old roué.

We are not suggesting the opposite, that Donne was fearful, timid, or dejected—the Lothian portrait, as well as his Cadiz expedition, rule this out, only that his mind was on other things. To put the matter baldly, a man this consumingly ambitious, secretive, learned, socially problematical, and dedicated to his place in the establishment, does not, except *en passant*, in an approved group style, engage in excessive public license. He is too vulnerable. In any case, he scarcely has the time. Brilliant poet though he was, Donne was establishing a career. Indeed, there is no evidence in the poem that the "sighes and teares" of the octave refer to romance and courtship. The allusion is congenial, but exceedingly loose. "My Idolatry" fits the early courtly love deity, but also the pursuit of his secular career, that consumed half his life, at enormous cost and to no purpose. So the sonnet finishes with a bitter awareness that he is in a jam, involvement trailing involvement, frustration frustration, nothing opening anywhere; so crime and punishment are one:

> . . . for, long, yet vehement griefe hath beene
> Th'effect and cause, the punishment and sinne.
>
> (ll. 13–14)

After the systole of Sonnet 3, Sonnet 4 eases into a diastole of solitary, but secure faith. The release here from the shadow of his dark career, is exceedingly dignified, and the more poignant therefore. For the first time in his poetry, Donne cites his dead father, departed when he was a baby and so swiftly replaced by another. He sees him now in the company of angels, despite the church barriers between them, and envisions his full felicity. Indeed, he would add, to his father's amplitude of felicity, the vision of himself valiantly striding over the gaping mouth of hell, faithful father and faithful son, in a chain of generations. He is only unsure if the dead perceive like angels, by a direct apperception of truth—in which case his father's felicity will increase—or only by circumstance, as do living people, as he can be sure of nothing. Beyond question is only his "mindes white truth." His cup of grace is finally presumed.

The abrupt reference to his father, closing a cluster of sonnets and simultaneous with a first pronouncement of his "mindes white truth," that "valiantly I hels wide mouth o'r-stride," corresponds with our general sense of Donne's poetic mind, dredging up loosely related areas and shaping their instinctual hungers and commitments into poetic form. One father, as it were, touched the other to life, God and John Donne, Sr., in a single sonnet, his innocence and his father's soul in heaven. A great process of integration is clearly under way, a mother figure in "La Corona," "A nocturnall," and elsewhere, his father figure in this sonnet. If Donne's actual mother is not touched upon, as is his father, it may simply be that the woman was still uncomfortably in the flesh. A saint in heaven is easier to express rapport with.

The sestet begins with a survey of worldly judgments, by opinion and circumstance. These are divided into three broad categories, "idolatrous lovers," "vile blasphemous Conjurers," and "Pharisaicall Dissemblers." These groups are caricatures, with tolerably clear references. "Idolatrous lovers" loosely describes the secularists, presumed hedonists and lovers all. By a strong continuity from Sonnet 3, "my Idolatry" (III, 5) becomes "idolatrous lovers" (IV, 9), "showres of raine" (III, 5) becomes "weepe and mourne" (IV, 9). One might gently protest, idolatrous lovers sometimes do other things besides hypocritically "weepe and mourne"; but something in Donne's psyche is blocking and fading away that entire world of experience. "Pharisaicall Dissemblers" who "feigne devotion" fairly straightforwardly caricatures the Puritans—Tribulation Wholesome would comfortably fit that crew. The "vile blasphemous Conjurers" who "call on Jesus name" would seem to refer to the Roman Catholic Church. Donne would thus seem strongly identifying here with the Anglican position. His invoking his father's soul in heaven cheek-and-jowl with calling the Catholic priests "blasphemous Conjurers" is somehow extraordinarily innocent and baldly open, also extraordinarily poignant, also very lonely.

The sonnet close is the most reserved of the sequence:

> Then turne
> O pensive soule, to God, for he knowes best
> Thy true griefe, for he put it in my breast.
> (ll. 12–14)

His soul is only pensive, not depraved nor insecure, yet caught up in an unnamed "true griefe," shared only with God. Its content is nowise hinted at. The poet's opaque dignity is not to be penetrated. He will only leave its responsibility in God's hands, who put it in his. This somehow reads as a personal, not theoretical matter, and of central importance, to merit the designation, "Thy true griefe." In so loose and open a sonnet, it could be anything, perhaps a premonition of his wife's coming death, extraordinarily touched on in the very next sonnet, beginning:

> Since she whome I lovd, hath payd her last debt . . .

Perhaps it is an anticipation of his eventual meeting in heaven with the family, Catholics, saints, and martyrs all, and he, the Anglican apostate. Perhaps it is an acknowledgment of the dust and ashes his early ambition has turned into. The man's silence is not to be penetrated. Whatever his "true griefe," his "mindes white truth" is not shaken.

Purely personal elements intrude upon this cluster of sonnets, as never before in Donne's lyrics, his reference to his father, his former "Idolatry," his "true griefe." Lyric poetry is no longer an inviolable plateau, but succumbing to the texture of Donne's personal life. Given the process of breakdown described in "The Crosse" and Sonnet 2, "I am a little world," his poetry would seem succumbing, like his secular ambitions, to his central concerns of soul. His magnificence remains; but it will henceforth have little to say in lyric poetry.

The first Holy Sonnet from the Westmoreland Manuscript, "Since she whome I lovd," involves some break, however brief, after the previous sonnets. It is the plainest statement in all Donne's lyric poetry, downright, dignified speech, less taut in equilibrium than Ben Jonson's elegies, with scarcely an image, and only an allusive cosmological reference. It was occasioned by the death of his wife, Anne, in childbirth. Many conventional elements of metaphysical poetry do not apply here. There is no colloquial plunge *in medias res*, no eccentric conceit, only a formal statement in dignified, plain, knowing speech. The phrase, "and my good is dead" (l. 2), recalls "nothing else is;" but its context engulfs its metaphysical reverberations. Yet the metaphysical shudder, as we understand it in Donne's work, begins to come alive in the second quatrain behind its formal dignity, gradually manifesting its dramatic immediacy. So, what began as the numb quiet of dignified mourning gradually becomes a shuddering declaration of love between man and God.

The continuity established here from Anne to God is an eerie variant on the dramatic situation of a proposal to a woman's best friend by her bereaved husband over her dead body, and this in serious dignity, with all the emotional complexity called forth. He even declares in naked seriousness, it was God in Anne he loved all along, that she directed him as a channel to God; yet God alone cannot satisfy him. He has Him; but that is not enough:

> But though I have found thee, and thou my thirst hast fed,
> A holy thirsty dropsy melts mee yett.
>
> (ll. 7–8)

So, standing ignorant before God's opaque will, with no panic stirring, the speaker expresses a numb truth of raw hunger for more, the dissatisfaction in his very tissues as a "holy thirsty dropsy." Indeed, his shudder of jealous, fretful hunger is now shared by God:

> But in thy tender jealosy dost doubt
> Least the World, fleshe, yea Devill putt thee out.
> (ll. 13–14)

Against its strain of deep mourning, this sonnet shifts about for an elemental continuity between secular and sacred love. The autonomy of the two lovers in "The Extasie" is here dissolved away. His wife, Anne, his good, is now dead; but even here on earth, the force of her attraction was not uniquely hers. She was rather the vessel by which the love of God descended on earth:

> Here the admyring her my mind did whett
> To seeke thee God; so streames do shew their head . . .
> (ll. 5–6)

We take this analogy to the head of a stream as literally as possible. As a stream shows its source by its direction, force, and quality of its stream, so the stream of her life showed its source by its grace, force, and direction. This is again an Augustinian narrowing of all grace to its divine origin, with human beings only its vessels and conduits. Gone is the fumbling toward a secular libido. Now the vessel has returned to its source in God, and with it has brought back the speaker:

> But though I have found thee, and thou my thirst hast fed . . .
> (l. 7)

The speaker is now addressing the source of all love; yet he is still thirsty. His piety does not satiate him. He longs for his wife, even as God "my thirst hast fed." Are the two lovers the same? Are they different? What does his soul know of such theological distinctions; as in a strange wonder, grief flows and dissolves into saintly passion.

So the sestet presents a dramatic mutuality between God and the speaker. The speaker hungers for more love, "A holy thirsty dropsy melts mee yett" (l. 8); yet God is as hungry for love as he. Indeed, God is the courtier, maneuvering to engage the speaker even in the shock of mourning:

> But why should I begg more love, when as thou
> Dost wooe my soule, for hers offring all thine:
>
> (ll. 9–10)

And God is a jealous lover. In an echo of the Protestant mistrust of overtones of idolatry in the Roman Catholic Church, the speaker sees God as impatient with a love shared with "saints and Angels, things divine" (l. 12), insecure "Least the World, fleshe, yea Devill putt thee out" (l. 14). The sonnet thus begins as a formal declaration of mourning, yet settles to a strange courtship dance of two jealous, newfound lovers, the speaker and his God, each jealously demanding love, each fanatically possessive. The distractions are gone, saints, angels, the things of flesh, leaving a mutual "holy thirsty dropsy." One will "begg more love," the other offer "all thine."

In the second Westmoreland sonnet, a certain nebulous, floating "she," flirtatious, motherly, ubiquitous, personal, comfortable, abstract, particular, universal, is teasingly fixed in the church, that is nowhere to be found. Helen Gardner's detailed elaboration of the specific references to the Catholics, the Lutherans, etc., seems quite valid. Our concern here is the dramatic thrust and structuring of forces the speaker comes to grips with in a bewildering world. The poem, in this regard, baldly and systematically overturns the entire courtly love tradition that so overshadowed Donne's lyrics.

The church is not simply referred to as a female; this is repeated in every possible way, calling her a "spouse" to Christ, "so bright and cleare," referring to her dress, her make-up, her daily habits, her reliability, where she moves, what kinds of lovers she prefers, sedentary Englishmen or adventuring knights, how she allows herself to be seduced, openly and with no evasion. This is "she," "she," "she," "thy mild Dove," courted by the speaker's "amorous soule," building to a heroic couplet of beautiful promiscuity:

> Who is most trew, and pleasing to thee, then
> When she'is embrac'd and open to most men.
>
> (ll. 13–14)

And all this is addressed to her husband, Christ, who is asked to be her usher, lest she prove difficult of access. Thus, the sonnet opens with a gracious, loving request that his amorous soul be introduced to his wife:

> Show me, deare Christ, thy spouse, so bright and cleare.

Moreover, Christ in the Holy Sonnets is repeatedly depicted as the speaker's brother, in the sibling rivalry of Sonnet 7, "Spit in my face yee Jewes," his presentation as adopted son alongside God's natural son in Sonnet 11, "Wilt thou love God, as he thee!" His good-natured solicitation thus glides over incest in its beatific release of abundance. In the realm of spirit, universal love is a gift of blessing, not a taint of sin.

Indeed, the tone of this sonnet suggests a loosely positive answer to the questions it asks. The church, a rather flirtatious matron, puts on costumes and disguises to intrigue her worshipers in many faiths; yet she remains herself, they but her costumes. Her purpose is beatific promiscuity. This echoes an antinomianism Donne expressed throughout his career from his early wavering between faiths to such a sentiment:

> Teach mee how to repent; for that's as good
> As if thou'hadst seal'd my pardon, with thy blood.
> (IV. 13–14)

Here, as elsewhere, Donne distinguishes the paraphernalia of church from the raw engagement of spirit in faith. We might remark, without questioning his sentiments here, that this ebullient dissolution of the Oedipal bond upon the death of his wife is most wistful, most poignant.

The closing Holy Sonnet defines his temperament in religious experience as a bundle of unpredictable contraries, and willingly accepts this as the best possible situation. The thrust of the sonnet is a flamboyant elaboration of the metaphysical shudder in his unpredictable presence. Indeed, he rises to an embrace of this condition: "Those are my best dayes, when I shake with feare." The metaphysical shudder is thus become a way of life. Settling for nothing paltry, nothing earthly, no structure of ideas, no framework of reality, he has the strength of soul to endure an intimacy with God.

# 18

# The Visionary Engagement

After many years exploring earthly experience, an occasional poetic master, in his last period, will strive to comprehend the gods, cosmic forces, and the stretches of the universe. So, in Shakespeare's *The Tempest*, Caliban and Ariel overshadow Ferdinand and Miranda. In Sophocles' late *Oedipus at Colonus*, Oedipus the tragic king becomes a divine constellation. In *The Divine Comedy*, Dante wings beyond all earthly welter into paradise. Donne also, at the last, sloughs off all human engagement to stir with the presence of God.

"Goodfriday, 1613. Riding Westward" rehearses the shape of the *Holy Sonnets*, as a spirit in disarray slowly attunes itself to God's will. Written about eighteen months before his ordination, it shifts from moods, fantasies, and orientations, to his order of secular and holy work. The *Holy Sonnets* projected a murky, static landscape, where visions are enacted; "Goodfriday, 1613. Riding Westward" shows bleak daylight, not a blade of vegetation in sight, as a solitary horseman rides away from his proper direction. The person of John Donne intruded in the last *Holy Sonnets;* "Goodfriday, 1613. Riding Westward" enacts such an intrusion; as on a particular Goodfriday, John Donne is out riding, on business, westward, away from Jerusalem.

The poem begins impersonally; as the *Holy Sonnets* began with a legal declaration:

> Let mans Soule be a Spheare, and then, in this,
> The intelligence that moves, devotion is . . .

A universe of mixed disorder is here projected, with no sense of anything beyond it, one analogous to Ulysses' speech on order in *Troilus and Cressida* (I. iii. 78–124), though here static. The opening passage could be entirely secular. The speaker and nature are one. Indeed, their identity gives them the same clumsy working pattern. Man's soul is another sphere, with its own intelligence, but constantly driven by foreign motions. His final cause, "devotion," has vague religious overtones, but is ineffectual, ebbing constantly, pushed by random efficient causes, "hurried every day" by pleasure or business. This universe is an odd halfway house, then, not a random cosmos, having its intelligences, yet not an organic universe either, being governed by foreign motions. Indeed, it suffers constant frustration, the spheres always bent awry. So he rides westward on Goodfriday when his soul is bent to the east, at odds with God's presence, a breathing contradiction, his back turned on the crucifixion.

This strong ten-line thesis evokes a four-line antithesis (ll. 11–14), rendering the divine, compressed, abstracted, delineated in ultimate terms, a language dense with puns and compressed contradictions. The pun on son—"Sunne" is piled on "rising set;" nightfall begets day, time eternity. The alliterations of "Christ . . . Crosse," "rise and fall" suggest the rocking of the deep, the shift of life and death. Yet rising and falling, nailed on the cross, contradicts all motion. Divine impossibilities thus close on "benighted," the ancient negative action of the eating of the apple. So the speaker perversely flees; Christ, against all order, rises and falls on the cross amid an eternal night of stagnant damnation.

Lines 15–32 begin a synthesis of the speaker and Christ, by a full rehearsal of the sight he is fleeing. He first justifies his flight as mortally necessary to avoid the suicide of a confrontation with God:

> Yet dare I'almost be glad, I do not see
> That spectacle of too much weight for mee.
> Who sees Gods face, that is selfe life, must dye . . .
> (ll. 15–18)

But the excuse tears loose his imagination. From lines 18–32, a strange division begins of his spirit from his body. His body is still subject to "forraigne motions," and is fleeing; but his spirit is turned full-face in in fascinated apprehension, simultaneously envisioning the crucifixion and insisting he cannot see it.

Several linguistic devices heighten and intensify the force of the division, and add frantic drive to the vision itself. Thus the repeated interrogatives fling the entire vision against his consciousness. Line 18 crackles with contradictions; the vision, the living experience, brings death, seeing God, who is life, die. Indeed, the equilibrium attempted in the *Anniversaries*, of mental grasp and panorama, is here achieved, the speaker projecting a repeated phrase in a refrain of gathering horror, "Could I behold," "Could I behold," "If on these things I durst not look, durst I . . . cast mine eye"; as his vision is pitched in a gripping horror. We are at once there, and inside the mind of the observer, much as in a cinema, when we watch a terrifying fire in the faces of its observers, the flames playing across their horrified cheeks and eyes.

Indeed, leaden negatives heighten the mental resistance, denying anything is seen; as the vision crackles forth: "I do not see that spectacle," "Could I behold that endlesse height?" "I durst not look," "These things . . . be from mine eye." Such questions, negatives, and mental blocks build up power as in a static electricity machine, grinding round and round as the pressure mounts. So the speaker, riding westward, clenches his mind against seeing; as the vision slams permanent that first tearing division, his imagination hanging back, his body riding from God's sight.

We mentioned earlier two modes of approaching Jesus, by his vocation of work and service, and by his crucifixion, miraculously bringing grace. Their balance here structures this vision; as the princely workman, Christ, whose vocation is the universe, has each aspect of his being systematically frustrated and torn to pieces. Thus, we begin with his tools and working crews, smashed by the crucifixion. His "Lieutenant Nature" shrinks; his footstool cracks; the sun, his emblem and badge, winks. His hands, "which span the Poles,/And tune all spheares," shaping and giving harmony to the universe, are visibly pierced with holes. Our eyes rise from his footstool, to his hands, to his full presence. What is being crucified here is the majesty of the cosmos, its rule, an "endlesse height which is Zenith" (l. 23), smashed and humbled.

The electricity tightens another notch, to reach fever-pitch. "That blood which is/The seat of all our Soules" (ll. 25–26) fuses both vocations of Christ in a single vision. Blood, the fluid of pain and redemption, compassion and grace, is "The seat of all our Soules," shaping the cosmos of spirit, as his hands shaped the cosmos of bodies; and it is made "durt of dust." The pitch cracks. The verbs come thicker, hissing, rasping out. He confronts his flesh, on the cross, torn apart, dead:

> that flesh which was worne
> By God, for his apparell, rag'd, and torne?
> (ll. 27–28)

Lacerated with affront, regicide, maculation, wanton, hideous destruction, his imagination stands fixed over the wreckage, "pierc'd," "humbled," "durt of dust," "flesh . . . rag'd," "torn," cosmos on cosmos wrecked for a drop of salvation. The four lines on Mary (ll. 29–32) already ease in tone. The pitchpoint of vision can endure no more.

Indeed, this vision of cosmic wreckage, though focusing on the crucifixion, the holes, the blood, the flesh raged and torn, entails a larger tearing. Thus, the references to "Nature . . . his footstoole . . . the Sunne," extend it across the cosmos. So "Could I behold those hands which span the Poles,/And tune all spheares at once" (ll. 21–22), simultaneously grasp them on the cross, and as they shaped a universe. So cosmic harmony is pierced with holes. But this is the very thrust of the *Anniversaries*, to grasp a universe rendered ghostly and imbecilic, indeed here a moment earlier, in the moment of the wound.

This larger reverberation makes possible the extraordinary force of these lines. The crucifixion not only brings agonized redemption to the world, but renders the loss of soul to the universe, the essential cracking of harmony and order, rendered in human form in the *Anniversaries*. Donne's rage to destroy the construct of order, his indifferent rejection of the physical world, his driving compulsion to expose disorder, his hunger to free and redeem his spirit, his death wish, his rage for maculation, here find a vessel sufficiently large, intense, and moral. Indeed, the very crushing of the instrument can propel him into heaven, let him only fuse with it. Gripped by the slashing, piercing, tearing vision, he cuts ballast with the physical world, and fixes his spirit on the crucifixion.

The parallel to Milton is striking here, as in "The First Anniversary." Both men moaned at the loss of harmony in the universe. Both saw the wound as painful, its results as irretrievable. Yet the contrast in "The First Anniversary" holds good here. Donne saw the cosmic disorder as pointing to a withdrawal to God, Milton to a "paradise within," the solitary path of a disciplined man in an imbecilic universe.

Lines 15 to 32 are the first accommodation of spirit to the presence of God. Lines 33 to 36 then consolidate this. Before, he simply rode westward; as Christ hung on the cross. Now his memory turns toward Christ; as Christ, hanging on the tree, looks toward him riding westward, in a harmony of muted endurance.

But the speaker veers yet closer, undertaking the labor of penance:

> I turne my backe to thee, but to receive
> Corrections, till thy mercies bid thee leave.
>
> (ll. 37–38)

His body and soul are now joined in God's service. The "forraigne motions" that impel him westward are but tools for his labor of soul, turning in perverse self-denial to receive correction. Was his entire life once bent on self-fulfilment? It is now one of patient self-correction.

From lines 33 to 38, the speaker is muted, reflective, after the surge of spirit in the vision of the crucifixion; but his spirit surges forward again in inchoate prayer, echoing the contrast of fire and water in the sonnet, "I am a little world made cunningly," asking for the radical fire of grace, where no human path will arrive at God. Donne's wheel is now come full circle.

In the earlier love poems, the god of love hung over his head, tantalizing, unnatural, enslaving, face behind face, God behind woman, making intimacy impossible, closeness a bondage, demonically making him a "rack't carcasse." Now, after the exorcism of the marriage poems and "The Extasie," the god figure returns; but it is God Himself. Instead of petrifying him, God now hangs Himself on the cross. He, not the speaker, becomes a "rack't carcasse." Now no one separates them. The illusory intimacy of love has become the utter intimacy of searing truth, the closeness of just punishment. Once his depraved isolation, "my rusts, and my deformity" be burned away, he and God will meet face to face.

So, at the close, they unite in a mysterious balance and equality:

> Restore thine Image, so much, by thy grace,
> That thou may'st know mee, and I'll turne my face.
> (ll. 41–42)

The speaker is now "thine Image," his "mee" unknown until God's image is restored within it. His true self is God, all else a rust and deformity. Let their identity be renewed; and he will turn, God's face to meet the face of God in ultimate godly intimacy.

Donne went as chaplain to Germany in 1619, two years after his ordination. His disengagement from the physical world had progressed in the six years since "Goodfriday, 1613. Riding Westward." There, he was indifferent to the countryside he traversed, but on some earthly spot, his body really moving in some direction. In "A Hymne to Christ, at the Authors Last Going into Germany," the physical world has sunk beneath its emblems; its substance, unto itself, no longer registers. He may embark in "What torne ship soever" (l. 1); all are emblems of his ark. He may be drowned in "what sea soever" (l. 3); all are emblematic of the blood of salvation. He is beyond fear and death. The world is like curtain material, all clouds hanging over his ship but angry masks of God. So the work of "Goodfriday, 1613. Riding Westward" has advanced a notch. Donne and his God are now turned face to face:

> yet through that maske I know those eyes,
> Which, though they turne away sometimes,
> They never will despise.
>
> (ll. 6–8)

In a great gesture of abnegation in Stanza 2, he sacrifices to God his land and those who love him. But his trip is itself a great emblem, a surrender of England and all it contains, for divine service as a chaplain. And in a now opaque emblem world, sea crosses sea, and parting parting. So, as he places a sea between himself and his beloved in England; let God put his divine sea of spirit between the speaker and his sins. So Stanza 2 presses on toward a radical either-or. As trees grow downward in winter, their sap seeking their root below; his winter growth is equally secretive, to push toward "th'Eternall root/Of true Love I may know" (ll. 15–16), the one great root of God's true love. By the image, man is underground to the world of spirit, reaching toward the divine root whose trunk stands in heaven, his sap, his spirit, seeking the root of God.

Stanza 3 renders the strange blending of the psychology of romantic love with a divine relationship, as in the sonnet, "Since she whome I lovd," and also its muted courtship dance; but the speaker is now in a state of harmony. Secure in an amorous relationship with God, he denies Him any control. So each now qualifies and demands love from the other. God is jealous, and would keep the speaker's love for Himself. The speaker insists upon his liberty to choose, and chides God, almost in a tease, not to deny him freedom, else there is no divine love:

> O, if thou car'st not whom I love
> Alas, thou lov'st not mee.
>
> (ll. 23–24)

The speaker seems comfortable here in the female role in this flirtation. God is possessive, exclusive, and jealous; he is amorous, and follows suit in jealousy. So he coyly defines the meaning of love to control what they will and will not do. So the religious relationship in Stanza 3 settles in a sentimental simplicity. God is jealous even of priestly paraphernalia; the speaker wants to be incarcerated freely.

Stanza 4 then seals his bill of divorce to all earthly values, "Fame, Wit, Hopes (false mistresses)." He varies the doctrine of the Holy Sonnet, "Since she whome I lovd," that human beings are but channels for divine spirit. Here he advances a hierarchy of love, the "fainter beames" of earthly love, the scattered loves of youth, yielding to full, adult, godly love. The religious either-or is sealed, complete. He plunges into darkness to see God in prayer, into everlasting night to escape the storms of earthly days. This shift of spirit to God is so total, the material world has slipped behind a free display of emblems; as a *fin-de-siècle* composer, a Mahler or a Charles Ives, he will freely rearrange conventional, even banal themes, disregarding their original context, for sources of power to reach his fresh intent.

The earliest date offered for "Hymne to God my God, in my sicknesse" is his illness of 1623, four years after "A Hymne to Christ, at the Authors last going into Germany." In those four years, his withdrawal into the world of spirit has heightened. In "A Hymne to Christ," the surrounding world was emblematic of the spiritual world. In "Hymne to God my God, in my sicknesse," believing literally in the resurrection of the body, he focuses entirely on his own body. Belonging in both worlds, it is more than an emblem. So he familiarizes himself with the instrument he must use in the divine service, rehearsing, as it were, and tuning up the instrument. "I shall be made thy Musique" shows his old metaphysical foreshortening; he will at once be the instrument, the musician, and the music played.

The old Renaissance adventures remarked in the earlier poems are here absorbed and made emblematic of the religious quest. His body is a cosmic map, a little world. The supreme challenge in Donne's day was not America, but the Orient, the seat of "The Easterne riches." The supreme exploration was the passageway, the "South-west discoverie." This challenge became emblematic of Donne's death, the world his passageway to God. The aura of the great circle is cast on the atmosphere of eternal life. East meets West on a flat map; death rounds out in resurrection. All end stops are straits to the riches of the Orient.

The great circle closes on the number one. The Pacific Sea, the Eastern riches, Jerusalem, shimmer about the resurrection. Anyan, Magellan, and Gibraltar are but ways to it, the lands of Japhet, Cham, or Sem. Paradise and Calvary are one place, the cross and the tree of knowledge one. The mystical one narrows from the earth to Paradise, then to Christ and Adam, and finally concentrates on the speaker's person, where both Adams meet, the sweat of labor and the blood of redemption. The overriding image in the speaker's person is of totality, satiation, abundance. He has passed the straits of penitential denial, and would have all adventure, all garbs, all crowns. An essence in the world of spirit, he would have grace.

The reference of "this" in line 29 is unclear. The speaker could refer to the closing line of the poem as his text, "Therfore that he may raise the Lord throws down" (l. 30). But his body and its sickness have preoccupied him here, an instrument, a world map, an emblem of resurrection, his occasion and subject. Thus, the poem tightens in structure, enriches in imagery, and embodies its emblems, referring "Be this my Text" to his body, sick and dying, as the living word of God, a fleshly sermon of his death and coming resurrection.

"A Hymne to God the Father," written during Donne's sickness in 1623, may well be his last lyric poem. We need not doubt Walton's word that Donne had it set to music. "Hymne to God my God, in my sicknesse" had a confidence and abundance, weaving lists of place names with tribes and mythic people, texts, sermons, and Latin phrases in a large harmony. "A Hymne to God the Father" keeps an ultimate, gray quiet. Its eighteen lines have only two rhymes, not a single metaphor, not one palpable object, not a single sensuous adjective, nor any adverb of feeling tone. In a sense, the first two stanzas weave verbs about the repeated noun, "sin." Its warp is God's steady capacity for forgiveness, its woof the speaker's turning and winding about, ever deeper in the world of sin. He grows entrenched, bogged down, from a first beginning in sin to a habitual running in sin, to a winning of others to sin, to making his sin their door to sin, hanging back at first, then wallowing in it. The poem builds, then, a formal, exceedingly sober music; as each stanza repeats the identical rhymes, a, b, a, b, a, b. Four pentameter lines tighten to a tetrameter, then a closing dimeter, a catch of withholding that releases to the same steady reverberation in the next stanza, its dignity restraining our sense of the fabric gradually sagging about the world of sin.

The first two stanzas weave an even texture. God's gesture of forgiveness hangs in a steady balance as the speaker evenly unfolds his condition, ending on the leaden refrain, "For, I have more." But the steady sag of confessional finally betrays his ultimate secret fear, a fear of loss of energy, of sluggishness, of spiritual failure:

> I have a sinne of feare, that when I have spunne
> My last thred, I shall perish on the shore . . .
> (ll. 13–14)

In perfect harmony with God's will, he yet has a catch of disquiet. It provokes a demand that God's "Sunne" shine on his deathbed, as it shines now, and he will fear no more.

Each stanza closes on a couplet with a last massive double pun:

> When thou hast done, thou hast not done,
> For, I have more.
> When thou hast done, thou hast not done,
> For, I have more.
> And, having done that, Thou hast done,
> I have no more.

The pun is, of course, on the poet's own name, Donne, and the maiden name of his wife, Anne More. Years after her death, he still longs for her, yet now feels it a worldly anchor, a catch in his turning to God. Whatever God's gifts, His grace, His love, He does not possess Donne, for Donne has More. But both the sonnet, "Since she whome I lovd," and "A Hymne to Christ at the Authors last going into Germany," have shown God as a jealous lover. The speaker then ties his diffidence to a fear he is essentially this-worldly, and at his death, will perish on the shore. Let a flood of grace assure him of eternity in the world of spirit, and God has Donne; he has no More.

This double pun is so nakedly simple, almost child-like, as to embarrass us; but only if we read the hymn as a structured lyric, where it jars the sober, unfolding thought. Here the hymn is closer to music, a patient weaving of himself and his wife onto a total union with God.

The artful elegance of poetry has more and more lost its sequestered excellence, its proscenium arch. The poet, his father, his mother, his wife, occasional events in his life, now wash across stage. The poet's hand, occupied with other things, will not hold firm inside its shaped structure. So the poet surrenders his island citadel and returns, not to any dukedom—that was never more than a cloud-capped dream, but to the jealous constancy of divine service. So the last religious poems bespeak the self-surrender of a Prospero:

> But this rough magic
> I here abjure; and, when I requir'd
> Some heavenly music,—which even now I do,—
> To work mine end upon their senses, that
> This airy charm is for, I'll break my staff,
> Bury it certain fadoms in the earth,
> And deeper than did ever plummet sound
> I'll drown my book.
>
> (*The Tempest*, V. i. 50–57)

# *John Donne*
# *A Selective Bibliography*

This is a select bibliography. Major editions of the poet's works, biographies, and important critical works have been taken into account. For further information see:

Berry, L. E. *A Bibliography of Studies in Metaphysical Poetry*. 1939–1960. University of Wisconsin Press, 1964.

Keynes, Sir Geoffrey. *Biography of Dr. John Donne, Dean of St. Paul's*. 3rd edition, 1958.

Spencer, Theodore, and Van Doren, Mark. *Studies in Metaphysical Poetry: Two Essays and a Bibliography*. Kennicat, 1939, contains (1) an account of scholarship on Metaphysical Poetry up to that date, (2) a section on "Seventeenth-Century Poets and Twentieth-Century Critics," (3) bibliography, 1912–1938.

White, William. *John Donne since 1900: A Bibliography of Periodical Articles*. 1942.

*The Year's Work in English Studies*, published annually, should be consulted for new writings.

## EDITIONS


Coffin, Charles M., ed. *The Complete Poetry and Selected Prose of John Donne*. The Modern Library, 1952.

Gardner, Helen, ed. *The Elegies and the Songs and Sonnets of John Donne*. Oxford University Press, 1965.

———, ed. *The Divine Poems of John Donne*. Oxford University Press, 1952.

Grierson, Sir H. J. C., ed. *The Poems of John Donne*. 2 vols., Oxford University Press, 1912.

Hayward, John, ed. *Complete Poetry and Selected Prose of John Donne*. Nonesuch Press, 1929.

Manley, Frank, ed. *The Anniversaries.* Johns Hopkins Press, 1963.

Milgate, W., ed. *The Satires, Epigrams, and Verse Letters*, Oxford University Press, 1967.

Potter, C. R. and Simpson, Evelyn M., eds. *The Sermons of John Donne.* University of California Press, 1953–1962.

Sparrow, John, ed. *Devotions Upon Emergent Occasions.* London, 1923.

Shawcross, John T., ed. *Complete Poetry*, Doubleday Anchor Books, 1967.

Simpson, Evelyn, ed. *Essays in Divinity.* Oxford University Press, 1952.

## BIOGRAPHY

Gosse, Edmund. *Life and Letters of John Donne.* 2 vols. London, 1899. (Helen Gardner comments, "Though highly unsatisfactory has not yet been replaced by a full scholarly life.")

Grandsen, K. W. *John Donne.* Longman and Books, 1952.

Hardy, Evelyn. *A Spirit in Conflict.* Constable, 1942.

Kermode, Frank. *John Donne.* (British Council Writers and their Works.) London House, 1957.

Le Comte, Edward. *Grace to a Witty Sinner.* Walker, 1965.

Walton, Izaak. *Life of John Donne (1675), Final Version.* World's Classic Series Edition. Oxford, 1927. (For a discussion of Walton's methods and his reliability as biographer see David Novarr, *The Making of Walton's Lives*, Cornell University Press, 1958.)

## BACKGROUND OF THE SEVENTEENTH CENTURY MIND

### *Primary Sources*

Browne, Sir Thomas. *Religio Medici and Other Writings.* Dutton, and J. M. Dent and Sons, 1951.

Burton, Robert. *The Anatomy of Melancholy.* Dutton, and J. M. Dent and Sons, 1932.

Castiglione. *The Book of the Courtier*, translated by Sir Thomas Hoby. Dutton, and J. M. Dent and Sons, 1956.

Hobbes, Thomas. *Leviathan.* Collier, 1962.

Hooker, Richard. *Of the Laws of Ecclesiastical Polity.* Books I–IV. Dutton, and J. M. Dent and Sons, 1954.

Montaigne. *Complete Works*, translated by Donald M. Frame. Stanford University Press, 1957.

Saint John of the Cross. *The Complete Works of St. John of the Cross, Doctor of the Church*, translated by E. Allison Peers, from the critical edition of P. Silverio de Santa Teresa. Newman Press, 1953.

*General Histories*

Baugh, A. C. *Literary History of England.* Meredith, 1948.
Bush, D. *English Literature in the Early Seventeenth Century.* Oxford University Press, second edition, 1962.
Grierson, Sir H. J. C. *First Half of the Seventeenth Century.* C. Scribner and Sons, 1906.
———. *Cross Currents in English Literature of the Seventeenth Century.* Chatto and Windus, 1929.
Ward, A. and Waller, A. R., eds. *The Cambridge History of English Literature.* Cambridge University Press, 1907–1916.

*History of Ideas*

Coffin, Charles Monroe. *John Donne and the New Philosophy.* The Humanities Press, 1958.
Craig, Hardin. *The Enchanted Glass.* Oxford University Press, 1936.
Harris, V. *All Coherence Gone.* University of Chicago Press, 1949, contains many references to Donne and Du Bartas, and considers the idea of mutability and decay; and creation according to Du Bartas.
Lovejoy, A. O. *The Great Chain of Being.* Harper, 1960.
Macklem, Michael. *The Anatomy of the World: Relations Between Natural and Moral Law from Donne to Pope.* University of Minnesota Press, 1958.
Mazzeo, J. A. *Reason and Imagination: Studies in the History of Ideas, 1600–1800.* Columbia University Press, 1962.
Nicolson, Marjorie Hope. *The Breaking of the Circle.* Columbia University Press, 1962.
———. *Mountain Gloom and Mountain Glory.* Cornell University Press, 1955.
*Seventeenth-Century Studies Presented to Sir H. J. C. Grierson,* 1938.
Spitzer, L. *Classical and Christian Ideas of World Harmony.* Johns Hopkins University Press, 1962. (Traditia ii–iii, 1944–1945.)
Tillyard, E. W. M. *The Elizabethan World Picture.* Vintage, 1961.
William, Cecil. *The Execution of Justice in England,* and William Allen. *A True Sincere Modest History of English Catholics,* Robert M. Kingdon, ed. in modernized text for Folgers Documentation, 1964.
Williamson, George. *Seventeenth-Century Contexts.* University of Chicago Press, 1961.
———. *Mutability and Decay in the Seventh-Century Melancholy.* (ELH ii, 1935).

*Criticism on Donne*

Alvarez, A. *The School of John Donne.* Chatto and Windus, 1961.
Andreasen, N. J. *John Donne: Conservative Revolutionary.* Princeton University Press, 1964.

Bald, A. C. *Donne and the Drurys.* Cambridge University Press, 1959.

Bennett, Joan. *Five Metaphysical Poets.* Cambridge University Press, 1966.

Ellrodt, Robert. *Les Poetes Metaphysique Anglais.* Yale University Press, 1954.

Gardner, Helen. *John Donne: Twentieth-Century Views.* Prentice-Hall Inc., 1962

Guss, Donald L. *John Donne, Petrarchist.* Wayne State University Press, 1966.

Heninger, S. K. *Handbook of Renaissance Meteorology.* Iowa State University Press, 1960.

Legouise, Pierre. *Donne the Craftsman.* Russell, 1928.

Leishman, J. B. *The Monarch of Wit.* Hillary, revised edition, 1962.

Louthen, Donophan. *The Poetry of John Donne.* Twayne, 1951.

Peterson, Douglas L. *The English Lyric from Wyatt to Donne.* Princeton University Press, 1967.

Praz, Mario. *The Flaming Heart*, Doubleday Anchor Books, 1958.

Spencer, Theodore, ed. *Garland for John Donne.* Harvard University Press, 1951.

Unger, Leonard. *Donne's Poetry and Modern Criticism.* Russell, 1950.

# Index